Endorsements for
Therapy Tales: Exploring relational process in practice

The 13 tales engagingly (and often movingly) recounted by Linda Finlay focus on what happens 'between' clients and therapists in their encounters. The 'relational space' that is created allows for mutual connection, disconnection and felt reverberation, which extends beyond the therapeutic relationship and onto all of the wider self, other and world relationships in both clients' and therapists' lives. Dr Finlay honestly and insightfully conveys the uncertain 'messiness' characteristic of relationally focused therapy. And, in doing so, she reveals its profound transformative impact upon all involved. *Therapy Tales* is a satisfyingly challenging book not least in its ability to remind its readers of the many complex and revealing existential possibilities that are awakened when we agree to engage in an honest and caring relationship.

Prof. Ernesto Spinelli, author of *Tales of Un-knowing: Therapeutic encounters from an existential perspective*

Linda Finlay is a true mastermind of relational therapy, and this new title, *Therapy Tales*, is a brilliant addition to her ongoing contributions. Looking at the magic of our work – the intangible power of the therapeutic relationship – this book explores the intricacies involved in relational work. Through simple, short stories the reader witnesses the nitty-gritty, in-depth process of therapy: the pain and the bliss; the ruptures and connections; the confusion and compassion; intensity and intimacy… and, if you think that sounds messy, you would probably be right. Therapy spaces can appear as microcosms of the 'outside world', and relational therapy at its best, is when moving with this sensitively and ethically; trusting in the robustness of the 'therapeutic frame'.

Finlay has an extraordinary ability to examine what constitutes as relational. What a treat to read a book that embodies all that is wonderful about the healing power of therapy!

Caz Binstead, integrative, relational therapist and supervisor. Also published author, speaker, visiting lecturer/facilitator and co-lead of #TherapistsConnect

Therapy Tales is an engaging book that is both accessible and thought provoking. Through 13 well-crafted stories, Dr Finlay brings the world of relational psychotherapy to life in a way that feels grounded and real. Each tale explores the connections between our past relationships and our present selves. These are not dry case studies but thoughtful, human stories of people working through their relational histories. This book makes a helpful distinction between therapy that simply involves relationships and therapy that is truly relational – where the dynamic between therapist and client becomes central to the psychotherapy process. This book is valuable reading for both trainee and experienced therapists alike, offering fresh perspectives on the relational dimensions of therapeutic practice.
Dr Peter Blundell, Senior Lecturer in Counselling and Psychotherapy Practice, Liverpool John Moores University

Therapy Tales is an absorbing, thought-provoking and rare book, one that many collections of clinical case material aspire to be but rarely achieve. From the very first story, it draws the reader into the lived intensity of therapeutic encounters, revealing how relational work is embodied, uncertain, emotionally charged and profoundly human.

It is a compelling, accessible, and deeply reflective book that brings the meaning of 'relational therapy' vividly to life. Through evocative clinical stories, Linda Finlay skilfully illuminates the layered, embodied and often messy nature of therapeutic work where loss, compassion, uncertainty and connection coexist. The book's integration of reflective, evidence-based discussion invites readers to critically engage with relational processes, ethical complexity, therapist subjectivity and self-care, while thoughtfully addressing contemporary issues such as trauma, neurodiversity, anti-racist and decolonising practice, interpreter-assisted and online therapy, and socio-cultural legacies. This contemporary breadth, which is discussed with nuance and accessibility, is what makes this book especially compelling. Insightful discussion questions invite deep reflection and make it particularly valuable for learning and supervision contexts.

This is an essential text rich in relational therapy, diversity, theory, and practice that belongs on every trainee and seasoned therapist's shelf.
Divine Charura MBE, Professor of Counselling Psychology, York St John University

The 'therapy tales' in this book are fictional scenarios illustrating how both client and therapist contribute to relational dynamics in therapy. They creatively showcase the diversity of relational therapy through a variety of social/cultural contexts: with respect to intersectional identities of all involved, including the supervisory relationship, different parts of selves including intergenerational trauma and organisational contexts for therapy. Finlay demonstrates the practice of cultural humility and openness, with commitment to disrupting dynamics of power. She encourages the reader to use the stories as prompts to think about our own responses, while clearly explaining approaches arising from various modalities.

This engrossing book is an invaluable corrective to the usual focus on the isolated therapy dyad, placing the lens firmly on the relational-cultural context of both client and therapist. A must-read for all students of relational therapy (including post-qualification).

Dr Gillian Proctor, Associate Professor in Counselling and Psychotherapy, University of Leeds

Therapy Tales by Linda Finlay provides a thoughtful and engaging account of relational psychotherapy in practice. Drawing on a series of carefully constructed clinical narratives, Finlay illustrates how therapeutic work unfolds within the shared space between client and therapist. The book pays close attention to process, highlighting both the client's experience and the therapist's reflexive engagement, including the role of supervision.

What emerges is a grounded and moving appreciation of therapy as a collaborative and evolving encounter, rather than a set of techniques to be applied. The nuance and complexity of the relational process is beautifully crafted, supported by insight, awareness and meaning-making. Finlay, as always, writes with clarity and relational sensitivity, offering perspectives that will be of value to both experienced practitioners and those in training. This is a hugely valuable and perfectly pitched contribution to our understanding of relational practice.

Prof. Andrew Reeves, Emeritus Professor in Counselling Professions and Mental Health, University of Chester

Linda Finlay offers another masterpiece. This is a warm, insightful and informative book about the many layers of psychotherapy and the complexity of being human. It is a must-read for both novices and experts – a book destined to be a classic.

Sofie Bager-Charleson, author of *Enjoying Research in Counselling and Psychotherapy*

THERAPY TALES

EXPLORING RELATIONAL PROCESS IN PRACTICE

LINDA FINLAY

PCCS BOOKS

First published 2026

PCCS Books Ltd
Wyastone Business Park
Wyastone Leys
Monmouth
NP25 3SR
UK

Tel +44 (0)1600 891509
contact@pccs-books.co.uk
www.pccs-books.co.uk

Therapy Tales: Exploring relational process in practice

British Library Cataloguing in Publication Data.
A catalogue record for this book is available from the British Library

ISBNs paperback 978 1 915220 78 3
epub 978 1 915220 79 0

Cover design by Ehsan Arjmand.
Printed in the UK by CMP (UK) Ltd, Poole, Dorset.

CONTENTS

Dedication

To Mel, for all our co-creations

About the author

Linda Finlay, PhD, is a practising existential, relational-centred integrative psychotherapist and supervisor based in York (UK). She is also an academic consultant and lecturer with the Open University, where she teaches and has written on various counselling and psychology courses.

She is best known for her many publications on integrative psychotherapy, occupational therapy, and also qualitative, phenomenological research and reflexivity, including *Relational Integrative Psychotherapy* (Wiley); *The Therapeutic Use of Self in Counselling and Psychotherapy* (Sage); *Practical Ethics in Counselling and Psychotherapy* (Sage); *Phenomenology for Therapists* (Wiley); and *Relational Counselling and Psychotherapy* (Sage).

Her particular research interests include applying existential and hermeneutic phenomenological approaches to investigate the lived experience of disability and trauma. Straddling clinical and academic fields helps her research and writing to be grounded in practice, while her practice remains informed by research. She trusts the therapeutic process and how the therapeutic relationship might be harnessed for healing and self-discovery – the topic of all her writings. For more information, please visit www.lindafinlay.co.uk

Acknowledgements

Special thanks go to all my clients and supervisees over the years, whose stories, struggles and courage continue to inspire me in my work, writing, and, most of all, in my personal growth.

Thank you also to all my colleagues (notably Suzanne Boyd, Divine Charura, Sarah Frettingham, Jameela Shabbir Khokhawala, Sally Openshaw, Jocelyne Quennell and Anna Robinson) who have critically read selected chapter drafts and offered affirmation and reality-testing challenge.

I remain uber-grateful to Mel Wilder and Susan Ram for their transformational editing and the way they have both supported my writing and prodded my critical thinking over the last 30 years.

Finally, regarding the publication process, I need to acknowledge both Sage and PCCS Books.

Chapters 7 (Liam), 8 (Taigh), 9 (Wei) and 12 (Kaleisha) are based on shorter case studies in Finlay, L. *Relational Counselling and Psychotherapy* (Copyright©2025 by Linda Finlay) and have been reproduced, adapted and/or extended with the generous permission of Sage Publications, Ltd.

Then, extra special thanks must be extended to Camilla Erskine, Editorial Director at PCCS Books, for her belief in this project, plus her expert and helpful eagle-eye edits, and ever-encouraging, thoughtful, responsive advice. Thank you also to the rest of the publishing team for seeing the manuscript through to publication. Of course, any mistakes and misunderstandings within this book are mine alone.

Abbreviations

ACEs	adverse childhood experiences
ACT	acceptance and commitment therapy
ADHD	attention deficit hyperactivity disorder
BPD	borderline personality disorder
CAMHS	Child and Adolescent Mental Health Services
CAT	cognitive analytic therapy
CBT	cognitive behavioural therapy
CFT	compassion-focused therapy
CoRT	complex racial trauma
CPD	continuous professional development
C-PTSD	complex post-traumatic stress disorder
DBT	dialectical behavior therapy
DTC	democratic therapeutic communities
EAP	Employee Assistance Programme
EMDR	eye movement desensitisation and reprocessing
FCT	family constellations therapy
GSRD	gender, sexuality and relationship diversity
FST	forensic schema therapy
IPT	interpersonal psychotherapy
LGBTQ+	lesbian, gay, bisexual, transgender and queer/questioning, plus other sexual orientations and gender identities
MBCT	mindfulness-based cognitive therapy
MBT	mentalization-based therapy
PTMF	Power Threat Meaning Framework
PTSD	post-traumatic stress disorder
TA	transactional analysis
TSD	therapist self-disclosure

Summary of chapters

Chapters	Key issues and focus of therapy	Therapeutic approach/techniques	Therapeutic, relational and ethical processes
1. Cally (and Tamara)	Counselling trainee's chronic shame, performance anxieties and attachment history; therapist's concordant countertransference	Long-term attachment-based *transactional analysis* (TA); creating a 'relational home' in both therapy and supportive supervision towards 'taming the shame' and offering relational healing	The evidence base around the power of the therapeutic relationship and how to work therapeutically with shame
2. Richard (and Tracy)	Depression and suicide risk given a life of emptiness and despair following death of abusive/controlling mother; therapy goal is to develop a meaningful life	Working within a medical model hospital context, implementing structured assessments, psychological 'formulation', safeguarding suicide risk and *interpersonal therapy* over 4.5 months; bodily attunement plus use of *Power Threat Meaning Framework* to help transition from hospital and nurture more nourishing social connections	The critical question at stake concerns the extent the therapist is able to work relationally given the medical model followed by the team
3. Claudia (and Sue)	Traumatic grief around a miscarriage; intergenerational trauma, shame and guilt	Short-term *grief therapy* that offers permission-giving space to explore bereavement; *gestalt* approach to dreamwork	Relational role played by care and self-care, given that both women had to manage trauma carried from their mothers

4. Lisa (and Michel)	Long COVID trauma; from 'bodily doubt' and dissociation to bodily trust; losses in work and social life; regaining a meaningful life	Long-term *existential psychotherapy*; phenomenological *Focusing* technique	Bodywork; therapist's (selective) self-disclosure
5. Darren (and Jon)	Violent impulsive behaviour, homophobia, toxic masculinity and substance misuse; forensic/prison therapeutic community context	Building of trust to counteract resistance initially; safety and emotional regulation promoted in the structured approach of *forensic schema therapy* and (psychodynamic and social cognitive) *mentalization-based therapy*	Relational commitments and relational challenges when working in a forensic context; negotiation of power involving a balance of acceptance and challenge
6. Morgan (and Diana)	History of suicide attempts; currently self-cuts as a way of managing emotions; turbulent trauma history of unsuccessful, toxic/abusive relationships; possible diagnoses of borderline personality disorder (BPD) and ADHD	Open-ended long-term weekly therapy; *dialectical behavior therapy* (DBT); use of AI, including a mindfulness app and ChatGPT; boundaried between-session telephone coaching towards emotional regulation; self-care managing risks of self-harm	Manualised therapies and the extent DBT might be relational; safeguarding

Chapters	Key issues and focus of therapy	Therapeutic approach/techniques	Therapeutic, relational and ethical processes
7. Liam (and Chloe)	Difficulties around sustaining long-term intimate relationships; trauma history of sexual abuse and losses/feeling abandoned; boarding school syndrome; issues around problematic pornography use	20+3 sessions: *Developmental-relational, psychodynamic integrative approach*; work with parts of self; *eye movement desensitisation and reprocessing* (EMDR)	Ethics around erotic cotransference and working with (class) privilege
8. Taigh (and Amanda)	Traumatic disenfranchised grief; neurodiversity (autism – being 'neurospicy')	Short-term *grief work* and *existential* exploration of intrapsychic and community relationships; *psychodrama*	LGBTQ+ affirmative therapy for non-binary client; reasonable adjustments made for autism; use of therapist self-disclosure
9. Wei (and Anne)	Secretive online gambling addiction; parental pressure/abuse with links to intergenerational (colonial Chinese) trauma legacy	Year-long, *pluralistic* approach; *mindfulness*; *systemic family constellations therapy*	Relational-cultural approach; online therapy via Zoom

10. Khalid (and Asha, Ali and Louay)	Refugee trauma, including profound loneliness and losses	Trauma-informed *multi-modal community-based psychosocial support* programme: time-limited 1:1 therapy (with interpreter) and longer term groupwork (a men's group)	Decolonising therapy and interpreter-assisted therapy; cultural competence, humility and openness
11. Ivy (and Karen and Otto)	Problematic young person's behaviour at home and school; ADHD; dyslexia; complex systemic issues	Multi-pronged/multi-agency *systemic* therapeutic approach: individual *person-centred counselling*, *family therapy*, medication, emotional regulation work with the school; use of apps	Layers of relationality; managing therapist emotional labour, burnout, supervision and self-care; ethics of privately funded family therapy and tutoring
12. Kaleisha (and Sarah)	Being bullied in workplace; racial trauma and rage around racism; ancestral wounds	*Pluralistic brief-therapy* (EAP) interventions relating to workplace bullying; year-long therapy on ancestral history, intergenerational trauma and rage using *transpersonal* 'ancestral circle'	Selective therapist self-disclosure; therapy to counter racism and to not be silenced; ethics of racial self-care and awareness of power and intersectionality
13. Neela (and Phil)	Fear of flying and avoidant behaviour; partner relationship tensions; complexities of being mixed heritage and 'light skin privilege'	*Integrative psychotherapy* (psychodynamic, TA, systemic, transpersonal) to explore Indian/British identity, belonging and colonial history; Parent Interview; use of cognitive behavioural therapy (CBT) apps	Extent of relational commitments; how to choose between therapeutic approaches; ethical boundarying regarding contracting and referring on

Preface

Therapy Tales aims to bring the process and practice of relational psychotherapy to life through 13 evocative and thought-provoking clinical stories. The stories are fictional, constructed accounts derived loosely from my experience as a therapist/supervisor.

Throughout the book, I emphasise how relational deficits and damage arise in relationships, so any healing needs to take place through relationships (Finlay, 2022). As Yalom's (1989, p. 91) often-quoted 'professional rosary' notes: 'It's the relationship that heals, the relationship that heals, the relationship that heals.' The connection between therapist and client, in relational therapy anyway, is the primary factor in facilitating positive change. Therapy is a relational encounter, one to which both client and therapist contribute, and which they co-create and figure out together as they progress (DeYoung, 2015).

Behind each client's story, there is another story lurking of the therapist's history and responses, and how they use themselves as part of the therapeutic relationship, as well as how they turn to their supervision relationship for support. Inevitably, therapists' worlds are involved as we draw on our own strengths and resources, sharing ourselves with clients while attending to what is in their interests (Finlay, 2022). With such intertwining, the 'between' can get complicated and challenging. We work with complex human beings who have complex needs and histories, while our own complex needs and histories as therapists are inevitably intertwined. It is important to be humble and reflexively curious about both our clients *and* us in relation to them. By encompassing the stories of both clients and therapists (and their supervisors), I've sought to highlight the fascinating richness, confusion, poignancy and power of what can happen in the relational space.

I like to use the metaphor of 'four-eyes' (cueing into the seven-eyed supervision model of Hawkins & Shohet, 2012). Here, the therapist's focus shifts constantly between thinking reflexively about: (i) the *client* – their process, history, experience; (ii) the *therapist* – their process, history, experience; (iii) what is going on *between* them relationally – transferences, impacts on each other; and (iv) the *social context* – their respective backgrounds and the current situation.

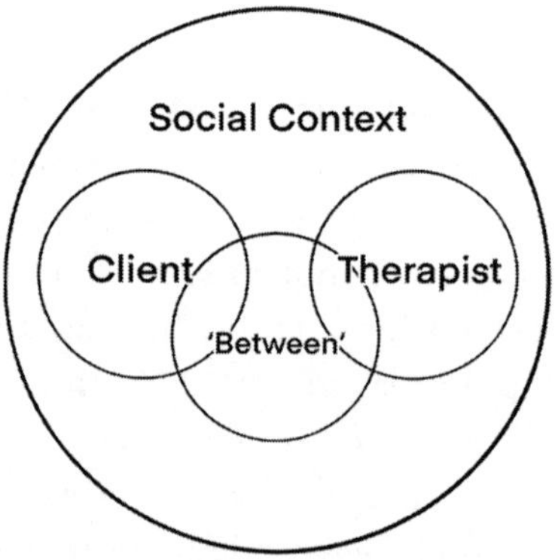

Figure 1 Four-eyes metaphor

More than involving problem-solving recipes, I view therapy in terms of *emergent processes*. In the words of Orbach (2018, p. 274), 'Therapy is a bespoke craft'. Both science and art are involved in the therapist's relational presence and intuitive clinical reasoning. There is a fascinating fluid quality to a therapist's work, with its varying levels of support/challenge, involvement/distance, containment/expression, empathy/indifference, certainty/unknowing. Therapists make deliberate choices about how and when to intervene, continuously adapting and pacing levels of 'tenderness, formality, spontaneity, emotionality, challenge, support, self-disclosure, intimacy, and directiveness' offered (Finlay, 2022, p. 3). Early in the therapeutic relationship, therapists might choose to engage more phenomenological inquiry or listen in quiet, empathic ways. A client's withdrawal might be supported and seen as self-stabilisation.

As therapy unfolds, therapists may become more energetic and inject more challenge or self-disclosure.

While I have tried to acknowledge alternative ways of working across different contexts and show both brief-therapy and long-term practice in action, my passion for working long-term on integrating 'parts of self', trauma and intergenerational legacies is inevitably foregrounded. As an integrative psychotherapist (Finlay, 2016a), I draw on various modalities to offer individualised therapy, where the therapeutic relationship can be harnessed for healing and self-discovery (Norcross & Goldfried, 2005). Across all the stories, however, I have tried to highlight alternative possibilities around how therapists might be relational.

My approach to working in this relational way fits the 'relational turn' over the last 40 years across all therapeutic approaches, where the focus has shifted from theory to examining the process of what is happening between client and therapist. In the *psychoanalytic* world (Mitchell & Aron, 1999), for example, there has been a significant move from developing insight into unconscious motivations and transferences towards exploring patterns of mutual intersubjective relating and 'cotransference' (Orange, 1995, p. 189). In the *humanistic* field, there has been a shift from exploring an individual's self-concept using a person-centred approach to focusing on here-and-now relating and growth that can be nurtured through having a real dialogic connection (Jacobs & Hycner, 2009). The relational turn is similarly seen in the 'third-wave' *cognitive behavioural* approaches (Hayes & Hofmann, 2017), which recognise that the relationship is an important mechanism of change. Then there has been the explosion of more *relational integrative* ways of working (Finlay, 2016a). Relational transactional analysis, melding psychoanalytic and humanistic relational approaches, is a case in point where the intersubjective relationship between therapist and client with an emphasis on mutual engagement, curiosity and exploration is emphasised (Fowlie & Sills, 2011). Finally, there are the various *relational-cultural* (Jordan, 2024) and *systemic* psychotherapeutic approaches (von Sydow et al., 2024), which take more constructivist and social constructionist angles, embracing layers of relationships (family, community, society).

In other words, there are diverse routes towards being relational. Relational therapy is not owned by any one modality and there isn't just one way of 'doing' relationality. There are contrasting understandings of what relational means across theoretical approaches. Therapists draw on different ways of being relational, even when they share the same theoretical orientation, and this is what I want to highlight in this book.

Structure of the book

The seven therapy tales in Part I foreground work with individuals' ***intrapsychic*** internal relational worlds involving embodied dialogical encounters, while the six stories in Part II apply a more explicit ***socio-cultural*** lens showing how our social worlds mesh. Of course, both elements constantly intertwine. Clients' lives are always layered and lived out in particular social contexts, and when in relationship with therapists, further dynamic layers are added. This is the basis of my four-eyes approach discussed above.

Each of my **narratives** begins with the client's first tentative engagement with therapy, typically a time of struggle to articulate needs, turmoil, shame and pain. As the therapeutic relationship deepens, client and therapist share moments of tension, conflict, contact, insight and breakthrough where important shifts might occur, often without forewarning. Eventually, the client's therapy ends, and both therapist and client need to let go.

Therapy can be overwhelmingly intense; it can be painful, puzzling and inchoate – for both therapist and client. As Adams (2023) so rightly pointed out in her *Myth of the Untroubled Therapist*, we can sometimes get it wrong, feel unsure, get stuck or feel overwhelmed with (dis-)stress, shame, rage, disgust and/or hopelessness. In the stories that follow, while I try to show reasonably effective therapy, the therapists are not perfect. They all have some uncertainties and vulnerabilities, and the limitations of their therapy are highlighted. Specifically, I emphasise a little of the **emotional labour** and emotional honesty that Shah (2023) generously gives as he highlights the torment therapists experience as we stumble into our psychotherapeutic encounters. We are routinely confronted by impossible choices and profound dilemmas, along with the challenge of sitting with another's pain. They tap on our heartstrings (Orbach, 2018). Our uncomfortable, sometimes disowned, processes are inevitably entangled – something that can both derail and support the therapeutic process. And therapy can also be intensely evocative and nourishing for *both* client and therapist.

In addition to weaving therapy tales, I've tried to offer a range of **practical applications** of relational empirically supported interventions. Here, numerous techniques and resources are suggested, including ideas for wording specific interventions (illustrated in passages containing explicit dialogue). Italics are used for emphasis and to highlight concepts or phrases related to the therapeutic approach or issues of concern. Bold is used to highlight key discussion points.

I also explicitly cue into **topical issues** around gender/sexuality, intersectionality, transgenerational trauma, neurodiversity, anti-oppressive practice and the use of technology. Each therapy tale touches on at least some of these themes – not out of political correctness, but because the way our socio-cultural worlds intertwine and collide is intensely relevant; context matters.

Concluding each story, I transition to a more academic register, offering **reflections** that highlight pertinent relational processes and ethical and evidence-based elements. I aim to show how practice depends on the situation and the therapist's chosen modality/approach (another therapist, in a different context, could well take the therapy in different directions). The point is to recognise there are debates around what effective relational therapy involves and how healing takes place. Often, we won't really know what is happening or how we may have helped our clients. We 'have to learn to live comfortably with mystery' as we accompany them on their journeys of 'self-discovery' (Yalom, 2015, p. 210).

As someone who prizes relational dialogue, I do not believe there is one correct way of doing therapy – a point highlighted by **common factors** research (Wampold & Imel, 2015), which demonstrates that competing approaches can be equally effective. However, my stories essentially embrace relational and integrative ways of working (sometimes in unspecified ways). These reflect favoured contemporary approaches to counselling and psychotherapy (and my own partiality), inspired by key writers in the field, namely DeYoung (2015, 2022), Erskine (2015), Gilbert & Evans (2000), Mitchell and Aron (1999), Orbach (2018) and Yalom (2001), among others.

Part 1

Intrapsychic relational worlds and embodied dialogue

Introduction to Part I

All seven chapters in this first part foreground the richly populated, poignant nature of people's intra- and intersubjective relational worlds. When clients embark on therapy, they bring with them an intricate mesh of internalised relationships, including ones deeply rooted in their past, along with different parts of themselves, such as their 'vulnerable child self' or 'confident professional part'.

DeYoung (2015, p. 2) captures the teeming internal world of the solitary client thus:

> When a client tells you a story as if there were no other people in it – last night he was desperately trying to finish a project without falling into his private pitfalls of perfectionism and procrastination – you know how thickly populated that scene really is. You know that just out of his awareness, there's how hard it is to please his father, and how his mother is on another planet, no help at all, and how his older sister can do whatever she sets her mind to. You keep the relational story in mind. It's as true for him today as it was 20 years ago, though different actors (a boss, a wife, a colleague) may be playing the main characters.

Just as the client carries multiple 'people' into the therapy room, so too does the therapist, and the clamour is intensified as the selves interact. In this, as DeYoung expresses it, 'thickly populated' encounter, who exactly is talking to whom?

As the intrapsychic worlds of client and therapist collide, interpretative understandings are born within the co-created embodied dynamic *dialogical encounter*, and this is what I try to highlight in the tales that follow. The relational component in therapy is thus made up of the teeming *intra-* and *inter*subjective mix of what happens as client and therapist connect and mutually influence each other (Mitchell & Aron, 1999). If a client is angry and attacks a therapist, the relational therapist tries to recognise what the client might be experiencing – being with them in that place, rather than retaliating, rescuing or falling into rote (disembodied) care-taking, responding not reacting. Then, the therapist's role is to invite exploration of what might be being co-created. Did the client's anger get triggered, for example, by the therapist withdrawing or becoming critical? What is happening in the 'between'?

Chapter 1 – Cally: Performance anxiety fuelled by chronic shame

Cally is a 23-year-old trainee on a psychotherapeutic counselling course. She is struggling with shame, performance anxiety and the stress of learning and deadlines. As part of her three-year diploma course, she is required to have ongoing, long-term therapy, and over time, she develops a deep relationship with her therapist, Tamara.

Tamara is four years older than Cally and qualified just two years previously. The model she has trained in (and thus favours) is attachment-based *transactional analysis* (TA). Unknown to Cally, Tamara has to work hard from the beginning of their relationship to contain her *concordant countertransference.* She, too, struggles with shame and performance tensions, and finds herself resonating with Cally's emotional state, raising questions about whose process is actually being worked on. Tamara turns to her supervisor, Dan, a hugely experienced practitioner, and leans heavily on him to help contain her vulnerability.

This chapter recounts and explores two intertwined stories of learning to 'tame the shame'. Both Cally and Tamara find significant healing through the therapeutic *relational home* (Finlay & Hewitt Evans, 2022) they discover in therapy and supervision, respectively.

At the end of the chapter, a reflective discussion explores the nature of *attachment-based* TA and the evidence base around the power of the **therapeutic relationship**. A final section explores some research on **working therapeutically with shame**. At stake is a particular question: Can a vulnerable, relatively inexperienced, insecure therapist still provide a secure base and a safe haven for their client?

Cally's story

Cally's ever-present struggle with feeling inadequate has been exacerbated by the demands of her counselling training course and the fact that her parents are both critical of and disappointed in her for not choosing a more academic, prestigious qualification. Feeling so flawed, she is keen to work on herself through the personal therapy she is required to have for her course.

Finding a focus and rhythm

'I want to use my therapy well to really learn,' Cally announces in her first therapy session. Tamara is delighted to hear this. Too often, in her experience, trainees seem half-hearted about their commitment to mandatory therapy. What Tamara initially misses is the depth of Cally's performance anxiety, where she is intensely afraid of being negatively judged, resulting in her overworking.

They contract a pattern of using the first 45 minutes of each therapy session to explore Cally's world, and their last 15 minutes to discuss relevant theory and applications of a relational approach. In the first few sessions, Tamara finds herself teaching polyvagal theory and how to regulate one's nervous system. She finds it hard to hold to their agreed-upon boundaries and is aware of Cally dutifully taking notes, as if eager to present herself as a 'good', if palpably anxious, student.

Discussing this in supervision, Tamara, to her chagrin, realises that she had been 'seduced' into being teacher rather than therapist. Her supervisor, Dan, is helpfully curious rather than critical.

'Fascinating. That sounds like a powerful process has pulled you, quickly and firmly, into teaching her.' He smiles. 'What do you think is going on between the two of you here? What part of this belongs to her; what belongs to you?'

Together, they use supervision to recognise the co-creation involved. Tamara acknowledges that she feels more comfortable talking theory; just two years qualified, she has a handle on theory but is less confident about applying it in practice. She surmises that

Cally, too, may feel easier talking theory rather than exploring her own anxiety. She also recognises the seductive power of a responsive, admiring student who hangs onto every word she speaks; it makes her feel valued and important. Such affirmations are a potent antidote to her own 'imposter syndrome'.

To Tamara's relief, Dan reassures her breezily that most new therapists feel this. A younger, vulnerable part of her expected Dan to be critical because she was 'not doing proper therapy', and she is grateful for his understanding. Her positive father-figure transference grows.

Simultaneously, Dan wonders if Tamara's retreat into theory suggests a pattern of avoidance. If so, what might she be avoiding – her emotions or intimacy in relationship? He shares these musings with Tamara, indicating that something *more* is going on for Cally, too. Perhaps they both find a retreat into theory stabilising – a defence mechanism to avoid uncomfortable emotions.

When Tamara starts to explore with Cally how and why they have fallen into head-level theory discussions, Cally's shame looms large. Cheeks flushed with embarrassment, she earnestly apologises for her 'mistake'. This opens space for Tamara to emphasise their *joint* process. Cally accepts this construct with uncertain relief. They move on to discuss how Cally often feels criticised and 'wrong'. Modelling on Dan, Tamara encourages Cally to put aside her self-abasement and be curious about the process to help Cally get some distance from her anxiety. How and why might they have co-created it? How does it relate to the way they are outside the therapy?

Their next few therapy sessions focus on Cally's performance anxiety and how it sometimes results in dissociation (her vagal 'shutdown'). Exploring what happens to her, they review the anxiety management and mindfulness techniques Cally is learning about in her course. Gamely, she resolves to test them out over the coming weeks.

They also wonder what might constitute the origins and triggers of Cally's chronic shame. Cally recounts how, throughout her life, she has felt pressure to succeed academically. An only child, she has never felt clever enough for her academically successful parents: a father who speaks seven languages and a mother who has penned several best-selling novels. She tells of how they would get on her 'case' if she failed to achieve top marks at school. Every assignment/presentation for her counselling course involves days of anxious preparation and sleepless nights.

'They are not impressed with my decision to become a counsellor, of course,' Cally says. 'Perhaps my failing will be for the best. They wanted me to be a psychologist, to get a doctorate, because that would have had more status. For them, of course, not for me. I chose this diploma course because it felt more human and less academic.'

'But, you want to do well in your coursework, don't you?' Tamara asks. 'It doesn't sound as though failure is an option in your family.' Tamara subtly acknowledges her own familiarity with the pressures and shame of studying. But she does so without revealing how much Cally's history resonates with her own childhood story and insecure attachment style (and difficulties with intimacy, trust and emotional regulation). She, too, was expected to excel in her studies, and she carries her parents' critical messages in her head constantly. At home, she was the youngest of five siblings, and she had always felt herself to be the 'dunce', despite obtaining many school prizes and a Master's degree in psychotherapy.

Cally now shares how stressed she has become with looming assignment deadlines. Her hands begin to tremble; tearing up, she shamefully admits that she hasn't even started to work on an essay due after the coming weekend. 'Somehow, I'm blocked,' she states. 'Every time I sit down to write, I go blank. I do everything I can to avoid studying. I even spring-cleaned my flat yesterday!'

'What's the essay on? Can I help?' As Tamara learns more about the assignment, she offers ideas on how Cally might structure her essay and get over her writer's block. She shares with Cally some essay-writing techniques that she has successfully used herself. Once again, Tamara finds herself in teaching mode. It is only when she is writing up her notes after the session that she realises what had happened. Adopting an academic stance was a helpful strategy to contain Cally's immediate shakes and tears. But was it also an unhelpful deflection that colluded with Cally's avoidance?

Making links in supervision

Although anxious about exposing her 'failure', Tamara pushes herself to book an extra supervision session and finds the courage to come clean about her 'mistakes'. She tears up when Dan puts her at ease and invites more self-compassion into the room. 'Instead of seeing your missteps as mistakes, be reflexive about how you might be caught up in a *process*,' he suggests.

Exploring what might be happening for both Cally and herself, Tamara is disconcerted to realise that her problem-solving approach may have fuelled, rather than eased, Cally's shame. Has she stepped into doing precisely what Cally's pushy, narcissistic mother would have done in a weird transference?

In response to Tamara's rueful, 'Oh, I've really messed up, haven't I?' Dan again offers some supportive words: 'Maybe this rescuing is another example of being pulled into enacting some dynamic – perhaps one involving projective identification where you became Cally's mother.'

They discuss how shame and self-criticism can lead therapists to direct their energy and attention inward, towards themselves, rather than outward, towards their clients, thereby missing opportunities to hear the client's concerns. Dan emphasises the importance of staying present when working with a client's shame and of modelling ways to face it. He explains how chronic shame fuels a sense of emotional dysregulation, and how it can arise in the presence of a dysregulating other. He then laughs, noting that he, too, has dropped into teaching Tamara, and suggests this may be part of a 'parallel process'. Tamara's own shame about teaching Cally is eased a further notch.

In the next therapy session, Tamara asks Cally how the essay writing went. Cally moodily admits that she had failed to get her assignment in: 'I had all weekend and just self-sabotaged.' She hangs her head with the ignominy of it. At this point, she clams up, and Tamara is concerned that their easy relationship seems more stilted. When she tries to find out what is going on, Cally shrugs and says she is 'having a bad day'. Tamara continues her gentle probing, but to no avail.

In the next session, Cally talks about things happening on her course but in an unengaged, unemotional way. Eventually, Cally's withdrawal speaks loudly enough for Tamara to comment on it explicitly. She asks if Cally is angry with her – perhaps for contributing to her not handing in the assignment. Initially, Cally denies feeling angry. But later on, she admits that she felt Tamara had been critical of her and had offered advice that suggested a lack of belief in Cally's ability to work it out. Some trust had been broken.

Tamara, for her part, is horrified that her attempt to support was received as shaming. She swallows her own shame and, in line with Dan's advice, strives to stay present to Cally's. Cally starts to express and explore her mixed responses more deeply.

At the end of the first year of the therapy, their alliance feels mostly repaired, if shadowed by mutual wariness. Tamara encourages Cally to own, non-judgementally, how she feels both bruised and wary while also trying to apply this advice to herself.

Nurturing an Integrating Adult

Over time, their connection and mutual attachment grow. Cally's trust deepens as she continues to share deeply personal information, saying that Tamara is the first person to have truly seen and accepted her for who she is. Cally blushes when she suddenly admits in one session that she wants her therapy with Tamara to go on 'for ever'.

Working explicitly through the lens of attachment theory, they recognise how, together, Tamara and the therapy have become a secure base for Cally: a reliable foundation from which to explore her experiences, thoughts and feelings safely and without fear of judgement or rejection. Tamara has also become a safe haven to return to when Cally feels overwhelmed or stressed. Somehow, therapy is helping her regulate her emotions.

Recognising the lurking danger of Cally becoming unduly dependent on Tamara, the two of them also develop ways for Cally to self-regulate and support herself when she feels anxious and dissociates. Rather than being didactic, Tamara nudges Cally to apply her mindfulness techniques with self-compassion and then report back.

In one session, inspired by Dan's suggestions, Tamara invites Cally to lay out toy objects and choose those that represent different aspects of herself. She selects a dragon to represent her internalised Critical Parent, a foal to represent her 'student part', some cotton wool to represent her 'dissociated self', a cracked, misshapen stone that is her 'shame', and a tearful baby figurine who is the anxious, vulnerable 'Adapted Child' self.

Leaning into TA theory, they also explore how quickly Cally can get caught up in *drama triangle dynamics*. Specifically, Cally and Tamara note how Cally goes into a 'victim' stance and how this can elicit others' movements towards becoming demeaning '**p**ersecutors' (like her parents) or disempowering '**r**escuers' (the position Tamara had inadvertently fallen into). Cally also learns how she enacts these dynamics internally, by persecuting her unwanted, insecure parts with her internalised Critical Parents. Together, Cally and Tamara explore ways Cally can engage a healthier triangle of holding her '**p**ower', being '**v**ulnerable' and '**r**eaching out'. By recognising that her insecure parts don't need further rejection, she learns to embrace them.

As Cally comes to know these different parts, she and Tamara look at ways to nurture a new 'Integrating Adult' (that holds and supports the different, disparate parts). They take opportunities to spot moments Cally might marshal this cohesive part of her here-and-now thinking-feeling-experiencing self – one that is free of contaminations from old Parent and Child scripts. Crucially, Cally learns that while she sometimes *thinks* she is in her Adult ego state, it is actually one contaminated by Child insecurities. In one session, for example, Cally describes receiving feedback from her course tutor on a presentation. While initially she'd thought she had reacted professionally, she later realised that she had heard only criticisms and had overlooked the tutor's appreciative comments. This proves a good example of how her belief that she is 'not good enough' shows up repeatedly, along with her tendency to collect data to support this belief while blocking out any balancing 'strokes'.

Over time, they continue to process Cally's chronic shame, where she doesn't just believe she has done something bad, she believes she *is* bad. The two of them discuss the disabling impact of this shame, particularly in the context of her ongoing studies. Tamara shares her memories of the shame she experienced during her training, and this allows them to identify similarities and differences in their process. While Cally's shame emerges mostly in her interactions with her course tutor (authority), Tamara's tends to surface in group contexts ('sibling' rivalries). They both undertake to read DeYoung's (2022) book *Understanding and Treating Chronic*

Shame (recommended by Dan) and compare their emerging understandings. Invoking their adopted mantra, 'name-claim-tame the shame', they laugh together about fun ways to befriend their respective forms of shame.

After almost four years, therapy is coming to an end. Cally feels that her Integrating Adult is strong and that she is more capable of emotional self-regulation. Both agree that it's time for Cally to let Tamara go. Although sad about this moment of parting, Tamara recognises the importance of being fully present with the ending, rather than avoiding it. While she will miss Cally, she knows this is the time to celebrate Cally's growth and let her go with grace.

Their ending session involves tears on both sides as they express mutual appreciation, exchange small gifts and hug goodbye. Cally is clear that she will carry Tamara with her for the rest of her life. What she doesn't know is that Tamara, who has been hit painfully by their ending, is going to carry Cally within her, too.

Later, Tamara acknowledges to Dan how important Cally has been to her – both professionally and personally. In professional terms, Tamara has grown hugely as a therapist through her work with Cally. With Dan's support, she has gained the ability to understand and handle powerful and challenging unconscious countertransferential processes. At the personal level, supporting Cally has helped Tamara with her own shame – something her own training hadn't really touched. She also admits to Dan that, somehow, Cally became the 'little sister' she had always wanted, and she rues the fact that this little sister has now departed from her life. It hurts that she may never know how Cally fares in the years ahead. Perhaps one day there will be a chance encounter at a professional conference…?

Reflecting on relational processes

Tamara's *attachment-based*, transactional analytic relational approach promoted a focus on the dynamic parts of Cally's self and her capacity to engage in psychological games such as the drama triangle (Karpman, 2014). Through Tamara's compassionate empathy, Cally gained awareness of her insecure attachment issues and tensions arising from her experience of critical, demanding parents. She learnt ways to manage her chronic shame (DeYoung, 2022) and nurture her Integrating Adult (Finlay, 2016b).

Their commitment to a **relational approach** was highlighted by their mutual disclosures, shared warmth/love, and readiness to discuss their therapeutic relationship and process explicitly. Both of them viewed the therapeutic relationship as the vehicle for change (Yalom, 2001; Mitchell, 1988).

However, Tamara's relative inexperience as a therapist needs acknowledgement. Of a similar age to Cally, she found herself experiencing a *concordant countertransference* identification (Racker, 1957) where she mirrored Cally's emotions. Here, both Cally and Tamara entered therapy with shame scripts and insecure attachment histories. Relational psychoanalyst Mitchell (1988) considers such countertransference as an inevitable and valuable product of intersubjectivity in the analytic relationship.

Little (2013) examined how to work through such countertransferences using a relational TA approach. He recommended looking beyond transference as a repetition of clients' patterns of relating to significant others from the past. He, instead, advises therapists to view transferences as showing how parts of the self and 'self-objects' (one's subjective experience of a relationship and its functions for the self) are enacted in the therapeutic relationship. Subjectivity – of both client and therapist – is thus implicated in this dynamic.

A key question arises from this intersubjective cotransferential process (Orange, 1995). To what extent can an insecure, possibly vulnerable, attachment-based therapist offer a **secure base** and **safe haven** for their client? Here, research suggests that once therapists can understand and regulate their own emotions, they are better equipped to build a relationship of mutual trust with clients, regardless of their own attachment security (Heinonen & Nissen-Lie, 2020).

In this story, Tamara made several missteps, particularly getting caught up in her own shame and transactional dynamics, causing her to misattune to Cally. However, this did not diminish the quality and impact of the therapy, nor did it compromise the relational depth and attachment they were able to achieve over their four-year therapy relationship. One could say that it was Tamara's humanness and imperfections, along with her readiness to face her own shame within the relational process that enabled both to heal.

The academically grounded reflections below consider the pivotal nature of the *therapeutic relationship* and the evidence base around *working therapeutically with shame.*

Therapeutic relationship

The relationship between Cally and Tamara was key to the effectiveness of Cally's therapy, and robust evidence supports this (Norcross & Lambert, 2019).

Research reaching back several decades confirms the key role played by **relational factors** (Cooper, 2008; Yalom, 1989) and how the *working alliance* often predicts therapy outcomes (Norcross, 2011; Norcross & Karpiak, 2017). The conclusion from 16 meta-analytic studies on aspects of the therapy relationship conducted by the American Psychological Association (APA) is that relationship factors, such as agreed therapy goals, getting client feedback throughout the course of treatment and repairing ruptures, are as crucial to positive outcomes as using the right therapy method (Norcross & Wampold, 2019).

Could human and relational factors be more important than theories and techniques? Writing from a developmental-relational integrative psychotherapy perspective, Erskine et al. (1999) recognise **inquiry**, **attunement** and **involvement** as significant components that nurture a client's growth. The literature also highlights the importance of the therapist's ability to hold a client safe and contain their process (Erskine, 2015; Finlay, 2022).

Another branch of relevant research inquiry is the humanistic, person-centred **relational depth** work of Mearns & Cooper (2005) and Knox et al. (2013). This concept refers to the profound mutual human connectedness that can emerge in therapy, a sense of affinity that enables the client to feel sufficiently safe to delve deeply into their experiences. In such moments, therapists respond from their own humanity, let go, and in the flow reflexively mine their own depths. This way of working emphasises the quality of the relationship between therapist and client based on principles like empathy, respect and partnership. The relationship itself is considered a key factor in achieving positive outcomes, with the individual seen as an equal partner in their own care and decisions. At the same time, they will remain aware that too much mutual self-disclosure may hinder client self-exploration (McMillan & McLeod, 2006).

There are certain commonalities here with the concept of therapy as a **relational home** (Finlay & Hewitt Evans, 2022). The metaphorical idea of relational home signifies a place of safety, shelter, groundedness, rootedness, familiarity, comfort, intimacy and ease. This is the 'secure base' and 'safe haven' underlined in Bowlby's (1988) theories.

Drawing on different literature, therapeutic relationships are also seen to potentially offer supportive social connections, helping clients regulate their nervous system (via their ventral vagal system). Here, interconnections between **neuroscience** and psychotherapy highlight brain-body-mind intertwinings, including how neurobiology underpins attachment theory, relationship and human empathy, along with offering neuroimaging evidence about the effectiveness of psychotherapeutic treatment. This research has spawned developments in mindfulness and nervous system mapping, as well as body-based approaches to trauma. Of particular significance is the work of Dana (2018), building on the polyvagal theory developed by Porges (2011). Dana points to how, in response to trauma, clients may move into fight/flight (hyperarousal) or shutdown/freeze (hypo-arousal) and how they may be helped to find a greater sense of balance, safety and social engagement.

Working therapeutically with shame

Shame is a painfully self-conscious emotional experience where one experiences judgement and unexpected or unwanted exposure by others, combined with profound internal, negative self-evaluations. There is a sense of being fundamentally flawed, deficient and defective (Bradshaw, 1988; DeYoung, 2022). In the therapy context, both the client's and therapist's shame are figural. Therapist shame arises when there is a felt threat to their sense of identity and they fear being exposed as an 'imposter'.

That both Cally and Tamara struggled with their shame and **insecure attachment styles** is significant. Research demonstrates that early attachment experiences can affect an individual's vulnerability to shame and their coping strategies for managing it. Attachment theory argues that *insecure* attachment amplifies shame-proneness while *secure* attachment protects against shame-proneness (Mitchell, 1988). Individuals with insecure (mainly preoccupied, anxious) attachment styles often struggle with self-esteem, problematic relationships and emotional regulation, making them more vulnerable to experiencing shame in relationships due to anxieties about being loved or accepted (Sedighimornani et al., 2020). Developments in interpersonal neurobiology confirm the significance early attachment has for the development of the human brain (Schore, 2019; Siegel, 2020).

Drawing on this research, Park and Shields (2023) recommend that therapists nurture their therapeutic skills in empathically receiving and expressing non-verbal communication and develop their ability to regulate their own emotions, which will help the client do the same. When relational ruptures are repaired, as was the case with Cally and Tamara, the therapeutic relationship can become a **corrective attachment experience**, with the potential to heal repeated misattunement that may have contributed to shame-proneness. Significantly, Tamara's relationship with Dan modelled some important processes that helped with the shame, including seeing Dan laugh when he caught himself getting caught up in the process. As DeYoung (2022) notes, *playfulness* is a helpful ingredient for overcoming shame.

There is also an interesting pool of literature on **trainees' experiences of shame** (Hauser, 2016). Research suggests that trainees often struggle to manage their insecurities, given the understandable anxieties associated with becoming therapists (Rønnestad & Skovholt, 2003). Findings emphasise that personal interpersonal experiences (in childhood *and* adulthood) and professional experiences of interacting with clients and colleagues are significant sources of influence on professional development (whether shame or confidence is elicited).

Importantly, research emphasises that shame and self-criticism have a negative impact on trainees' therapeutic work, as they can deflect attention from their clients onto themselves. However, self-compassion or compassion from others can help therapists counteract negative feelings and promote greater resilience, wellbeing and clinical effectiveness. For supervisors and training schools, the message is that more needs to be done to incorporate lessons around managing shame – both for trainee therapists themselves and for those they work with (Karris & Kim, 2022).

Conclusion

In this therapy tale, both Cally and Tamara struggled with their (historic and current) *chronic shame* (DeYoung, 2022). The parallels between their respective experiences were palpably present, with shame threatening to derail their attachments and relationships.

Cally's long-term *attachment-based transactional analytic therapy* with Tamara helped her focus on – and to an extent overcome – the performance anxieties and shame amplified by her counselling training.

For her part, Tamara found herself falling into various traps. The lapses in her attunement, which involved her rescuing, being the 'expert', and over-identifying with Cally's shame, were potentially counterproductive. It was important for her to separate out what belonged to her and what belonged to Cally. Tamara laboured to manage her countertransference (Shah, 2023). She used her relational supervision with Dan well to help her stay present and face her shame. Her positive transference and the therapeutic element in their supervision was necessary to help her unravel herself from undue confluence with Cally.

Arguably, it was her preparedness to own her human vulnerabilities – and use these in the service of Cally's development – that ensured an authentic therapeutic relationship and strengthened the quality of the therapy.

This chapter has highlighted a key understanding of relational work – namely, that as psychological issues such as shame arise in relationships, healing similarly needs to take place through relationship (Mitchell, 1988; Finlay, 2025). In this story, the dyads of Cally's therapy with Tamara, and Tamara's supervision with Dan, constitute *relational homes* – safe places to be seen, accepted and affirmed. In such protective spaces, both Cally and Tamara learnt to regulate their vulnerabilities, tame the shame and achieve some measure of relational healing.

Discussion questions

1. In what ways might the therapist's own attachment style influence the therapeutic alliance and client outcomes?
2. Note the numerous times when Tamara self-disclosed and held back from self-disclosure. To what extent do you agree with her choices, and why?
3. The horizon of loss when ending therapy can present a challenge for both client and therapist. Explain.

Chapter 2 – Richard: To live or die?

Richard, a 60-year-old man who for many years cared for his ailing mother, finds himself feeling depressed and suicidal two years after her death. He is admitted to a private rehabilitation hospital, where he is treated by a multidisciplinary team of professionals, first as an inpatient for six weeks, then as an outpatient for another three months. On the team is Tracy, a counselling psychologist, who offers Richard *interpersonal psychotherapy* (IPT) – an empirically validated, structured, time-limited therapy. The team engages in a comprehensive assessment, and care is taken to evolve a psychological formulation of Richard's mental state and treatment recommendations.

For Richard, the primary challenge is to decide whether to live or die. He also needs to find ways to reframe his past relationships towards nourishing new ones.

Tracy also confronts a challenge: that of working relationally with Richard as part of a team that adheres to a medical model orientation, which favours evidence-based protocols for the management of depression. This is not her preferred way of working, but having newly moved to the area, this job seems to offer much towards expanding her continuing professional development. So, she compromises by injecting a *relational-social* orientation that ensures a dual focus on Richard's intrapsychic-relational world and his community-social roles.

The more academic reflection section of this chapter considers the extent Richard's therapy can be seen as **relational practice** and the challenge of **countering formulaic medical model** practice.

Richard's story

At the weekly ward round, the multidisciplinary team learns that Richard has been admitted with a diagnosis of 'major depressive disorder following a serious suicide attempt'. He had been the sole carer of his wheelchair-bound mother with multiple sclerosis, who died two years ago. Her death has left him isolated, without any other friends or family, and without structure or meaning to his day. The team plans a six-week admission, gradually moving to day-patient status over three months.

The initial team strategy involves a comprehensive assessment process, which includes applying a battery of standardised assessment scales. A range of therapies is then offered, including medication, ward activities, art therapy and exercise therapy, plus supportive group therapy and social skills training with an occupational therapist.

The (newly appointed) counselling psychologist, Tracy, engages *interpersonal psychotherapy* with Richard. The focus of this therapy is on how relationships affect mental health, particularly depression. The therapy addresses issues such as grief, role transitions and interpersonal issues to enhance social functioning and reduce symptoms of depression.

Assessment and formulation

In the first couple of weeks following Richard's admission, the psychiatrists and nurses use a range of standardised assessments. These include the *Beck Depression Inventory* (to measure characteristic attitudes and symptoms of depression); the *Beck Scale for Suicide Ideation* (BSI) (a tool to evaluate suicidal thinking and help identify suicide risk levels); the *Hamilton Rating Scale for Depression* (HAM-D) (a clinician-administered scale used to assess the severity of depression); and the *Patient Health Questionnaire* (PHQ) (a self-administered scale that reflects the DSM-5 criteria for depressive disorder).

As she receives the results of these assessments, Tracy is concerned at the degree to which the medical model is followed in the unit, led by the consultant psychiatrist. At the next ward round, she feels uncomfortable being asked to join the formal assessment process by implementing the *interpersonal inventory* (a structured assessment tool used to explore a patient's current and past relationships, identifying potential problem areas and goals for therapy) as the basis for her psychological formulation. Reluctant to follow the practice of the psychologist who was previously in post, Tracy plucks up her courage to take a stand and says that she would prefer to postpone any formal assessment at this stage and simply begin her therapy with Richard with regular IPT sessions. Encouraged by what seems to be the team's acceptance of her approach, she suggests that a Power Threat Meaning Framework (PTMF) might be a useful, structured lens for formulation as an alternative to diagnosis.

Tracy eventually meets Richard during his second week at the hospital. He politely agrees to go with her to what will become their therapy room, but it takes time, as he is moving slowly. Facing him at last, she sees a withdrawn, hunched, immobile, softly spoken man staring listlessly out at the late autumnal landscape. 'I feel… like those… dead trees. Barren… devoid of life… with shrivelled leaves… decaying at the roots.' His speech is slow, with frequent pauses, and he has difficulty making eye contact. Tracy wonders if his slowness is a result of his depression or of the sedating effects of his medication (she resolves to question the team on this). She moderates her approach, slowing her speech and keeping her tone gentle.

'But the trees are not actually dead, are they, Richard? They trust in the arrival of spring when they will blossom again. I believe you will blossom, too. All the staff here hold that hope for you.'

Tracy then introduces herself more fully. She explains that she is not going to ask him about his depression, given he has already answered such questions several times over since his admission.

'I'm not complaining,' Richard eventually says in a tired tone. 'Everyone is… kind to me… kinder than I deserve.'

'Let's agree to disagree on that one – this is not about being deserving,' Tracy replies. 'I believe you've been brought low, and we need to work together to find a way to get you through this. I would like to get to know you as a person and hear your story first. Then I want to help you find a more liveable life. Will you meet with me for an hour every week for personal therapy, just the two us?'

Richard agrees to having weekly sessions – at least while he is in hospital. It strikes Tracy that, by agreeing, he's being compliant rather than actively committed. Nonetheless, she is relieved: even a lukewarm commitment acts as a 'protective factor' – an implicit acknowledgement that he is probably not intending to take his life in this period. The fact that, in hospital, he's being watched over by the nursing team offers additional protection. There is safety in being so sedated, or when a one's energy is so low. However, it is on leaving hospital and/or when energy returns, that the risk increases and more exploration of 'precipitating factors' might be needed.

In their second session, Richard appears more responsive. Although he remains hunched and his movements are still slow, Tracy decides to be more direct. 'Can we talk about your suicide attempt, Richard?' she asks, pleased that she has managed to be so compassionately direct – a skill she has been developing with supervision.

'I… shouldn't have done it. I have caused so much… bother. It's different now; I told the doctor, "I'm not going to do anything." My mother would be really… angry with me. She'd say… it was a sin against God.'

'What is *your* view?'

'Err, I don't know really. I think the Church is, err, much more… accepting these days and I know our vicar would be kind.' Richard pauses; Tracy waits, implicitly inviting him to say more. 'I used to… go to church a lot with my mother, but I stopped going after… she died… there didn't seem to be any point.'

'Your vicar sounds kind, but I'm interested in you, in your feelings. Do you still think about killing yourself?' Tracy wonders about Richard's deflection. Is he so unused to thinking about what *he* feels?

After a long pause, he admits, 'I don't, I don't… really want… to die. But, err, I do think about death often.'

Tracy explains that it's not uncommon to have thoughts about death, particularly when bereaved. She also reassures him that many people have passing thoughts about suicide or have a small part of themselves that wants to die, even when they generally want to live.

Richard's reply is thoughtful. 'I really don't want to, err, kill myself. It's more… I feel, err, I feel… I don't deserve to live.'

This starts a longer exploration of how unworthy and undeserving Richard feels. And then there is an extended silence between them. Tracy notes that Richard doesn't look uncomfortable with this withdrawal. Undecided about what to do, she tries to tune into what is happening. She experiments with mirroring Richard's bodily being by pulling herself in. She has an odd sense of blending into the background and slowly disappearing. She wonders if this is what Richard had to do in the face of his mother's powerful presence. Interestingly, in their silence, as she becomes smaller, Tracy senses Richard becoming more solid. She decides to share her embodied experience and together they experiment with what happens to him when Tracy becomes 'bigger and stronger' or 'hunches inwards'. Richard learns that he loses his sense of self unless he is given space. Together, they agree that a silence between them invites Richard to come forward, while Tracy agrees to try not to swamp Richard.

Over the next session, he tentatively describes how empty, dark and pointless his life has been since his mother died. He explains that she had been in a wheelchair for 20 years with her multiple sclerosis and had required much practical care, which she would only accept from him. He tells of how his mother had ruled him all his life; it had always just been the two of them in their family home. Now he wonders if he could have offered better care, and maybe it was his fault she died.

Tracy is somewhat shocked to hear that he had never been separated from his mother overnight except for a few hospital admissions. 'How about university or school trips? How about relationships outside the home?' she enquires, trying to communicate interest rather than judgement. Aware of having to curb some irritation at Richard's passivity, she pushes her compassionate voice to the fore.

Richard hangs his head and explains that, since school, he has never really had any friends. He had wanted to attend university, but his mother had insisted he do an online degree instead.

'So, your mother was always the centre of your life?' Richard nods, sighing. 'She feels very big in her presence even here, now. Can we make more space for you? I'm hearing you say that you're no longer going to church. Is there anything that you do just for you?'

Richard is taken aback. 'Well, err… I've always worked. For the last 10 years I've been with a big international legal firm as an online legal consultant. Mostly, I proofread and edit legal documents to ensure their accuracy and clarity. I have an eye for detail. I'm diligent,' he adds modestly. 'My mother never really knew what I did. She would, err, disparage me, saying that I was useless. If I worked too long, she'd tell me to quit playing with my computer and do some proper work or attend to her in some way. So, I would work around her, mainly when she was sleeping. She slept a lot, which helped.'

Without hearing details of their life together over the decades, Tracy intuits that the weight of his mother's dominance (if not active abuse) has left deep scars. Yet, without his mother, Richard appears lost and purposeless; he seems trapped in a void of isolation, meaninglessness and despair. Tracy gently reflects back to Richard that it seems his empty life had become so unbearable that it led him to a dark place where he saw no way out. Hanging his head, he slowly nods.

Together, Richard and Tracy eventually agree that the focus of therapy is to help Richard find a new life separate from his mother's influence. They recognise that his particular challenges derive from his lack of relationships. The fact that he is going to be discharged in three weeks and attending as an outpatient gives more urgency to their work.

To further reinforce this understanding, Richard agrees to a formal assessment of his social situation using the structured self-report *Inventory of Interpersonal Problems-64* (IIP-64) (Horowitz et al., 2000).

Tracy first draws two concentric circles and invites Richard to write in the names of people he is connected with. The inner one represents Richard's 'intimate' support circle and the outer ring any 'close supports'. Outside the circle are more distant individuals. Richard's completed sheet has few names on it, and none in the inner circle. Outside the circles, he has noted his work colleagues, church acquaintances and the staff and patients in the hospital.

After they have discussed the quality of these different relationships, Richard and Tracy then run through further questions – for example, 'It is hard for me to be firm when I need to be [choose the closest answer]: Not at all; A little bit; Moderately; Quite a bit …'.

After completing the assessment, Tracy invites Richard back into relationship with her and to discuss his experience of the exercise itself. Has he learnt anything about himself from doing it?

'It made me see how isolated I am and how I lack confidence dealing with people.'

Addressing the identified problem areas

Richard and Tracy work together on drawing up the formal formulation report Tracy will share with her team:

> Much of Richard's current depression arises from his mother's death and the loss of a meaningful role as her sole carer and the absence of supportive social relationships. His sense of worthlessness is profound, leading him to feel that he doesn't deserve to live. However, he is committed to the therapy being offered in the hospital and his valued work as a legal consultant is an additional protective factor. Interpersonal therapy is recommended (initially as an inpatient and then as a day-patient) to help him explore his past relationship with his mother and to develop his confidence towards having more nourishing future relationships. [Extract from Tracy's report]

Over the next few sessions, Tracy helps Richard explore the depths of his hurt. Together, they chip away at his negative self-beliefs while Tracy helps him untangle the complex emotions tied to his mother's memory.

When she asks him about his childhood, he initially says that he doesn't remember much and that he only remembers his mother, as his father left when he was a baby. He seems reluctant to discuss his relationship with his mother in any real depth or detail. But slowly, over time, a picture of their toxic relationship emerges. Richard begins to recognise how many years he spent under his mother's control, believing her harsh words and feeling unworthy of love or happiness.

As she listens to Richard telling his story in his faltering way, Tracy has to remind herself to curtail her impatience (something she has been working on in her own therapy) and allow him to tell his story in his own time. As she stops herself from pushing him to open up more quickly, she is aware of feeling a huge hollowness in her abdomen. This sensation is amplified each time Richard withdraws into silence (several times each session). Tracy is at first unsure whether to let these silences continue until Richard opens up of his own accord. However, mindful of the limited time and sessions available and with encouragement from her supervisor, she learns to ask prompting questions. For example:

> 'Is it difficult to say what you're remembering and feeling now?'
>
> 'What is happening for you right now, inside you, as I say this?'
>
> 'I'm sensing you expect me to be critical and harsh.'

Together, they build a picture of Richard's tortured inner world. Acknowledging his extreme sensitivity to the slightest whiff of criticism, Richard learns to trace his shame more directly to his fault-finding mother. In one session, Tracy asks Richard to repeat his mother's disapproving words out loud – with energy – a couple of times, and he begins to see how belittling and unjust they are.

As they begin to unravel Richard's story of shame, despair and aloneness, Tracy finds her compassion for Richard growing. Part of her wants to rage at his mother – who, in her mind, is a monstrous woman. She tries not to let her anger with his mother leak out and, instead, focuses on Richard's feelings and perceptions. She acknowledges how difficult it had been for Richard to have any real warmth and contact with his mother: 'You did all you could to try to stay in this relationship by pushing down your needs and feelings and making yourself as invisible as you could. That was your gift to her – your personal sacrifice.'

Richard is stunned by this new perspective and begins to see that maybe he didn't deserve the treatment his mother had meted out after all. He begins to recognise that his own self-criticisms had become louder over the years as a way to pre-empt hers and to keep the peace. To help counterbalance the negative messages, Tracy invites him to step back and view his behaviours more compassionately.

Preparing for the end of therapy

After a few weeks of attending the hospital as a day-patient, Richard is encouraged by the team to wean himself off the support given by both staff and patients. He owns that he feels quite different now: more ready to stand on his own feet as he faces the world outside.

Richard and Tracy turn to reviewing his progress and exploring ways he might meet his future. More than simply deciding to live, he contemplates how he could live a more enriched life.

Richard notes that he has begun to feel easier around others in social situations. Importantly, he has learnt how his compulsion to retreat from the world isn't his only option and that there is a difference between being 'withdrawn' (potentially unhealthy) and being 'introverted' (more acceptable). He now recognises that he could choose something different. He and Tracy explore how he can take a more active part in the world and perhaps form some new relationships. Tracy also reinforces his hobby interests, including new home-based activities like reading and gardening. Although solitary, he finds them nourishing. As they brainstorm other possibilities, his interest builds. They discuss how he might get involved in community activities, including participating in weekly Pilates classes and joining a walking group on weekends. He also resolves to become more regularly involved with his local church (his attendance at Sunday services stopped after his mother's death). Richard also shares that he has been working on his skills to engage in small talk with others in his ward group, and he notes his growing confidence.

As he is leaving the therapy room for the last time, Richard turns to Tracy. 'Do you remember your first words to me?' He smiles at Tracy's puzzled look. 'I was looking out at those trees that had seemed so dead, and you said that you'd be holding hope that, like them, I would blossom. And, yes, I think I am like those trees after all.' He points to the cherry blossoms in full bloom outside the window. 'You know, my mother hated cherry blossoms. She said they were not native to the UK. But she was wrong, many varieties are, in fact, native. I never told her that. Anyway, I've decided that I like them and I'm going to the garden centre this weekend to buy a couple of trees to plant in my garden.'

Reflecting on relational processes

In Richard's therapy, the spotlight was on his relationship with his dominant, controlling mother, while his wellbeing was enhanced by evolving relationships – both within the hospital and in the community. The move from concentrating on Richard's internal relational world to considering the wider community relationships over the course of treatment is a logical progression that characterises much relational work (Finlay, 2025; Spinelli, 2007). The critical question at stake concerns the extent Tracy engaged *relational practice* and *countering formulaic medical model practice.*

Relational practice?

From the beginning, Tracy's relational approach was evident in her compassionate **bodily attunement** to Richard's story and what was happening between them in the silence. Throughout, she worked to contain her irritation and impatience with Richard, and anger at his 'monstrous' mother.

Her collaborative use of '**we**', as in 'we need to work together to find a way to get you through this', was a significant relational move as well as being a component of managing suicidal risk. That she subtly distanced herself and their therapy from the rest of the team's approach by inviting Richard to focus on his life story more generally, rather than on measuring symptoms of depression, amplified the idea of a shared project.

The team's focus on **suicidality** needs addressing. Of course, attention was required around whether or not Richard continued to pose a suicide risk. However, government guidelines (NHS England, 2025) emphasise that rather than relying on risk prediction (unreliable because suicidal thoughts can change quickly), practitioners need to focus on understanding the individual's situation and managing their safety. Of note is the guidlines' advice *against* using risk assessment tools or scales to predict future suicide or repetition of self-harm.

Current research from a relational perspective tends to take issue with the continuing emphasis on standardisation and defensive risk-factor-based suicide assessment. Espeland et al.

(2021, p. 9), for instance, call for a 'fundamental change in suicide prevention towards an emphasis on relational aspects'. Their qualitative research argues that while formal risk assessments may be a helpful tool, evaluations tend to simplify the situation and may ignore contextual factors, to the detriment of suicide risks. Risk assessments help to facilitate conversations about suicidality, they note, but it is the relational focus that increases the client's sense of safety and connectedness.

In this context, Tracy's direct discussion with Richard about his suicidal thoughts and wider situation is significant. Her permission-giving, non-judgemental approach is likely to have been helpful; it normalised the fact that it is not unusual to think about death (or even having a small part of oneself feel suicidal), particularly after a significant bereavement. This normalisation, combined with attention to risk, is important, while Tracy's relational approach gave her a language to be with Richard with his ambivalence, which would also have helped him feel less alone.

Tracy's priority in getting to know Richard would have helped him feel less alone. A relational approach was highlighted in their second session, as Tracy attempted to tune into Richard's bodily experience empathically and invite a discussion about what happened between them in their silence. However, the primary thrust of Tracy's relational approach lies in her use of IPT, which emphasises how current relationships and social interactions have an impact on mental health. The evidence base demonstrates the effectiveness of IPT in the treatment of depression (Bian et al., 2023). However, it is not clear that IPT has greater efficacy than other psychotherapies, including CBT.

That said, the extent to which Richard's therapy was actually relational is up for debate; it could be seen as an example of 'light-touch' (as opposed to 'deeply committed') relational work (Finlay, 2025, p.17). For one thing, despite Tracy's efforts to be collaborative, the focus of the therapy was on Richard and his spheres of relationships (Horowitz et al., 2000), rather than the therapeutic relationship per se. Tracy seems to have dwelt less with examining how she and Richard were being in relation to each other. Other more committed relational therapists might have chosen to engage this dialogic (humanistic) and/or transferential (psychodynamic) realm more. Arguably, the hospital context and the time-limited nature of the therapy may have ruled out such deeper relating.

Tracy's determination to engage a more relational approach was evident in her avoiding a focus on traditional psychiatric diagnosis. Instead, she favoured a formulation that drew on the PTMF (see Box 2.1). Her formulation seems to have drawn on this framework in recognising the oppressive power of Richard's mother and her belittling, controlling behaviour.

Box 2.1 Power Threat Meaning Framework

The PTMF (Johnstone & Boyle, 2018; Gallagher et al., 2024), developed by the British Psychological Society, focuses on understanding emotional distress and/or challenging behaviours by considering the **power dynamics** (interpersonal, economic, ideological) *and* the **individual's meanings** around their experiences.

Helpful therapy questions in this framework would involve making sense of Richard's experiences through questions like:

- 'What has happened to you?' (How is Power operating in your life?)
- 'How did it affect you?' (What kind of Threats does this pose?)
- 'What sense did you make of it?' (What is the Meaning of these situations and experiences to you?)
- 'What did you have to do to survive?' (What kinds of Threat Response are you using?) (Johnstone & Boyle, 2018, p. 9)

Countering formulaic medical model practice

Tracy works in a **medical model** cultural context where team members favour scientific, evidence-based approaches. As a member of this team, she needed to respect others' views and appreciate the place for the medical-psychiatric understandings and knowledge about the course and prognosis of mental disorders. This context offered Richard the crucial containment he was unable to give himself. The point that medication (and a biological focus) is largely effective for people with severe and enduring mental health problems is also important. For instance, the evidence shows reductions in suicide rates are correlated with higher rates of antidepressant use (Mann et al., 2023).

However, Tracy also seeks to avoid **reductionist labels** and collusion with dehumanising practices. Taking diagnostic systems and protocols too seriously may 'threaten the human, the spontaneous, the creative and uncertain nature of the therapeutic venture' (Yalom, 2001, p. 5). Tracy's values seem to mirror Yalom's, as she resisted the push to join her more medically minded colleagues and, instead, selected a relational approach from the start of therapy, prioritising relationship-building over standardised protocols. Relational-centred therapists believe that if excessive emphasis is placed on diagnosis, therapists may selectively attend to aspects that confirm the 'problem' and may pathologise certain client responses (such as grief responses or having stray thoughts about death/dying).

One way to work relationally within a medical model context is to view the multidisciplinary approach taken by the team as a whole, where combining team members' contributions allows for a more holistic **bio-psycho-social approach**. While the medical model primarily focuses on pathology and individual/psychological factors, a relational approach recognises how social determinants of health can significantly affect a person's health. This wider lens then becomes a focus for any *formulation* (a working hypothesis of what has contributed to and maintains the client's presenting problems, rather than diagnosis).

The commonly applied 5 Ps approach to **formulation** developed by Macneil et al. (2012) embraces:

1. *Presenting problem* (thoughts, feelings and behaviours that the individual finds hard to manage)

2. *Predisposing factors* (biological, environmental or personality considerations increasing the person's vulnerability)
3. *Precipitating factors* (triggers for the presenting issues)
4. *Perpetuating factors* (internal and external factors that maintain the presenting issues)
5. *Protective factors* (both internal and external resources and resiliency that help to maintain the individual's emotional health).

A greater degree of relationality can be deployed within the overall programme to ensure that the client/patient is seen as an individual who needs to be actively involved in their treatment choices and decisions. Instead of presenting the client/patient with a predetermined treatment plan, a relational approach would encourage shared decision-making: for example, discussing the pros and cons of different options and taking the patient's values and preferences into account when considering treatment options. In other words, clients/patients have the right to make informed choices about their care, and a relational approach respects their autonomy by providing them with accurate information and support in making decisions. This includes respecting their right to refuse treatment, even if it is recommended (Avasthi et al., 2022).

Taken as a whole, the combined input of all the staff offering care to Richard, including doctors (to manage medication), nurses (to hold and monitor him), the occupational therapist (to offer socialising opportunities) and Tracy (to provide psychotherapy), was crucial. The hospital context offered a holding/containing **safety-net** and safe haven to help Richard stabilise, particularly given his initial vulnerability and the risk of suicide.

Conclusion

With the help of the containing hospital support, Richard slowly and painfully clambered out of a profoundly lonely, empty, withdrawn existence, shadowed by thoughts of suicide. By the story's end, he had taken wing; a new life full of possibilities beckoned. The vital step Richard took during this journey was to relinquish the shaming wounds left by the oppressive, toxic relationship with his deceased mother. Richard decided to live, to allow himself to blossom, to *be*.

For Tracy, the principal challenge was to find a way of working relationally with Richard while being part of a multidisciplinary team embracing a medical model orientation. She found a way to fit into the team by going along with their use of a formal assessment (*Inventory of Interpersonal Problems*) and a form of therapy (*IPT*) that are both empirically validated. At the same time, she also held out for a more explicit (light-touch?) relational approach by asking for a delay in producing her psychological formulation of Richard's mental state and treatment recommendations.

While Richard's diagnosis was informative, it overlooked the broader context of a depressing life situation lacking human warmth and intimacy. Tracy's formulation focused on his avoidance and withdrawal, where his loss of purpose and role had led to his emptiness and despair. Throughout the therapy with Richard, she remained true to her relational model (guided by the PTMF and her attempt to attune to his experience bodily) to ensure his active collaboration and involvement. Their work helped to hold Richard as he transitioned from the safe haven of the hospital to moving back into his world. Together they worked to nurture supportive social networks – something we all need.

Discussion questions

1. What are the arguments for and against Tracy's move to distance herself from the team's focus on 'depression' early in the therapy?
2. If there is a requirement to engage standardised tests, what steps can a therapist take to prioritise the therapeutic relationship while ensuring reliable assessments?
3. How useful (or not) was the *formulation* that Tracy and Richard agreed, and why?

Chapter 3 – Claudia: Beneath the surface

Claudia, aged 30, embarks on 12 sessions of therapy following a miscarriage six months previously. While she understands that miscarriages are a common occurrence, she still feels in some way responsible for losing her baby and is inconsolable.

This story recounts how Claudia's initial presentation (grief around her miscarriage) becomes the starting point for a much deeper exploration of her trauma, including its relationship to painful family history. We see how much *more* may be involved in what may appear to be a clear-cut therapy story. Therapists need to take care not to inadvertently dismiss experiences or make assumptions that something is or is not a problem.

Similarly, it is important not to dismiss therapists' experiences inadvertently. Lurking behind Claudia's story, we also hear something of her therapist's – Sue's – history and how she is affected (even traumatised) by the therapy, as well as how she manages this challenge.

The reflective, evidence-based discussion following the story of Claudia's *relational gestalt therapy* emphasises the importance of **care**, including **therapist self-care**.

Claudia's story

Aggravating her grief, Claudia feels overwhelmed by a sense of guilt, but it's confusing for her. She has a sense that she is somehow responsible for her baby's death. At the same time, she worries that she is letting her husband down with her emotional overwhelm, as she 'should have moved on'.

Initial stages

In her first session with Sue, Claudia gives some basic details about her background, namely that she is married (without children), works as a dental hygienist, and generally has a supportive group of 'lovely' friends and family around her.

Claudia describes her shock when, 19 weeks into her pregnancy, she was told during her second ultrasound check-up that her foetus had probably been 'malformed' and was now dead, requiring a dilation and curettage (D&C) surgical procedure. Claudia and Sue explore what this surgery meant to Claudia. They talk about how her turbulent emotions may be partly down to the double trauma (miscarriage and surgery) as well as her disrupted hormones.

The loss of Claudia's baby becomes the focus of the next few therapy sessions. Claudia's grief still envelopes her. Sue is gently reassuring as she explains that grief takes time to be processed and that everyone's grief experience is unique. She outlines the goal of therapy in these early stages as offering Claudia a space to express the grief and have it witnessed without judgement. She reassures Claudia that she will not attempt to lessen it or find ways to reframe it. Sue also acknowledges how grief often involves both the bereavement loss and the loss of what might have been (i.e. Claudia becoming a mother). That reassures Claudia, who now accepts that it is understandable that she is currently feeling a bit 'lost-in-her-loss'.

Beyond her shock and sadness, Claudia begins to own some feelings of guilt. She wonders what she might have inadvertently done to damage her baby. Was the miscarriage a 'sign' that she is unsuited to being a mother or doesn't deserve to be one? She worries whether she will ever be able to have a child in the future and feels guilty that her relationship with her husband is suffering. She is uncertain if he is willing to go through another cycle of pregnancy with her, or if he even wants children.

With this turmoil of questions to the fore, Claudia expresses relief at having a permission-giving space to share her worries and cry freely – something she feels unable to do elsewhere: both her husband and her wider family have become impatient with her failure to 'move on'. Affirming Claudia's grief, Sue explains that it will take time to move on, given the trauma involved and that Claudia needs to do it in *her* time. At the same time, she nudges Claudia to share some of what she is processing in therapy with her husband.

Pivotal processing

In one particularly turbulent session, Claudia sobs as she connects with a sense that her lost baby is 'haunting' her. She tells of a recent nightmare where she was sifting frantically through piles of dead, malformed baby bodies to find her baby.

Sue decides to take a *gestalt* approach to analysing the dream. Gaining Claudia's consent to help process the dream, she starts by inviting Claudia to describe the dream in the first-person as if it were 'happening right now'.

Claudia talks of getting lost in a building full of corridors and how she opens a door tentatively, only to see this pile of dead baby bodies. She speaks of her desperation and panic as she sifts through it with her guilt to the fore.

Sue then invites Claudia to retell her dream sequence from the perspective of one of the babies, again speaking in the first-person. Here, Claudia expresses a sense of the baby's lostness as they call out to be found. The baby cries out, 'Why did you discard me?'

With each iteration of the dream taking on different perspectives, Sue invites Claudia to tune into the emotional tone of what is being expressed and to expand on the sensory dimensions present (e.g. sights, sounds, sensations, smells).

Finally, she invites Claudia to have a dialogue between her 'digging' self and the baby. As they process the sheer horror and meanings of this nightmare, Claudia suddenly remembers a long-buried family secret. When she was 10 years old, she had comforted her mother, who had just had an abortion. Apologising to Claudia for making it impossible for her to meet her 'younger brother', Claudia's mother made her daughter swear that she would never reveal this abortion to her father. Claudia has kept this promise to this day.

Aided by Sue's sensitive attunement, Claudia recognises how this secret has haunted, corroded and contaminated her; carrying the secret has always felt shameful and shaming. Sue offers the interpretation that Claudia might be carrying her mother's shame and guilt for her, and that some of her feelings aren't actually hers.

It takes a couple of sessions for Claudia to return to these themes and feel more grounded, integrating this new awareness.

Later stages

Through their processing, Claudia experiences mixed feelings of anger, sadness and compassion for her mother. She comes to understand that memories around her mother's shame and guilt (that she had mostly repressed), and her own grief around losing a brother (whom she had secretly named 'John'), have been triggered by her miscarriage. These are the deeper wounds lurking beneath her reactions to the miscarriage.

In their 10th session, Sue invites Claudia to engage in an enactment where they have a naming-cum-funeral service for her miscarried child, and also for 'John' and the place he has had in Claudia's life. Tearfully, Claudia agrees.

Claudia starts by lighting two candles while she whispers a message to both babies. She expresses love for her baby, whom she names 'Sara', and tells 'John' how she had always wanted a brother. She then says her goodbyes, telling both that she is sorry she won't be able to see them grow up, but that she is comforted by feeling they are now together.

Sue, for her part, finds this work on the miscarriage and abortion triggering. Though it had been challenging to stay with Claudia's weeping, she was comfortable processing Claudia's grief and anxiety about not conceiving again and becoming a mother in the future. This all felt reasonably distant to her, and she could maintain her professional boundaries. However, with the abortion material, she finds herself getting pulled in as she attunes to Claudia, and at times, she finds it hard to know if what she is feeling are her own or Claudia's feelings.

Sue is particularly affected by nightmare images of dead babies, which continue to intrude. Flashes erupt in a couple of harrowing nightmares of her own. She herself had a traumatic abortion in her teens decades ago, as had her mother before her. Sue takes these 'ghosts' within her memories to both therapy and supervision, so as not to contaminate Claudia's story (of her miscarriage and her mother's abortion) with her own (and her mother's) experience.

In the last couple of sessions, Sue and Claudia move towards ending therapy. Sue encourages Claudia to look beyond her grief towards her wider life – now and in the future. Now able to move beyond mourning, Claudia can see more clearly the impact her miscarriage is having on others, including friends who have also had miscarriages but have gone on to have successful pregnancies. Nudged by Sue, she talks with her husband, who reassures her that he is equally committed to trying again for a family. Claudia's dream of becoming a mother remains a possibility. She expresses feeling more positive and hopeful for the future.

Reflecting on relational processes

The story of Claudia's therapy illustrates an unfolding of healing that may have occurred naturally over time. However, extra relational support can be helpful towards easing more profound anxiety, depression and/or trauma that can result from miscarriage. Research (e.g. Barat et al., 2020) shows that being enabled to have a space to explore their personal miscarriage experience supports women to reflect on their loss and helps them decide when and how to move on to and deal with possible future pregnancies.

While this therapy started with a focus on the bereavement, deeper traumas emerged. Sue attuned to Claudia's wide-ranging needs and feelings of lostness-in-her-loss (B. Brown, 2021). She appears to have intuited that there was something *more* underlying Claudia's grief and she made sure there was time to go exploring with Claudia safely.

With the dream enactment, Caviglia (2021) distinguishes between three different varieties of dream work: dreams as unconscious infantile expressions, dreams as a function of thinking and mentalization, and dreams as a dialogue that can include dissociated aspects of the self. Sue chose to take the latter *relational gestalt* (rather than a psychoanalytic or cognitive) approach, which assumes that dreams hold existential messages for us while representing fragmented parts of ourselves. Unlike traditional methods that decode symbols through interpretation, the gestalt view is that everything in the dream, including other characters, inanimate objects and the atmosphere generally, is seen to express an aspect of the dreamer.

The discussion below focuses more explicitly on the relational role played by *care* and *therapist self-care*.

Care

Most, if not all, professional codes of practice emphasise the importance of therapists' **duty of care**. This means placing clients' best interests to the fore. Care starts with the therapist being fully aware of the potential power of therapy and, on that basis, ensuring an appropriate focus, ideally one that is mutually negotiated, along with an appropriate level of containment. Research (e.g. Levitt et al., 2016) confirms that therapists' care enables clients to feel safe enough in the therapy space to set aside defences (such as repressing memories) and allow themselves to be vulnerable during their therapeutic journey of self-exploration. However, if a therapist is working in a setting offering only a handful of counselling sessions, it is essential to be cautious not to delve too deeply and risk opening up a *Pandora's box*. The therapist, too, needs to be ready and able to deal with whatever might emerge.

Initially, Sue provided Claudia with a safe, **permission-giving space** in which to cry – this is the essential hospitality we ideally offer. Initially, therapy seems to have focused on Claudia's immediate grief and loss (of the baby and what might have been) and other feelings about the miscarriage. Then it was about creating a space that allows vulnerability to be freely expressed/owned without judgement (Finlay, 2019). I like Kapitan's (2003) words here:

> The guest… client comes seeking sanctuary, a safe place of protection where wounds can be carefully cleansed and healed. But, where is the sanctuary, if not fundamentally in the heart of the host or therapist who is willing to face this living encounter and courageously open to it? (2003, p. 74)

As the level of intrapsychic contact deepened in the therapeutic space, Claudia was enabled at last to acknowledge and **be present** to her momentous nightmare involving malformed babies as *Sue stayed present to it too.* By holding both Claudia and the dream safely, Sue helped Claudia connect to deeper historical trauma, which she had repressed. In the process, Claudia's less obvious grief regarding her absent brother ('John') could also find space and expression. Opening these wounds allowed Claudia to separate the grief of her miscarriage from the grief associated with family secrets, loss of a sibling and shame regarding her mother's abortion. The naming–funeral enactment allowed further acceptance and a sense of completion.

Finally, Sue enabled and validated Claudia to find solace over time, and this was helped by a **hope-filled attitude** of realistic optimism – i.e. that Claudia just needed space to process her trauma and then would be ready and face her future (Wojnar et al., 2011). In the latter stages of therapy, they transitioned from intrapsychic exploration to consider Claudia's wider support systems – an approach consistent with research recommendations.

Therapist self-care

Part of the care a therapist needs to demonstrate is therapist *self*-care. In the therapy tale narrated above, it was important that Sue's own history (in particular, the trauma surrounding her own abortion) did not contaminate Claudia's experience. At the same time, it was hardly surprising that Sue was triggered by Claudia's nightmare (given the horrific explicit images), to the extent that her own past trauma began resurfacing in the form of nightmares.

Throughout the therapy, then, Sue needed to manage her own responses. Orbach (2018) suggests the art of therapy is to hold onto clients' emotions with **curiosity** and **compassion**, long enough to make sense of them without getting taken over by them. At the same time, more than empathy, as therapists, we need to draw on our own histories as Stolorow (2014, p. 82) recommends: 'If we are to be an understanding relational home for a traumatized person, we must tolerate, even draw upon, our own existential vulnerabilities so that we can dwell unflinchingly with his or her unbearable and recurring emotional pain.'

In this sense, Sue's experience of not being sure of whether her traumatised feelings were hers or Claudia's (or Claudia's mother) is relevant, as is how she handled it. Sue had a choice about whether or not she disclosed her past to Claudia. Such a move could be seen as being ethically dubious and unnecessary. Instead, Sue opted to work through her issues in her own therapy/supervision. Rather than show herself to Claudia as a real person with her own vulnerabilities, Sue was aware of the differences separating her experience from Claudia's. While such self-disclosure might be helpful in other circumstances, **containment** of Claudia's experience seems a more helpful intervention (Finlay, 2016a); there was no need to contaminate Claudia's world with Sue's trauma – particularly given this was short-term therapy.

Drawing on psychodynamic theory, Schore (2019) argues that the mother/therapist must contain her own arousal before being able to contain the child/patient. Appropriately, Sue took her vulnerability to her own therapy and **supervision** to help her understand and manage emerging processes, including separating out what might be received from the client but actually belonged to her.

Another therapist, with a different history, will have had other issues. Simply listening to Claudia's nightmare would have been harrowing for any therapist – and especially so for a therapist who herself has been pregnant. Alternatively, a therapist with strong views against abortion might face a different challenge. All the more reason to take our feelings to supervision. It's an ethical imperative to be reflexive about such processes and use supportive opportunities (therapy, CPD, supervision) to hold and contain us (Finlay, 2019)

Conclusion

Claudia's story alerts us to the deeper disturbance – even trauma – that may lurk within apparently straightforward, though still distressing, stories. This therapy tale of grief following miscarriage highlights what can emerge in unexpected ways if space is given to enable deeper exploration. It shows that layers of trauma are inchoate and often only revealed in fragments of dreams and memories. These dreams and memories were mostly pushed down in Claudia's case, only to erupt after the miscarriage.

Both Claudia and Sue experienced the painful intrusion into their present lives of elements from the past (including intergenerational components). Both were contaminated with intrapsychic parts that feel shame and guilt. Claudia's own lost baby and miscarriage was the starting point. But what of all the other lost babies where traumatised mothers have to find a way to manage their grief, shame and/or guilt? This is the *more* that underlies clients' stories as well as the profound, powerful, emotional, even mystical, resonance that can emerge in therapy.

Both Claudia and Sue had to manage their personal histories *and* those of their mothers. They both needed a safe space to process these, particularly those emerging through their respective nightmares. Challenged by her own reactive trauma responses, Sue knew she needed to contain her own process and avoid undue self-disclosure about her own nightmares and history.

Discussion questions

1. In Claudia's case, might it have been beneficial for her and her husband to engage in couples therapy? Or do you think individual therapy was the better starting point for her?
2. How do you practise your self-care as a therapist? Is there something more you could do that would be helpful?
3. How might a therapist's past wounds or trauma be explored ethically in supervision without transgressing boundaries where the supervision tips into being therapy?

Chapter 4 – Lisa: 'Bodily doubt'

Lisa is a 61-year-old woman suffering from the effects of long COVID-19 and the loss of her previously healthy body. She feels 'depressed' and 'reduced' three years after her original illness and takes the step to seek therapy. She wonders what lies before her other than bodily ageing, forced retirement and an empty life.

Seeking an experienced, well-credentialled *existential therapist*, she approaches Michel, a middle-aged Frenchman who has been practising in the UK for 20 years. Importantly for Lisa, he has published some research into Covid experiences, while his international background adds to his appeal. They agree to have an initial contracting session with a view to having longer-term, open-ended therapy.

Lisa's story, and the discussion that follows, highlights **body therapy** and the value of attending holistically to a person's body, and the therapist's use of **boundaried self-disclosure** while maintaining ethical boundaries.

Lisa's story

There is an existential character to Lisa's struggle. How might she discover new life within the limitations of this new post-Covid body, which remains so alien, so diminished? What can be reclaimed of her previously exciting, meaningful and taken-for-granted life? Such questions concern anyone confronting dramatically reduced capacities and the destruction of valued life roles as a result of ageing, ill health or trauma.

Multiple losses

'I can't do this on my own anymore,' Lisa announces at the start of their first session. She is holding herself tightly; her voice is tired and flat, her movements stiff and slow.

Michel replies gently, 'Take your time to tell me your story.' He is also listening carefully for any possibility that Lisa may not want to live anymore.

'Thank you.' There is a pause. Then, 'I don't know where to start… And I don't know if you can help me, but I know I need help.'

Reassured by her reaching out and not wanting to be alone on her journey, Michel invites her to say more: 'So, what has brought you to this moment?'

'I think I'm probably depressed. My life feels like it has ended already; I'm living a half existence on automatic… There is no… joy, no nothing. I'm just empty, no motivation; nothing interests me.'

'I'm hearing your lack of joy and empty life. That would be enough to create depression. You said on the phone that you've had long COVID. Is this all linked?'

'Definitely,' she replies with a tired smile. She goes on to describe her debilitation, naming a host of physical symptoms: 'brain fog', fatigue, joint pain, respiratory issues and breathlessness during any physical activity. Before Covid, she explains, she was a travel journalist jet-setting round the world and staying in stylish locations. Now she is stuck at home, isolated and struggling to find the energy to get through each day.

'The contrast with your full, exciting old life and current low-energy, empty life is marked,' Michel replies. 'I can see why you don't feel you're still living.'

As Lisa is leaving at the end of their first session, she turns to Michel to ask, '*D'où venez-vous?*' [Where are you from?]

'*Vous parlez très bien français*', [You speak French well] responds Michel, impressed and taken by surprise. Seeing no need to hide this personal information, he replies in English: 'I grew up in Pau in southwestern France, near the Pyrenees mountains.'

'Oh yes, I know it well – wonderful history and culture, as well as hiking and skiing in the mountains. You must miss the stunning scenery.'

Michel sidesteps the issue of missing his native land. Instead, he brings the focus back onto Lisa by acknowledging her expertise: 'I hear your travel-writing experience.'

'Indeed, I did a two-article spread for a major woman's magazine on health spas and saunas around Pau. I spent a glorious month researching and simultaneously polishing my French.'

Despite this tantalising glimpse of Lisa's dynamic, energetic former self, Michel is aware that they are over time. He makes a mental note of this flexing of the time boundary; he will need to hold it better in future.

In the next session, Lisa is clearer about the emptiness of her current existence. 'This is no life,' she explains. 'I have just the energy to unpack my delivered groceries and do basic cooking before I crash and binge-watch mindless TV re-runs from my couch. I don't see friends, and they stopped calling me long ago. I don't have the energy for small talk and I'm no fun at dinner parties anymore, so invitations have dried up. I go days now without talking with anyone other than my cleaner. She does loads for me. Thankfully I can afford her.'

'No family or other supports?'

'Just distant cousins, but no partner, siblings or children. That's one life decision I might have got wrong. I remember talking with an old grandmother in Gambia who had had eight children. She told me they needed the extra insurance of more children to make sure some survived to take care of the old folks.' Lisa is lost momentarily in her memories.

'Do you wish you had children?' Michel probes, bringing her back.

'No – too busy enjoying my glamorous life. A husband and children would have held me back.'

'I'm hearing how your freedom and independence are fundamental to you. I can't help thinking how your limited state now must be doubly challenging.'

In the next session, Lisa and Michel continue to probe the 'death' of her old life and the emptiness of her current one.

'You've had so many losses since becoming ill, it must feel unbearable,' Michel reflects. 'Not only have you lost your old body, but also your friends, lifestyle, work, life.' When she doesn't respond, he continues: 'It's really not surprising that you feel depressed. Can we slow down here and think of the magnitude of what you have lost? More than your body and lifestyle, it's also the loss of your sense of wholeness, certainty, control, freedom to act, and the loss of your whole familiar world.'

For the first time, Lisa puts aside her tendency to deflect via witty comments. She begins to cry. 'God, I never cry. And, certainly never in front of others!'

'Therapy is a different sort of space,' replies Michel, gently smiling. 'We do and say things here we would rarely say outside. Do you think we could free this *vulnerable Lisa*? Give her the space to express herself while *strong independent Lisa* listens in? Could you handle that?'

Lisa manages a watery smile. 'As long as it's our secret.'

Bodywork

Over time, Lisa begins to recognise how difficult she finds it to be vulnerable. Slowly, her guard drops, and she manages to express her anger at 'this body that has let me down'. To emphasise this point, she strikes her legs in frustration.

Michel finds himself torn. Should he follow her anger or stay with her body? He decides to maintain the focus on her body and comments that it seems that Lisa has been battling continuously with her body ever since her Covid battle had eased. 'Is your body the enemy, *peut-être*?' [maybe]

'Yes. No. Oh… I don't know.' She shakes her head, confused. 'The fact is, I don't know this body. It's new, strange, kinda like it isn't mine anymore. It's my enemy because it controls me; I can't control it any longer.'

'These are important insights, recognising the body that you're living with is strange and challenging for you.' Michel can't help but note that this also applies to himself and his ageing, arthritic body. He redoubles his focus on Lisa, drawing her attention to her posture, noting how she's sitting tightly, seemingly tense.

'Hmmm.' She muses for a moment. 'I guess I don't want to waste my energy.'

'But I'd say it's more than that, Lisa. My sense of your body…' Michel pauses, trying to follow his intuition. 'It's like you're holding stuff in, holding your whole self together. Do you relate to that?'

'I guess so,' she acknowledges. 'I'm so stiff these days. At one time I was a graceful dancer and mover; I would swim often. Now I limp around, with all my aches and pains, and can't even walk around the block without suffering for it.'

'So, with all your aches and pains, you feel apart-from this new, post-Covid body?'

'You're right. I'm distant from it. I don't want this body – like I didn't want Covid.'

'Tell me about your actual Covid experience in more detail. You've said it was really tough for a time, but I'd like to feel it with you.'

'I didn't know if I was going to live or die. I… I couldn't breathe.' Lisa tells her story hesitantly, finding it hard to face those memories.

'I had this image in my head of the virus with those strange crowns of club-shaped, spiky tentacles that were breeding inside me, multiplying. They reminded me of the sea mines used in World War II with trigger mechanisms all over, waiting for something to bump into them. Those weapons were alive inside me, bombs that left destruction in their wake… Covid killed me. It did really… I had no way to fight back, nothing to fight with… The only fight I could attend to was to breathe, to keep breathing. I longed for blessed sleep but if I slept too long, I'd wake up gasping… A week was an eternal week with my body screaming for air… My cleaner was a darling, she'd bustle round – socially distanced, of course. Every day she managed an hour or more as her mother fetched her children. She left hot soup in a flask for me and was my lifeline. I just lay there sorry for myself and binge-watching old TV programmes. I was a spectator living a horror movie of my own. Somehow, I still haven't left it.' She mocks herself as she subsides into silence, overwhelmed again at the grim enormity of her experience.

A long, respectful pause follows as Michel waits for Lisa to rebalance herself and perhaps say more. Eventually, he finds some words. 'I can't imagine the terror of feeling that you couldn't breathe.' He pauses, wondering if this is the moment to go deeper. 'If I try to tune into those feelings, it seems like endless suffocation with odd snatches of air – like torture drownings by interrogators. Constant suffocation, constant attack. Was it something like that?'

'Yes. Exactly right! I was being suffocated, it felt like an attack – an invasion by this unseen bloody virus, which I surrendered to. But it played with me, not quite killing me and I had no way to fight back.'

'Suffocating and surrendering to an unseeable attacker. It's not you, is it?' Michel then names it. 'This was a full-blown *trauma*, Lisa – both physical and emotional – and I'd say, part of it still haunts you.'

She reflects on this new perspective. 'I hadn't thought of it as trauma, but you're right, of course. Do you know, I've tried not to think about it; but part of me is still stuck in that sickbed. I think you would say, "*Je broie du noir, j'ai l'impression de vivre dans les ténèbres, j'ai perdu le sourire*" [I'm feeling down, I feel like I'm living in darkness, I have lost my smile.]'

'Yes, that is what we'd say in French. *Tu parles très bien français. Et je me sens triste. Ton sourire qui a disparu.* [You speak French well. And I feel sad. Your smile that disappeared.] I feel so sad hearing that you've lost your smile.' By using this French expression of 'tu', Michel has moved to a more informal and intimate style of communicating with Lisa.

Michel suggests that she could well have post-traumatic stress disorder (PTSD) from her Covid experience. He is initially tempted to offer her a role in a new research study on long COVID that he is involved in. He quickly thinks better of it: the ethics involved would be tricky to navigate, and the dual relationship of being both therapist and researcher would be problematic. Instead, he decides to offer some psychoeducation. Aware of the risk that this intellectual approach may distance him from Lisa, he still decides to share this academic/theoretical part of himself. He rationalises that he is being relational by sharing an important part of himself, and anyway, she may view the information positively and find it helpful.

He asks Lisa if it's okay for him to say something about the nature of trauma. She nods and he shares something from current research around *polyvagal theory*. After explaining how survival responses to stress/threat of 'fight, flight, freeze or flop' are essentially 'natural phenomena', he tells her that the focus of current thinking is on the 'window of tolerance' that enables individuals under stress to cope with everyday life.

'This thinking is useful for us,' he says, 'because you may have gone into hypo-arousal "flop". This leaves people feeling depressed, shut down and disconnected from their lives and bodies.'

For the subsequent few sessions, Michel encourages Lisa to tune explicitly into her body and let it speak more directly.

'Why don't we slow down and see if you can sense something more within your body. When you are sitting stiffly, like now, what might your body be saying – to me, to you and to the world?'

Using the technique of *Focusing*, he invites Lisa to listen inwards to her body, sense her way into it in search of anything that calls for attention, and then speak *from* her body in the first-person. The aim, Michel explains, is to help her develop a new relationship with her body and discover how to appreciate its wisdom.

Lisa surprises them both with her body's hesitant answer: 'I… I mustn't move… I'll die if I move… I don't want to breathe and let more germs in.'

Recognising the anxiety now held in Lisa's body – the body she has sought to reject and ignore – Michel encourages her to breathe deeply: in for a count of 4 and out for a count of 6. 'Breathe to take in healing; breathe to let every cell in your body expand with the oxygen it has been deprived of,' Michel explains. 'Care for your body; give it the healing oxygen it needs. I think it wants to live.'

They practise this breathing technique together and Lisa agrees to do regular breath work exercises at home. They also explore her experience of 'bodily doubt', a philosophical concept that recognises her sense of discontinuity with her body and her loss of faith and trust in what it can do. Their project, says Michel, is to help Lisa learn to trust her body again.

Moving again

Over time, Lisa acknowledges that, contrary to her previous thinking, she actually wants to return to the 'land of living'. Together, they plan different ways to get her body moving, get it living again. Lisa plans daily exercises and weekly treatments of either massage or osteopathy. She also joins a local somatic movement class, which promotes mindful movement, breathing, body awareness and trauma release. Perhaps most healing of all, she resolves to return to swimming daily, increasing the number of lengths she does each week. Michel cautions her to take it slowly and be realistic.

Their goal is for Lisa to 'make peace with' the body that has battled Covid on her behalf and deserves credit rather than anger. She agrees. 'No more battle-against my body – instead, a new partnership.'

Michel shares some ideas from Sartre, his favourite French philosopher, about the concept of 'bodily transparency', where one's body is '*passé sous silence* – passed-by-in-silence'. 'Listen to your body, make friends with it and check in regularly to determine what this "newly-old lady" is fit for and what might prove too much for her today.' He doesn't share how severe arthritis in his knees and his resulting disability has negatively affected his own sense of potency and how ageing and Sartre's words has been on his mind.

Over the next few weeks, a visibly more contented Lisa reports progress and how her body is reacting positively to her gentle adventures. She also notes an improving capacity to focus and concentrate. Best of all, Lisa feels a growing desire to write. Michel cheerleads from the sidelines as he follows her progress. He had always wanted to encourage her to write but had held onto that thought, because the motivation had to come from her. Now he can respond spontaneously:

'*Formidable!* That's wonderful to hear. Are the germs of an idea bubbling?'

'Yeah, well, I can't travel, but I can still write. Somehow, I'd forgotten that.' She mocks herself but then softens. 'Now I've got an idea for the novel I have always had a yen to do.'

After several months, as her health and movement improve and her novel writing takes off, Lisa admits to Michel how she has missed social, and more intimate, contact. She acknowledges her need to both give and receive love.

'I'm an old woman now, of course, so you will probably think I'm past it. Would it shock you to know that I have a racy past?' Her provocative glance at Michel is distinctly flirtatious.

'Oh, you're not so old really, as you well know, and you've been growing steadily younger these last few weeks. And, for the record, I'm a man of the world, Lisa – virtually unshockable!' His eyes dance but he knows he needs to step carefully, wanting to enable Lisa to share more while retaining a professional distance.

'A century ago,' Lisa continues, 'I would have been doing the can-can on nightclub tables while my lovers drank champagne from my slippers.' Michel smiles at her evoked image and an appreciative glint in his eyes encourages more. She tells him that she has embraced many affairs as part of her enjoying bisexual polyamory.

Michel does not reveal his Christian values about monogamy and against promiscuity and how she has rather shocked him. He is sceptical about polyamory and, if pushed, might say that often such relationships reveal fears of commitment or intimacy. However, with judgement set firmly aside, he tries to stay open to this suddenly flowering Lisa. 'So, you are mourning your lost sexuality but perhaps ready to bring *Eros* back to life? Are you ready to reach out to old party friends?'

Lisa smiles, nods slowly. 'Yes, I need a reminder of who I used to be.' She pauses, then asserts with more certainty, 'My body deserves more.'

'I like hearing of your care for your body, and it's good to hear you get in touch with more of your old self. You and your body both deserve more. *Tu as fait du chemin pour arriver là où tu en es aujourd'hui.*' [You've come a long way to get to where you are today.] He checks that Lisa understands this colloquial reference..

Reflecting on relational processes

The following discussion delves into two pertinent ethical dimensions of Lisa's *existential therapy*: the evidence base for **body therapy** and therapists' use of **boundaried self-disclosure**.

Body therapy

Body therapy (also known as body-orientated psychotherapy or somatic psychology) encompasses various therapeutic practices based on polyvagal theory and/or approaches that focus on the body's sensations, movements and expressions, to promote healing/wellbeing. Therapists might introduce exercises such as breathing exercises, body scans, shaking, relaxation, humming, self-holding and dance, among others.

Acknowledging the mind-body connection, bodywork recognises how our bodies can store memories, tensions and emotions, and how these might be released and processed. Unlike traditional talk therapy, body therapy engages the individual more directly and experientially (for example, through the use of touch, movement and/or mindful breath work). Specifically, T. Brown (2025) highlights the process of 'body listening', where a therapist might direct a client's attention to parts of the body and talk directly to it. Another approach, taken by the gestalt therapist Ruella Frank (2023), involves identifying six fundamental movement patterns that babies use to connect with their environment: grasping, reaching, pulling, pushing, releasing and yielding. Her approach argues that these patterns set a template for everyday relating. Can I support myself and reach for what I want, or yield to receive you, or do I back away…?

In their systematic review and meta-analysis of research on the effectiveness of body psychotherapy, Rosendahl et al. (2021) are optimistic about the potential of such work. Other research indicates the efficacy of body psychotherapy for chronic pain (Monsen & Monsen, 2000), depression (Röhricht et al., 2013) and trauma (Langmuir et al., 2012). Westland (2018) suggests that positive therapeutic change can result from body psychotherapy without interpretation or cognitive understanding.

The extent to which bodywork is *relational* is up for debate, as it depends on how it is applied. In this therapy tale, the existential body-orientated approach revealed itself mainly in the work undertaken to promote Lisa's relationship with different parts of herself, especially her body, and also in the way she and Michel both recognised the impact of physical-emotional trauma. Michel used a body listening technique rather than a movement pattern approach when he asked Lisa what her body stiffness might be telling them. He asked, 'What might your body be saying?' This invited Lisa to tune phenomenologically into the space held by particular sensations and speak from there in the first-person – the approach taken in **Focusing** (Gendlin, 1981). While Focusing can be practised alone, here the relationship between Lisa and Michel was crucial for facilitating her contact with different parts of herself (including her sick body self, her international journalist self and her sexual being self), moving her out of stuckness.

Beyond explicit bodywork, Michel helped Lisa get in touch with her **sexual body-self** through showing his awareness of her as an attractive woman (though keeping it ethical by not getting seduced) and encouraging her to talk about her sexual needs.

He did not engage touch as part of his relational approach, whereas other therapists might have used touch to energise or help Lisa connect with her body more. As T. Brown (2025) explains, **therapeutic touch** (as opposed to erotic touch) involves different qualities and intentions, namely for contact, comfort, containment or to show expertise, energise or explore. Depending on how it is engaged, it can both be healing and have a shadow side. Of course, touch should only be used with the fullest consent, and professional ethical codes would advise limiting touch except when used in a specialist way. Such codes emphasise how an explicit line needs to be drawn where therapeutic touch may be misinterpreted as being unduly intimate, intrusive or sexually invitational (Finlay, 2019).

Boundaried self-disclosure

As with touch, therapist self-disclosure must be **selectively applied**, carefully timed, and invoked to serve the client's needs. Decisions about when, whether or how to self-disclose should only ever be made with the client's interests and/or the therapeutic relationship to the fore (Finlay, 2019).

Hill et al. (2019) emphasise the importance of using self-disclosure sparingly and for appropriate reasons only. In their qualitative meta-analysis of 21 studies exploring the clinical consequences of therapist self-disclosure (TSD) and immediacy (Im) in psychotherapy, they found that appropriate disclosures enhanced therapeutic relationships and improved client functioning and insight. *TSD* was associated more often with improved mental health functioning and better therapy relationships, while *Im* was associated more often with clients opening up and being more immediate with their responses.

The value of self-disclosure lies in its ability to enable therapists to reveal themselves as genuine, transparent human beings who can be fully present as individuals (Finlay, 2019). Artful, intuitive judgement is involved when deciding what personal information might be appropriate to disclose. As therapists, we need to be aware of *when* we are tempted to self-disclose, and *why*. What is our primary motivation? Might it be our need to express something or to charm our client? And if we allow the focus to shift from the client to ourselves, might this not breach a precious boundary?

The therapist's chosen **modality** is also relevant. For example, a Kleinian psychoanalytic or behavioural therapist would be less likely to self-disclose than a humanistic or relational integrative one.

Michel self-disclosed several times in ways that seem to have been helpful:

- At the end of the first session, Lisa asked Michel where in France he was from. He answered factually, while aware that both time and personal boundaries were being tested inadvertently. Some therapists would have been reluctant to give this **personal information**. Others would have refused to engage because their time was up. Michel chose to respond, bending their time boundary, which enabled the forging of a shared connection around a love of France and speaking French. Michel's sidestepping of whether or not he missed his native country maintained an ethical boundary, keeping the therapeutic focus on Lisa.
- As their relationship deepened, Michel used self-disclosure as an intervention. He shared **here-and-now responses** like 'I feel sad at hearing you've lost your smile.' This has the effect of modelling authenticity and presence while simultaneously reflecting back Lisa's messages.
- Michel self-disclosed his philosophical, phenomenological **knowledge** when sharing lessons from Sartre and Focusing (Finlay, 2011).
- Lisa and Michel's occasional use of **French idioms** – another form of self-disclosure – is interesting. Research (e.g. Byford, 2015) suggests that using a client's first language in psychotherapy can facilitate deeper emotional exploration and a stronger therapeutic alliance. At the same time, a second language might offer a different perspective or emotional distance, either of which might help or hinder the processing of difficult experiences by constituting a

> defensive or creative adjustment (Cook, 2019). Research (e.g. Rolland et al., 2021) also shows that multilingual clients can benefit from expressing themselves in more than one language. Significantly, Michel tended to respond to Lisa's choice of language – mirroring her – rather than initiating language switches. However, their occasional forays into French appear to have facilitated deeper connections. As Byford (2015, p. 345) puts it, 'something valuable is *gained* in the translation'.

However, in certain situations, Michel also showed **professional restraint**. Firstly, he didn't reveal his Christian views about monogamy nor his lurking judgements about polyamory. He found a way to sidestep that debate while still inviting dialogue through his claim of being 'virtually unshockable' (even though he had been shocked). By not imposing his personal morality on Lisa, he helpfully kept the focus on her. While his disclosure of being a 'man of the world' could be seen as a professional breach (because it implies sexual experience), in this instance, it seemed to maintain the relational-professional boundary.

Secondly, he did not reveal issues around his own body fragility and ageing journey despite sharing some of Lisa's experience of frustration of the body letting oneself down. He kept the focus on Lisa's embodied being.

Thirdly, Michel resisted the temptation to invite Lisa to join his research project in order to keep their therapist–client boundaries clean. Of course, cases of dual boundary flexing do occur – and might be a positive development. But every situation needs to be carefully and collaboratively evaluated.

Finally, Michel contained his hopes for Lisa. Although he had wanted to encourage Lisa to write as part of her recovery, he waited for her to take the initiative. If he had pushed, he might have shamed or overwhelmed her, to the detriment of ongoing therapy. The artfulness of therapy thus reveals itself in the *timing* of interventions, where we follow our intuitive hunches, as much as the interventions themselves. Such clinical intuition involves a relational process (Arnd-Caddigan & Stickle, 2017).

Conclusion

Lisa's journey involved a movement from 'bodily doubt' to 'bodily trust' (Finlay, 2020). Her Covid trauma had destroyed her confidence, leaving her with a profound, pervasive sense of bodily doubt, uncertainty, dissociation and distrust (Carel, 2016). In her recovery, she developed a growing awareness of her 'new' body; she was able to make a relationship with it as she learnt to breathe and move again.

Michel's holistic, relational approach, combining *existential body therapy* and *Focusing*, proved valuable. He encouraged Lisa to re-integrate her fragmented identity by attending to her body, mind, emotions and social being. While their collaborative focus on energising her body was their initial project, the long-term nature of the therapy allowed a broader canvas to be worked with. Here, they could confront losses in her work and social roles. Their relationship was additionally supported by their mutual bilingual interests and Michel's non-judgemental openness to Lisa's history and preferred ways of being. Michel's carefully considered use of self-disclosure, while also containing himself in the service of Lisa, underlined the relational approach taken.

Discussion questions

1. Justify how you would handle a client's request for you to share personal details of your life.
2. How do therapists know when to disclose personal or political values, and when not to?
3. When attending to clients' bodies, what might therapists do to minimise the potential for turning the body into an object, which might invite shame into the room?

Chapter 5 – Darren: Taming the 'brute'?

Darren, aged 35, has been transferred from a secure prison to a prison-based therapeutic community (see Box 5.1) for the final half of a five-year sentence for grievous bodily harm (GBH) and violent assault of a gay man.

His transfer follows an incident where his cellmate accidentally killed himself when using spice (a synthetic cannabinoid). Like many inmates, Darren has dabbled with both spice and skunk (high-potency marijuana) because of boredom and the absence of alcohol (his drug of choice). His cellmate's death has proved a wake-up call: Darren has decided to give up drugs as one target towards a hoped-for recommendation of early release.

He also agrees to a long-term programme of one-to-one therapy with Jon, a senior counselling psychologist, also aged 35, who is part of the therapeutic community's close-knit team of professionals. The team includes another counsellor, prison officers, probation officers, nursing staff, a social worker, an occupational therapist and a multi-faith chaplain. Jon works in a *pluralistic* way (Cooper & McLeod, 2011) and likes to use relational *forensic schema therapy* (FST) (Bernstein et al., 2019) when appropriate. This is what he offers Darren.

The story below focuses on Darren's individual therapy; I have omitted the more substantial story of his life in the therapeutic community (TC), which has undoubtedly played a significant role in his growth. The individual therapy is shown to be a challenging experience that requires Darren to stay with painful feelings and memories of past trauma. Their first step is to build a relationship based on mutual trust. Darren has to learn to trust Jon and know it is okay to show vulnerability. Conversely, Jon has to learn to trust Darren to control his impulsive anger and not hit out violently when Jon touches on sensitive areas. On top of this, Jon, who is gay, must find a relational way to be with Darren despite his history of violence against a gay man.

Reflecting at the end of the chapter, the focus is on the **relational commitments** and **relational challenges** around being relational in a prison context and when a client is resistant and quick-tempered.

Box 5.1 Evidence base supporting forensic therapeutic communities

There are currently 14 democratic therapeutic communities (DTCs) operating within the UK prison system, spread across five prisons. They are based on the idea that living together and participating in shared activities can be therapeutic.

While DTCs have a long history and are used in various settings, including substance abuse and forensic contexts, existing research often falls short of the standards required for inclusion in NICE guidelines.

However, the evidence demonstrates that DTCs reduce re-offending rates and promote positive psychological changes in individuals with a history of offending (Shuker, 2010; Capone et al., 2016).

In a synthesis of resident experiences of prison-based therapeutic communities in the UK, Fernandes et al. (2025) searched five databases of qualitative studies published between 1962 and 2023. Residents shared that the safety provided by the community enhanced their sense of belonging and encouraged respectful acceptance between residents and staff, which in turn helped them build trust. However, residents from ethnic minority backgrounds facing racial or sexual hostility had harder struggles to integrate; some felt disconnected and isolated. The authors recommend culturally informed interventions within prison-based DTCs to help reduce 'toxic masculinity' while assisting inmates to tune into their emotional vulnerabilities.

Darren's story

Forensic therapeutic communities operate on the principle that individuals' social environment is a key factor in rehabilitation. The community is still a prison, and resident inmates are subject to the same security constraints as they would have in prison. However, everyday life is less regulated and residents are able to make significant contributions to day-to-day procedures, allocations and activities. The TCs are managed on democratic lines, with prisoners agreeing to their own rules, restrictions and punishments. Regular groupwork provides space for them to explore and control their own anti-social and violent behaviours, while structured daily routines of occupational/educational activities, gym/sports and social events keep them active and engaged.

In this particular unit, all residents have weekly therapy. Two weeks into this new environment, Darren begins his therapy with Jon.

Laying the groundwork

Darren ambles into the therapy room, led by a prison guard. He chooses to sit on a chair backed against a wall. He leans back, legs splayed, arms folded across his chest, tattooed biceps straining the seams of his prison-issue shirt. He exudes caged energy primed to pounce, simultaneously bored and belligerent. His deep-set eyes flicker with calculation and challenge. The air contracts, taut with possibility and threat. It's not a promising start.

'You made it here, then – hello and welcome.'

Darren is not impressed by Jon's friendly greeting. ''Have to be here, don' I?' he snorts. 'I'm not a 5150, a nutter. So you ain't fixing me.'

'Therapy isn't like that. It's one part of your participation in the community where you're working out what you want to change in your life. Some people find it easier to talk one-to-one rather than in a group. This is our space to use in whatever way will help you most.'

Silence from Darren. Jon lets the silence hang a while before gently breaking it. 'It's okay not to talk. But can I ask, how are you settling into this new, somewhat weird, environment, Darren?'

'Beats the other place. Them f***ers treat you like animals.'

'Well, if you think this unit is a soft touch, you won't last long. Not with that attitude.' Jon injects some toughness: Darren needs to understand that he won't be walking over him.

'No, yeah, I get it.' Darren suddenly abandons his tough guy stance. 'I want to be here. I asked to be here. Bad shite happened in the last place. Made me think. Something's gotta change. I get it. They ask a lot of us here and it'll be tough.'

'You're right, Darren. It will be tough in many ways. But you'll be treated like a human being, and I appreciate your clarity and honesty about wanting to change. You okay to talk about what happened at the last place that got you here?' Jon already knows much of the background, but he wants Darren to share it.

'My celly (cellmate), Karl, he OD-ed. Freaked out with the spice.'

'Tell me about Karl.'

'Good bloke, Karl. Didn't belong in prison, I reckon. Set up, he was. We all say that, I know, but it was true about Karl: he was sensitive, like, and lock up was too rough for him. That's why he took to dope.'

'That's a sad story; and I'm sorry about Karl. He obviously didn't deserve to die like that… And you've lost your friend, which must be hard.' Darren replies with a grunt, but his aggressive stance is less evident. 'It sounds like your mate needed support and he didn't get it.'

'Yeah, so I'm here to get that support for me *and* him.'

'Karl is here with us too, then? That's nice.' A trace of a smile from Darren acknowledges Jon's gentle humour. 'I'm good with you and Karl here together. What would he say right now?'

'Yeah, Karl would want to come here where drugs are less available; that would help. And he'd work hard for a different life after prison.'

'I'm hearing you're in that place, too.' Since Darren doesn't deny this, Jon is encouraged to push on. 'What would you like to be different for you when you leave here?'

Their initial conversation culminates with Darren accepting Jon's invitation to get started on their therapy. Darren uses his time with Jon to talk about what it's like for him to be in this new community and the unfamiliar challenges posed by groupwork.

Expressing feelings

Three sessions on, Darren expresses, yet again, his frustration and anger at the 'f***ing rules of the unit'. He struggles with the daily 'thoughts and feelings meeting', where the whole community (staff and residents) meet to sort out what's going on for them and share anything that's bothering them.

The previous night, Darren had become the focus of the community meeting after an incident when he smashed a chair. He was required to account for himself. Replaying the events with Jon, he shares his shock and confusion that it had been the inmates rather than guards who 'gave out' at him.

'What did you hear them say to you?' Jon enquires. 'I was there, but I want to know what you made of it.'

'They told me I had to find another way. That I was too quick to react and needed to learn another gear, not just rage or shutdown.'

'What do you think about that?'

'I guess they're right. I need to *think* before smashing up.'

Hearing this story, Jon becomes even clearer that a key goal of this therapy is to get Darren to mentalise and think things through. Jon also grasps the importance of standing up to Darren and listening fearlessly to his ranting: he needs to be one of the few people who don't flinch at Darren's rage – or worse, who avoid it.

Jon's approach seems to work. After a few more sessions, Darren actually admits to feeling comfortable with Jon, whom he describes as 'okay; tough, but fair and steady'. When invited to say more about what is happening between them, Darren points out they are the same age and, indicating Jon's muscles, notes that Jon must work out like him.

Jon takes the opportunity to highlight a further similarity: that, like Darren, he has had 'alcohol problems' in his time. This revelation, a surprise for Darren, opens the door to a deeper focus on the way Darren has abused alcohol (and occasionally drugs) in the past. They talk about the importance of alcohol in Darren's life, and how his social life revolves around the local pub, where his quick temper (especially after a few drinks) has precipitated numerous fights.

While Jon feels okay about revealing that he has unspecified 'alcohol problems', he decides against giving further details to Darren at this early stage of their therapy. Generally, he chooses not to disclose his personal life to anyone at work. He worries it could mess with his prison relationships, and he also believes in his right to keep it private.

As they continue exploring Darren's drinking, Darren expresses surprise that Jon hasn't told him he has to 'stop' drinking. Jon underlines that such decisions belong to Darren himself. It is his decision and his responsibility to change his drinking habits – or not.

'Do you *want* to stop your drinking?' Jon enquires. When Darren shakes his head, Jon asks a key question: 'Okay, do you want to at least change your old drinking habits?' Darren gives a slow, reluctant nod.

Over time, their discussions develop along mostly fruitful lines. But sticky moments arise. On one occasion, when Darren is recounting one of his many pub fights, he tells of how proud he and his mate had been at 'beating up a pansy'.

'What happened to make you want to beat him up?'

'He was new in town – a teacher, we'd heard. He came in with a couple of homo friends and that kind are not welcome in our boozer.'

'How did you know they were gay?' Jon keeps his tone neutral.

'He had one of those rainbow pins on his jacket. But him kissing the other bloke when they sat down – that was too much.'

'So, are you saying that you were justified in beating him up?'

'Yeah, he needed to know he didn't belong in our boozer.'

'That kiss seems to have been a bit of a trigger for you.'

'He deserved being molly-whopped. And it worked, 'cos they didn't come back.'

'I'm hearing that you don't regret the beating. But what about the future? Are you saying you'll want to beat up every gay guy you meet? How is that going to work out?'

At first, Darren shows confusion. 'Probably, well; maybe, no.' Then he drops back into comfortable territory. 'They just need to stay away from me and my territory. You'd do the same, wouldn't you? Would you want them taking over your pub?'

At this point, Jon begins to struggle with his own demons, and his mind goes blank. His therapist self has momentarily checked out of the room. Jon knows himself well enough to recognise that his dissociation is a defensive mask that covers his anger at homophobia in particular. He plays with the idea of asking Darren how he feels about having a 'pansy' for a therapist, but that would not benefit Darren and would probably wreck their relationship.

The contrast between Darren's complacent lack of remorse and his own simmering thoughts makes Jon long to strike back at Darren. 'Your kind is not welcome in my therapy room,' is what he wants to say, his therapist self seemingly replaced by a Darren clone. He pushes that urge away, keeping his facial expression as neutral as possible. He knows he mustn't respond to Darren's bigotry by losing his own control, and there is a futility in challenging Darren's prejudice head-on. But what to do?

Conscious time is passing, Jon is aware of the need to say something constructive. He looks at the clock, grateful their session is almost over.

'We need to end soon. But we're talking about you, Darren, not me. I hear you protecting your space but I think the issue is about you flipping abruptly from calm to violence without any thought of self-control or alternative action. There are other paths you can choose. Maybe that would be a good focus for us next time. Perhaps between now and then we can both think about other options for you.'

Darren nods his agreement as he saunters out.

Supervision

Following that session, Jon requests an extra supervision. His supervisor, Victoria, is an experienced, older woman. She starts by appreciating Jon's trust in bringing his turmoil to supervision. She then acknowledges that although they have worked together for over a year, she never knew he was gay, which shows how much he prizes his privacy. Alert to any whiff of homophobia in his supervisor, Jon is relieved to feel her acceptance and curiosity.

When Victoria affirms Jon's handling of Darren, he sheepishly admits that part of him 'hates and despises' Darren; he feels disgusted and sickened by Darren's 'arrogant, narcissistic smirk' and the way he 'oozes toxic masculinity'. Embarrassed, Jon draws back. 'I mean, don't get me wrong: that's just one part of me; I also have a compassionate side. I'm just sharing. I love men – all shapes and sizes of men. It's just that Darren pushes some buttons. Is it possible for me to work with someone I feel so negative about? Would it be more ethical to refer him on?' Jon hangs his head. 'I don't know how to manage Darren's brutish side, and maybe I need to think about my own!'

'I don't blame you at all for having this cocktail of feelings, and you're entitled to the brute part, too. Remember Winnicott's wise observation that no matter how much we might love our patients, we also hate and fear them? I'm not sure I'd be able to manage as much self-control as you did if I had been face-to-face with Darren at that moment, not with your equanimity, for sure. You seem to have managed much better than you might have done.' Seeing Jon is soothed by her words, after a pause, she probes. 'And these are strong emotions you're expressing. Does Darren remind you of someone from your past?'

Jon takes a long thoughtful breath: 'Yup. Unsurprisingly, I guess. My homophobic father is around. He died before I came out. A good thing probably, finding out would have killed him. I've talked about him endlessly in therapy!'

'Okay, so what we need to underline is that your father is a powerful figure in the field; right now he is present alongside Darren. That's important. But I'm also thinking about the power of your own silencing process and how difficult it must have been for a younger you to come out. I'm wondering if that silenced part of you is struggling with Darren, too.'

'Yeah, you're right.' Jon lets out a breath. 'I hadn't made that link. I'm feeling silenced and I resent it. And there's more. Darren reminds me of all the bullies from school. I was slow to grow physically, and they picked on me, calling me "Girly". No surprise that I got into bodybuilding.'

'Painful stuff, Jon; I'm sorry you've had to live through all that. I can see that it won't help you to share all this with Darren.

I appreciate you not silencing yourself here though.' Holding eye contact, they share a special moment of connection, each registering and acknowledging the deepening of their relationship.

Victoria eventually breaks their silence. 'I'm guessing from Darren's muscles that he grew up in an environment like yours, where masculinity was rigidly defined and where anything soft, effeminate or showing softness between men was seen as weakness or deviance. Perhaps you could explore that with him sometime when it doesn't feel too close to your process?'

Jon shakes his head.

'I can see that that doesn't feel right,' Victoria says. 'So maybe we're allowing the homophobia to distract us? Maybe your focus should tend towards Darren the bully, more generally?'

Something eases in Jon, and he nods, allowing their strategising to move forward. They agree that Jon should strive to empathise with Darren's anger and lead him towards less extreme reactiveness. They speculate about using a forensic schema therapy approach more explicitly.

Victoria also recommends that Jon reads one of her favourite books, *The Devil You Know: Stories of human cruelty and compassion* (Adshead & Horne, 2021). In it, she explains, Adshead recounts her experiences as a psychiatrist working with 'monsters' in prison. 'Her capacity to find empathy and compassion is almost as shocking as the offences she describes.'

Jon thanks his supervisor for being so available and constructively offering tips and extra readings, which help both his client and his own growth as a therapist.

Managing the 'bully'

Over the course of the next few months, Jon teaches Darren schema theory. During their sessions, Jon becomes aware of Darren's tendency to embrace a '*bully and attack mode*' characterised by overt, reactive anger, and lack of empathy. Jon also picks up on other modes Darren admits are familiar to him: '*predator*', '*conning-manipulator*' and '*self-aggrandiser*'.

Over time, Darren learns that the threats, intimidation and aggression, which have characterised much of his life, represent attempts to pre-empt, dominate and control others – in ways that keep others on the defensive and to hide his own vulnerability and feelings of inadequacy. Therapy enables him to understand some of the triggers for his bully-attack modes and to learn the difference in fight responses between assertion and out-of-control aggression that creates more problems.

The two of them begin by exploring how Darren acts out when triggered within the therapeutic community. Darren starts to own the way he has used threats, aggression and intimidation in the past to get what he wants and pre-empt possible threats. He begins to recognise how bullying makes him feel strong.

As they explore some of the violent incidents from his past, Darren begins thinking about other ways in which he might have reacted. In one particularly significant session, they scrutinise the time he had beaten up his live-in girlfriend, after she had tried to leave him. She had landed up in hospital with a broken nose. While Darren admits to not feeling any particular remorse now, he is able to recognise that his behaviour had been 'triggered'.

'I'm impressed with your insight, Darren. What was the trigger, do you think?'

This seemingly simple therapeutic question inaugurates some deep processing on Darren's part. He reveals more about his girlfriend – in particular, his feeling that she was 'abandoning' him, *just like his mother did*. He talks about his father's regular beating up of his mother that continued until the day, when Darren was at school, she disappeared, leaving Darren alone with his violent father. A year later, he was taken away and placed in a care home.

Listening to this, Jon experiences rage and disgust, his own father replacing Darren in his mind. However, he just about manages to keep his own history to one side.

Histories involving domestic abuse are common enough in the unit. Jon is aware of the part of him that is disengaged, deadened, and he wrestles with his urge to leave the room. His own abandoned child-self struggles to stay focused on Darren's story. But Jon reveals none of this to Darren. Instead, he communicates compassion for the suddenly abandoned child who had had to cope with this violent and terrifying father.

Although Darren has taken an important step by recounting this story, Jon feels it is too soon to focus directly on Darren's complicated relationship with his father. He suggests they continue to focus on Darren beating up his girlfriend and her decision to leave. With hindsight, could he have adopted other responses?

Darren hesitates. 'Think, Darren,' Jon continues. 'Say this happens in the future and you have a girlfriend you really like and are thinking about a future together. But it's not going to last, is it, if you keep beating her up? She'll go away like your mother, like the other women you've known. Also, next time if this happens, you could get the police onto you, and with your record it doesn't look good. So, is that what you want?'

Darren tries to speak several times during this tirade, but Jon is not ready to let up. 'If you want to change, start here, start NOW. Try thinking about and talking about other ways to live that do not rely on being a big bastard in your ever-shrinking world.'

Darren listens without storming out or becoming aggressive. Sensing the time is right, Jon pushes on. He asks Darren for a detailed account of what exactly happened with that girlfriend as they prepare to look at what Darren could have done differently.

Darren begins his story, 'When she said she was leaving, I shouted "Oh no, you're not!" I grabbed her top and smacked my fist into her face. Just once. But blood poured from her nose and she fell bang against the TV. There was blood everywhere and she ran to the bathroom. I went back to watching the footie on TV. I'd missed the start, which didn't help my mood: I like the build-up, you know. Anyway, she got to bed eventually, with icepacks on her face. Next morning, a friend took her to hospital where the doctors realigned her nose; they were worried about brain damage. They wouldn't let me see her… Her brother took her away and she never came back.'

'Okay. Let's work with this. Did you ever apologise?'

'I never apologise to anyone. It's weak… Except… except *you're* not weak and *you* don't mind apologising.' Darren looks a bit confused.

'Thanks, Darren, I appreciate you recognising an apology isn't necessarily weak. Let's work with that. What else could you have done instead of punching her? Could you have said something?'

After a pause, Darren finds some words. 'I dunno; something like, "I don't want you to go, errrm, can we talk about it?"'

'Brilliant.' Jon points out that while Darren's 'bully self' may always want to hit out, his 'sad, scared child self' always feels upset at rejection. 'But now I'm hearing a new Darren,' Jon adds. 'A Darren who isn't just hitting out in pain. A Darren who can find words to explain his feelings. That's definitely something that the new Darren – you – could do if a girlfriend threatens to leave you in the future.'

After this successful processing, they use the same approach when considering other violent incidents in Darren's past. Darren develops the ability to recognise that others have a right to their own thinking and life choices.

The ice broken, their work moves on to explore Darren's childhood: his ways of coping with his violent father, the trauma of being taken into care, and his unsuccessful placements with foster parents. Jon acknowledges how tough Darren's childhood had been, with so many painful abandonments, separations and losses. Through Jon's mirroring of his pain, Darren begins to feel compassion for his younger child self.

Further avenues for exploration open up around the way Darren's younger selves were pressured to suppress emotions such as sadness, fear and vulnerability. Instead, they were encouraged to express themselves through violence. 'What chance did your child selves have to do anything else, Darren?' asks Jon, compassion to the fore.

In another session, Jon invites Darren to say what he would have liked to say to his father now as 'new Darren'. Darren tells him straight: that he was a bully and that his treatment of both his wife and his son was 'out of order'.

Towards release

The latter part of Darren's therapy, both within the community and in its one-to-one form, focuses on continuing to develop the skills and strategies Darren needs for his post-prison future. These include managing stress, building healthy relationships and resisting negative influences. One particularly positive aspect of Darren's two-year stay is his growing interest in horticulture, something he wants to pursue professionally once he is released.

Aware that other team members are working with Darren on his employment options, Jon focuses on his social drinking. Jon speculates that when, after his release, Darren finds himself back down the pub with his mates, it's more than likely that alcohol-fuelled 'gay bashing' will be on the agenda – more so since Darren will be drawn to impressing his long-lost friends.

This remains a delicate topic for Jon, who still struggles to contain his own festering rage and fear. Is this the moment, he wonders, to share with Darren the anguish of his experience of facing the homophobic violence? Should he reveal the distress people have caused him over the years? Would this help Darren discover some compassion for his 'victims'?

Jon takes these questions back to Victoria, who confirms that there are no clear-cut correct answers. Jon tells of his fear that disclosing the fact that he's gay to Darren could damage their relationship, shatter their bond and result in Darren losing his respect for Jon. He notes that while Darren has made many gains through therapy, his homophobia remains entrenched.

The two of them eventually agree there is good reason for Jon *not* to self-disclose being gay to Darren. Thinking of future clients, however, he might want to take a different approach if he finds that self-censorship affects his ability to be present and authentic.

In his next therapy session with Darren, Jon reveals that he regularly attends AA meetings as part of his ongoing support process. Darren expresses his respect for Jon's strength, even in vulnerability, and earnestly debates the possibility of doing that himself. They use this as a springboard to discuss other strategies (including the possibility of drinking alcohol-free beer) that might help him avoid a return to his old ways.

Reflecting on their therapy, Jon notes that Darren has absorbed the concepts and lingo of therapy and can 'talk the talk' in his head. For all that, Jon sees only a 50:50 chance – at best – of Darren being able to 'walk the walk' in the real world. What happens when the next gay man walks into Darren's pub? With luck, Darren's bullying demon won't emerge as quickly or violently as before.

Jon keeps his doubts locked away, only to be expressed in supervision. As he and the rest of the community bid Darren farewell, they stay focused on hopes for his ongoing growth and future happiness.

Reflecting on relational processes

The exploration below identifies significant *relational commitments* and *relational challenges* arising in Darren's therapy with Jon.

Relational commitments

Jon's relational approach was evident from the start, particularly in his readiness to listen and ask **open, non-judgemental questions** and when he invited Darren to check in about what was happening between them. By posing '*what*' questions rather than '*why*' questions, he strove to elicit detailed descriptions rather than explanations (Bateman & Fonagy, 2013). By not sharing too much of his perspective, Jon kept the focus squarely on Darren rather than on their relationship. While this could indicate that his therapy was *less relational*, such a conclusion is negated by his recognition of therapeutically appropriate titrating of their intimacy.

The relational component is also evident in Jon's awareness of his **countertransferences** and at those crucial moments, when he managed to stay calm and compassionate, rather than dissociating or retaliating in anger, disgust or fear.

Jon's approach drew on **relational schema therapy** (Žvelc, 2009). This theory integrates the concept of schemas with transactional analytic ego states, script and games theory. Applying this, Jon aimed to explore how Darren's early life experiences, particularly within relationships, might provide a blueprint for the reshaping of core beliefs and behaviours (schemas) that influence current relationships.

We also might say that Jon drew implicitly on ideas from (psychodynamic and social cognitive) **mentalization-based therapy** (MBT) (Bateman & Fonagy, 2013) and this offers another relational angle. With this approach, the focus is on improving a person's ability to understand their own and others' mental states. MBT emphasises the role of relationships in shaping mental health and uses the therapeutic relationship as a space to practise and develop these skills by continually bringing attention to mental states and their impact on behaviour.

Jon could equally have chosen to use another therapeutic approach, though the empirical evidence around evaluating psychological interventions delivered in forensic settings is patchy

(Gilling McIntosh et al., 2021). However, there is evidence that indicates positive outcomes using CBT for anger and aggression in forensic mental health populations (Morris et al., 2024).

In line with the philosophy of the therapeutic community, Jon strove to activate Darren's own **motivation for change** rather than being didactic. He respected Darren's autonomy, including his right/freedom *not* to change, while making it clear that Darren had choices. This is in line with the practice of motivational interviewing (Miller & Rollnick, 2002) with its four guiding principles, presented via the acronym RULE:

- Resist the righting reflex
- Understand the patient's [client's] own motivations
- Listen with empathy
- Empower the patient [client].

Jon's relational approach was also evident in his selective **use of self-disclosure**. While he opted to foster a sense of connection with Darren by disclosing his own history with alcohol, he decided against revealing his sexuality, which he saw as likely to hurt their therapeutic relationship (as well as being too exposing and unsafe for him personally).

Relational challenges

While Jon's choice of therapy for Darren in many ways proved beneficial, Jon found himself facing significant relational challenges while working with an individual with a violent, homophobic and misogynistic history (Morrison et al., 2021). Jon was tested by having to maintain several **contradictory positions**:

1. Clients who are violent or have a violent history are among those who provoke the most anxiety on the part of therapists. Many therapists struggle to maintain a therapeutic alliance, particularly when there is an immediate threat of aggression. To help Darren *emotionally regulate*, Jon needed both to keep himself regulated and to safely contain any threats, irrespective of any turmoil he experienced.

2. Jon sought to humanise Darren: to see him as a *whole person* with strengths and weaknesses, rather than as simply a violent bully who perpetuated hate crimes and domestic violence. He needed to see Darren as a lonely, abandoned victim of child abuse. It is important for clients with violent histories to feel that there is a safe therapeutic space where their therapist can receive and hold the double story of being both victim and perpetrator.

3. To work positively and relationally with Darren, Jon needed to hold in check his own trauma history and negative emotions about Darren's homophobia. He similarly needed to *contain* his own anger and feelings of hatred/disgust around Darren's toxic masculinity (exposing this would have put him in an antagonistic position). However, he also found that silencing those parts of him triggered memories of being silenced in his relationship with his father.

4. Jon needed to act with both softness and firmness, empathy and authority. While he couldn't show too much vulnerability, it was important for him to *model strength in vulnerability*, such as showing that apologies needn't be seen as a sign of weakness. He couldn't be too bland or else he wouldn't be congruent with himself. He needed to choose when to challenge and when to back down and how to do it. It would then be useful to process how any challenge landed.

5. While *acknowledging his similarities* with Darren (being physically strong masculine men in their mid-thirties, with alcohol problems), Jon also needed to distance himself from Darren's violence, teaching him the difference between understandable and contained assertion/aggression/anger versus impulsive violence/rage.

6. Jon had to find a way of *democratising*, levelling, his interactions with Darren, in line with the philosophy of the unit. He strove to do this in the context of the real disparity in their power positions (Jon, the professional, versus Darren, the incarcerated inmate who could be transferred back to ordinary prison at any time).

The complex relational challenges that arise in work with clients with histories of violence and abuse require that therapists have their own support. In Jon's case, **supervision** proved crucial, and being part of a supportive team would also have helped.

Conclusion

In this story of individual therapy, layered relational processes were involved in helping Darren take responsibility for his violent urges and tame his bullying, brutish side. His therapy (both one-to-one and in the therapeutic community) encouraged him to think before reacting. It helped him regulate his own emotions and enhanced his capacity to mentalise (understanding his own and others' perspectives). As he understood more about his process, different paths and ways of responding to triggering situations opened up.

The story also illustrates the demanding nature of therapy for both Darren and Jon. Their first task was to build a relationship based on mutual trust. This was a challenge given Darren's tough guy persona and the need for Jon to stay safe while interacting decently with Darren despite his own lurking rage. As their relationship grew stronger, they negotiated a more comfortable way of interacting while containing complexity and contradiction. Jon needed to see Darren as both abusive adult and abused child; Darren needed to feel he had autonomy and would be treated as a human being, despite the constraints and skewed power relationships involved in incarceration.

This chapter highlights some of the *challenges* of doing relational work, particularly in a prison context. In this story, it was taxing for Jon to be a gay man working with a homophobic client. He needed to find a relational way of being with Darren, despite his feelings of rage and disgust around Darren's toxic masculinity. There was a limit to how authentically present Jon could be with Darren. Therapy involved a delicate balance between acceptance and challenge, between empathy and holding boundaries, between acknowledging Darren's worldview while simultaneously challenging harmful attitudes and behaviours.

Helped by supervision, Jon was able to tap into his compassion for Darren as an abused, abandoned child. His use of relational schema therapy helped to anchor him and enable him to be present for Darren. While Jon worked relationally, he also kept his distance from Darren, limiting both their intimacy and his self-disclosures to keep himself safe while preserving their alliance.

Discussion questions

1. Do you agree with Jon's choices around selective self-disclosure?
2. How well would you handle being faced with toxic masculinity and/or a client's violent history?
3. Mirroring a client's language (words and vernacular) in therapy is important for building rapport, enhancing understanding, and facilitating communication. Discuss with reference to Darren's and Jon's use of prison lingo and other expressions.

Chapter 6 – Morgan: Finding emotional balance

Morgan, aged 32, is a lively, party-loving beauty therapist. Back in her 20s, however, she was briefly hospitalised following a serious suicide attempt. She received a diagnosis of borderline personality disorder (BPD) but failed to engage with the therapies offered. Since then, she has avoided further serious suicide attempts but cuts herself regularly as a way of managing her emotions. A recent toxic break-up has resulted in Morgan feeling her emotions are out of control, so she seeks therapy but this time resolves to follow through.

Morgan agrees to open-ended long-term weekly therapy with Diana, an experienced integrative psychotherapist. Diana specialises in working with people who struggle to control their emotions and/or have a history of unstable relationships, and she has a postgraduate qualification in dialectical behavior therapy (DBT).

The reflections that follow Morgan's story explore the evidence base for **manualised therapies** and ask, '**Is DBT relational?**'.

Morgan's story

Morgan experiences intense, unstable emotions and has a fragile sense of her Self. Her difficulty regulating emotions frequently results in impulsive self-harming behaviours, and that includes getting involved with the 'wrong men'. Despite a turbulent history of unsuccessful, often abusive relationships, she has a wide circle of friends and has carved out a successful career in the beauty therapy industry, where her creative nail technician services are in high demand.

First moments

Morgan breezes boldly into the therapy room, wafting perfume and clad in designer clothes. Her make-up embraces fake tan, thick black lashes and glossy, plump lips; her acrylic nails are a work of art. Undeniably beautiful, she commands attention, while wearing her make-up like armour.

Diana keeps her expression as warm and inviting as she can manage, hiding her personal distaste of the cosmetic overload.

'I have BPD,' announces Morgan as her starting salvo.

Biting back her wary response to such diagnostic labels, Diana mildly enquires, 'What does that mean to you?'

'It's more what it means to you,' Morgan retorts. 'The last therapist I called refused to treat me when she found out! I've come because you were recommended as being a therapist who treats BPD. I was officially diagnosed, you know; I'm not just making this up.' Morgan's eyes narrow, her stare proclaiming she is ready for battle.

'I hear you, Morgan, and I'm taking you seriously. However, I work with people, not labels. I want to understand what BPD means for you and also something about your life story.'

Morgan proceeds to list multiple traumas and current issues, hardly stopping for breath. 'People who know me would say I'm "fun but f***ing crazy", a "drama queen". I get uber emotional and have intense mood swings; I lose it; I never know how I'm going to feel minute to minute. I might be fine one minute, then freaking out in rage, or else depressed and suicidal in the next; and then feeling nothing at all. When I first meet people, they love me, I love them, it's like we're soulmates; I'm a good "party girl" so I get invited places; then – poof – it gets ugly, and they end up screwing me over. I just wish someone would understand me, just once, without me having to explain myself. I hate myself and I just can't be like this anymore. It's time I did more "adulting". I'm not coping.'

Morgan takes a breath, allowing Diana to get in a question: 'When you say you're not coping, what's happening for you?'

'I'm all over the place; it feels bad and seems to be getting worse. Just last weekend I had to escape from this man's house – I thought we were going to have a nice time but when he took me home after a group of us went clubbing, things got "sus", the creep. Drinking helps – I like my wine, or I binge on chocolate. Once I start, I can't stop. Last week, I ate an entire box of Quality Street in one sitting. I can't do that because I need to watch my weight and figure for my business. So, then it's major dieting time. But I'm better on my drinking now. I used to party hard and get really trashed and not remember stuff. Now, I don't want the girls to see me like that. Mostly now, when I drink and binge myself into a coma, I'm alone, my rep intact.'

Before Diana can get a word in, Morgan switches registers again. This time, however, she looks more reluctant to share. 'If I'm honest,' she says, 'when I'm seriously stressed, I cut myself.'

Diana looks for evidence of scarring on her arms but finds none. 'I cut my thighs mainly or upper arms so it can't be seen,' Morgan explains. 'It's my little secret. I work in a beauty salon, I'm a nail technician, you know, and I do make-up for weddings and so on. I'm in demand and getting a name – I've worked with some rich and famous local people. So, I have to look professional and – anyway – my cuts are always hidden. Most of the girls don't know about that side of me. I've a rep to keep up.'

'It sounds like quite a successful career, and you've managed to protect it. Can I ask how often you cut-up?'

'One or two times a week, maybe – it depends what's going on. More if there is s*** happening. Cutting just kinda helps pull me together. When I bleed it's like all the bad feelings flow out and, for a while, I don't feel much. It's bliss. And then I have a whole ritual of taking good care of my cuts so they don't get infected. I know what I'm doing. I'm not trying to kill myself. Been there, moved on. Now I just want some peace from the noise in my head; some place where no one can hurt me. The cutting isn't that big a deal really.' Morgan catches Diana's extra-questioning look. 'Well, okay, maybe it is. Maybe it's another addiction like chocolate and wine?'

Overwhelmed momentarily by the many different avenues she could take to respond to Morgan, Diana gathers herself to focus. She decides to ask Morgan about her wider relationships; there will be time later to explore Morgan's self-harm, assuming she engages therapy. 'I can hear you take care of yourself, even when self-harming, and that's important,' Diana says. 'But it also seems like other people hurt you a lot.'

'Who doesn't? Everyone. Some of the girls are nice and supportive. But it's men. They all screw me over eventually. My boyfriends – and I've had a few, I admit – they cope with me for a while; some might even stay for a couple of months. But the end is always the same. They leave. Or they give me s*** and beat up on me, so then I leave. It never works out. Even back in school, there was a teacher I had when I was 17. Yeah, I had him! He gave me stuff for having sex in his car. He said he loved me, and we'd get married when I left school, but it turned out he loved others the same time. One student in the year below me reported him, and he was arrested. Lost his job; I never saw him again. Never said anything. Don't judge me, I know what he did was illegal, but I'll deny it if you say anything.'

Diana feels that Morgan is testing her, perhaps to see if she is shocked or able to take everything in her stride. She adopts a temporising, neutral approach rather than taking an official, 'child protection' stance, given the time that has passed and his arrest. 'I'm hearing that you've had some really tough times in your relationships, and we'll need to get more into that, assuming you decide to work with me. For now, it helps me to hear how things are for you now. What about family or people around who support you?'

'That's another whole can of worms. How much time do you have? My friends are my family. I don't have family – at least none that I know about. It was all a mess as a child. My father died when I was 4, then my mother lost it and became a druggie, addict; she was often comatosed or out scoring. I was 7 when I realised if I was hungry, I would have to cook and feed myself. Sometimes, school would get involved and things would be better for a bit, or I'd get passed on to various "aunties" who weren't aunties, or I'd stay at different friends' houses. When I hit my teenage years, I think the aunties were worried about their husbands hitting on me, so they refused to have me. One lodger, I don't remember his name, was always asking me to touch him or give him oral sex. He was actually quite fun as he'd sneak me alcohol which, aged 12,

I thought was cool. They all just want one thing. It's all sus, can't trust 'em.'

Morgan pauses for breath briefly. 'Sometimes I have to hold my tongue when I'm working with these blushing brides who are so in love. Little do they know it's all crap and the husbands will do stuff behind their backs. Do you know, I was taken on a fancy long weekend once to Spain. He was rich and handsome, and I could have fallen for him. Turns out he just got married three months earlier. What the f***?! I got well played.'

Engaging, planning, contracting

Diana sees an opening to build the therapeutic alliance. 'I hear you say you don't trust people, especially men – and you have lots of good reasons to not trust them. Yet you've come in here this morning and shared all sorts of personal details with me, even though we only met barely 30 minutes ago.'

'Yeah, yeah, my verbal diarrhoea – I'm famous for it. Likely have some ADHD too.'

Again, Diana bites back her negative response to such labelling, something she is seeing more frequently.

'I sense that it's hard for you, Morgan, to decide when to draw the line; to know what's safe and what's not.' Morgan narrows her eyes again, but this time in appraisal, rather than battle readiness. Eventually she nods, and this encourages Diana to carry on. 'I think you also need me to hear you; to hear your story calmly without shock or rejection. Is that about right?'

'Yeah, I guess so.' Morgan pauses. Then, 'Ya goin' take me on, then?'

'Let's talk about that.' Diana avoids the direct answer as she is still undecided. 'What do you want to work on in therapy?'

'I want to feel better, be happier. Can you do that?'

'Actually, no. I'm not going to make easy promises. I want to be honest with you. Therapy comes in many packages. Sometimes it's about listening. Or it can involve teaching you skills to cope and level out your emotions. Sometimes it's about working through past trauma. And there are other choices to be made. For example, which would be best for you: individual or group therapy? For now, individual work might be good to ensure that you are safer and harm yourself less. What do you think about me saying that?'

'Yeah, I guess. It's time. My life isn't really liveable at the moment. I can't go on like this, and if I lose it at work I'll lose everything. Something needs to change. I want to be less crazy.'

'So what does a "less crazy", "liveable" life look like? But also, what would you understand if I told you that therapy is not about making you *feel better*, instead it's about *better feeling*?'

'Sounds a bit weird.'

Sensing that Morgan might be ready to listen, Diana describes something of her therapy philosophy. 'Mostly, therapy is not about getting relief from negative emotions; it's about improving self-awareness so that you understand more about your emotions and behaviour. Then, with that knowledge, instead of just acting out and reacting in habit, you will have awareness of other – different – possibilities about how you could choose to act. If we decide to work together, my job would be to help you to think about and test out alternative ways to be with and respond to different situations. I want to go with you on this journey of discovery and together we'll try to make sense of this puzzle called Morgan.'

Diana stops to let her words sink in. No instantaneous and sharp retort from Morgan? Diana begins to feel they may get somewhere.

'What do you think about what I'm saying? Different from what you expected?'

'I guess. Dunno. You're different. If you're prepared to take me on, then that would be dope.'

'That sounds like we might be able to move forward, then.' Diana responds gently but she needs more from Morgan before committing to this contract. 'When therapy gets hard you may want to bail out. But it's important you try to hang on and keep coming each week. There aren't any quick fixes. How about you think about all this and come for one more appointment next week? Then we can discuss what you would like to work on with me. If we still both want to work together, we can agree our contract.'

As Morgan leaves, Diana sinks into her chair and releases the long, deep breath she has been holding. Morgan's testing provocations have left her feeling struck by an express train. What a trauma history! From child to woman, an endless string of abuse and neglect experiences... Diana has heard such stories of multiple abuse events before, but hearing them all at once has been emotionally flooding. Can she contain this?

Slivers of anxiety run through her when she thinks of the potential child protection issues around some of those men in the shadows. The extent of Morgan's secretive cutting is also worrying but addressing that is for another day. What's clear is that their contract around risk will have to be carefully negotiated and agreed. At the same time, Morgan's dissociation is already clear; she knows her public life to be a performance, and her feelings are screwed down so hard that she self-cuts to obliterate them.

Diana wonders – how she is going to get Morgan to slow down enough to focus and allow herself to *feel*? How can she gain Morgan's trust, given her history of being abandoned and let down? And will she, herself, ever be able to trust Morgan in turn? As all these questions tumble around her head, Diana allows herself a wry smile: it seems her own thinking process is reflecting Morgan's turmoil.

Despite her aversion to labels, Diana recognises that Morgan's presentation and snippets of history sound like classic BPD with perhaps some ADHD. She has worked with a number of women with similar chaotic histories – with varying degrees of success.

What might help Morgan to engage fully, to commit? A DBT skills group would be an option to consider at some point. But for now, maybe one-to-one might be their best starting point. *If* she turns up.

Slightly to Diana's surprise, Morgan does reappear – and is ready to engage.

Reviewing progress

Six sessions later, Diana invites Morgan to review their progress.

Their sessions so far have all followed a similar pattern. The first half is always taken up with Morgan offloading about current and past relationship dramas, shot through with random references to her traumatic history of multiple abandonments and rejections. Diana then has to work to hold a safe, empathic frame and help ground Morgan. To Diana's relief, this approach seems to be working, as Morgan mostly leaves in a calmer, more focused state.

They both agree that it seems that Morgan is beginning to trust Diana, and commit to therapy. Morgan says she finds the offloading space helpful: a bit like having a 'binge', as she puts it. She also expresses appreciation for Diana's kindness, protectiveness and listening.

Diana is touched when Morgan shares this, particularly as she often feels Morgan is in drama 'performance mode' and is not really aware of her except as an audience. Diana sees a glimmer of hope. 'I appreciate your trust in me, Morgan, and all that you've shared. I like working with you, too.'

This leads on to a conversation about deepening their work together. 'I think it's time now for us to start working on how to manage your emotions outside and to look for patterns and triggers in your life,' Diana says. 'This will involve us continuing to explore stuff from your past but then doing some homework exercises to think about how you can take responsibility for your current self-destructive patterns. In other words, instead of focusing on your past traumas, we'd concentrate on looking at managing yourself more effectively now and in the future. Are you up for that?'

They agree that, in addition to the weekly therapy, Diana will offer 5–10 minute 'as-needed-between-session telephone coaching'. These extra mini in-vivo coaching sessions will seek to bridge the gap between therapy and life by helping Morgan receive support when applying DBT skills to real-life situations. However, Diana advises Morgan that such sessions are only for working hours. Moreover, while Diana will try to be available, Morgan can't assume that she always will be. In situations where Diana is not available, Morgan should note down her experiences so that they can be explored at the next session.

Diana gives Morgan a handout detailing other sources of support she can consult out-of-hours. These include her friends, the National Suicide Prevention Helpline, A&E, the police and even ChatGPT.

Learning to emotionally regulate

Morgan engages well with their deeper therapy. She attends sessions regularly and on time, demonstrating a readiness to learn. Diana grows to enjoy being with her; she warms to Morgan's exuberant directness and the vulnerability lying beneath the confident veneer.

Over time, Morgan blossoms under Diana's validating gaze. For her part, Diana remains calm (at least on the surface) when 'express train Morgan' holds forth. Compassionately listening, she models the 'self-acceptance' she has been teaching while also offering rational challenges that encourage Morgan to be less reactive.

Over the next four months, Diana offers a fairly standard DBT package:

1. Morgan is taught *mindfulness* techniques and starts using the set routines regularly with the help of an AI app. These include: a) paying attention to thoughts, feelings and physical sensations without judgement; b) putting her observations into words and trying to describe her feelings; and c) doing her 'mindful breathing' by focusing on the sensations of in-and-out deep belly breathing.
2. Morgan is invited to fill out *daily diary cards* to track her emotions and behaviour. Morgan brings her diary cards each week to therapy so she and Diana can discuss triggers and patterns. The aim is to help Morgan learn to *feel* rather than perform, and to understand the complex layers involved in her emotions. Systematically, they work through the triggers for her self-harm and bingeing (on both alcohol and carbohydrates), with Diana validating Morgan's feelings of shame or anger while challenging the assumption that self-harming/bingeing is the only way to cope.
3. To specifically tackle the *self-cutting*, Diana encourages Morgan to take a step back when she gets the urge and think about what she wants to achieve and why. Does she really want to cut or might she express her feelings some other way? Could she do a distracting activity or even imagine cutting without actually doing it?
4. Similarly, Morgan learns to take a step back and 'respond' in a more choiceful way rather than 'react' impulsively in her *interactions*. The two of them focus on Morgan learning how to say 'no' while communicating her needs in positive ways.

5. Morgan is also prompted (partly modelled by Diana) to be generally more *self-compassionate*, acknowledging her thoughts and feelings without labelling them 'good' or 'bad'. Through this, she learns to challenge some of her noisier internal criticisms and be more self-accepting.

While Morgan engages reasonably well with this DBT programme, it isn't all plain sailing. Her emotional intensity and frequent crises, plus her intense fear of being abandoned, make the work challenging. She continually tests Diana's boundaries, and Diana often has to check her strong countertransferential reactions of feeling inadequate and helpless while regularly swallowing her frustration.

One issue they battle over is Morgan's tendency to text Diana late at night – usually when she is drunk and distraught. On one occasion, Diana finds herself particularly worried about Morgan's safety, and she texts back, *against their contract*. This simply evokes a flurry of further texting over the following nights.

Diana owns her mistake, and they have to work extra hard to re-establish the agreement set out in the contract, that Diana will only respond to texts during work hours and only when she is available. Diana has to remind Morgan, too, that while short phone calls, lasting 5–10 minutes, are permitted, they can only occur during work hours, subject to Diana's availability.

At one point, the pressure to have more short phone calls becomes overwhelming, forcing Diana to put in a relational boundary: 'I want to keep supporting you with our little phone calls, Morgan. However, if you overuse this, I start to feel used, even a bit abused, and it's not sustainable. I don't feel you're really working with *me*. It also doesn't help you develop your own resources.'

This challenge proves helpful, with Morgan agreeing that she has been too reliant on Diana. They agree to begin a process of reducing the times Diana will be reachable by phone, allowing Morgan to develop her 'response versus reaction' skills further.

However, on occasions when therapy is interrupted by Diana going away on holiday for a couple of weeks, Morgan returns to previous unhelpful acting-out patterns and steps up her bingeing and self-cutting. She describes feeling angry at being 'abandoned' yet again, even though the two of them have discussed other sources of support during Diana's absence. It takes two or three sessions for her anger to subside.

However, over time, Diana's holidays become less of an issue. Morgan starts to respond more thoughtfully and take some responsibility, rather than react impulsively. Specifically, she learns to use AI apps, selectively and responsibly, including a mindfulness app on her phone and she also off-loads her emotions onto ChatGPT, which she has programmed to give her soothing responses. ChatGPT also supports by offering responses that help Morgan recognise unhelpful patterns of self-criticism or 'all-or-nothing' thinking.

At times when Morgan feels 'too much' for Diana, she turns to her supervision group for support. In this group, three experienced, qualified DBT practitioners meet once a month for an afternoon of mutual bolstering where they share therapeutic strategies. Morgan provides much 'fodder' for their dialogue, while Diana receives some steadying validation to keep holding and containing Morgan. It was her group who, in their own protective mode, encouraged Diana to put in some more boundaries for the extra phone calls, which had begun to feel too demanding. Diana appreciates their wise counsel, recognising the need for boundaries parallels what she is trying to do with Morgan.

Ending

Three years later, the therapy ends. While Morgan has learnt much in terms of coping skills and being more level in her management of feelings, the last months of preparing to end prove fairly turbulent, with Morgan behaving in unpredictable ways. Diana suggests Morgan might be finding ways to sabotage their ending (by perhaps rubbishing their relationship or, worse, ending unilaterally).

Acknowledging Morgan's attachment to Diana, the two of them work explicitly on her dependency. This 'weaning off' process takes place over a period of 15 months, with Diana constantly reminding Morgan that she now has within her the resources she needs for the rest of her life. In her calmer moments, Morgan agrees. She admits that simply visualising Diana's eyes helps her feel calmer. She also starts to report handling crises herself rather than being reliant on Diana.

Diana has hoped to let Morgan control the ending process by gradually extending the time between sessions. In the event, Morgan does not initiate any movement towards separation, and Diana has to nudge Morgan, reminding her that she wants to be independent.

What helps their ending the most is an unpredictable external factor – a new love interest. Morgan is happy to announce that for the first time in her life she may have found a 'healthy relationship' with an older man (aged 48) who is kind and supportive and seems to truly love her. With Morgan's new relationship awareness and skills, Diana feels some hope for her future.

Rather than the tears Diana is expecting at their last session, Morgan talks excitedly about the world cruise she and her man are going on. Nonetheless, she embraces Diana enthusiastically in a bear hug at the end.

Reflecting on relational processes

Acknowledging Diana's effective use of DBT, the discussion below critically probes the nature of *manualised therapies* and *if DBT is relational.*

Manualised therapies

Empirically validated standardised therapies follow a structured, clear, focused approach outlined in a treatment manual. They include versions of: DBT, CBT, acceptance and commitment therapy (ACT), mentalization-based therapy (MBT) and interpersonal therapy (IPT), among others. Other approaches, such as cognitive analytic therapy (CAT), might be considered structured but not standardised or fully manualised.

One of the most widely applied manualised therapies is **dialectical behavior therapy**. This is based on cognitive behavioural principles developed by Linehan in the early 1990s for the treatment of parasuicidal (i.e. suicidal or self-mutilative) behaviour in women with BPD. It incorporates the 'dialectical thinking' of Zen practice, such as seeking a balance between acceptance and change. Standard DBT involves various components, including weekly individual therapy, weekly group skills training, as-needed between-session telephone coaching, and weekly therapist consultation team meetings. The focus is on enabling:

- mindfulness
- distress tolerance
- emotion regulation
- interpersonal effectiveness.

NICE (2009) guidelines, following Linehan et al. (2006), recommend that DBT should be considered for individuals experiencing self-harm, suicidal thoughts and high-risk impulsive behaviours (particularly those with BPD). The evidence base is persuasive (e.g. Hernandez-Bustamante et al., 2024; Gillespie et al., 2022; Storebø et al., 2020).

While DBT is widely recognised as the gold standard of treatment for people living with BPD (Stoffers et al., 2012), in the UK, therapists trained explicitly in DBT remain thin on the ground. Research suggests other structured, manualised therapy may be equally effective as DBT with particular groups: for instance, CBT for binge-eating disorders (Lammers et al., 2022), 12-step programmes for substance use disorder (Giannelli et al., 2019), and MBT for adolescents (Jørgensen et al., 2021).

Deciding *which* manualised therapy to follow involves **clinical judgement** about what would be a helpful priority focus, as well as pragmatic considerations (including the team approach and resources available). While MBT and DBT have both been found to be effective psychological treatments for BPD, they differ in their theoretical underpinnings and approach: DBT focuses on skill-building to manage intense emotions and improve relationships, while MBT emphasises improving the ability to understand mental states (one's own and others') to regulate emotions and behaviour.

In practice, therapists tend to mix various approaches pragmatically. As Stoffers-Winterling et al. (2022) note, different approaches can be used in complementary ways. DBT may be particularly useful in early stages of treatment linked to reducing self-harm, while mentalization aspects may come into their own in later stages. Therapists may also supplement standard CBT and mindfulness interventions with other techniques, perhaps drawing on neuroscientific, humanistic, psychodynamic or systemic ideas.

Is DBT relational?

Relational therapists tend to be critical of protocol-driven therapy, arguing that such treatments undermine therapists' clinical artistry and creativity, and pay insufficient attention to clients' particular needs. The promotion of particular 'schools' of psychological therapy, along with the opaque motivations of creators, who may focus on the positive potential of their approach while downplaying its limitations, is a further source of concern.

How can therapies like DBT be relational if a therapist is obliged to be directive, even controlling, to fulfil set protocols? Probably most of the therapists in this book would eschew manual-based therapy in favour of more intuitive practice. However, some therapists work in contexts and countries that demand standardised evidence-based practice. So how can they ensure such procedures are implemented in more relational ways?

A good **therapeutic relationship** in DBT is, in fact, understood to be paramount. Viewed as both a tool for treatment and a therapeutic factor in itself, such a relationship is considered essential for effective treatment characterised by validation, acceptance, and a balance between change and acceptance strategies.

Therapists **challenge** clients' limiting beliefs or behaviours and aim to encourage self-reflection. They are more empathic than confrontational, helping clients identify inconsistencies and move toward change. Typically, challenges will involve questions like 'What evidence do you have for that?' or 'I've noticed a pattern of x. Does that feel familiar?' or 'How would it be to just sit with those feelings instead of pushing them away?' or 'How did that land with you, that I offered that challenge?'... The point is to stay relational within the challenge.

A strong therapeutic relationship, built on trust and respect, helps clients engage with the therapy process, manage difficult emotions and ultimately achieve therapeutic goals (Linehan, 1993). However, if the focus is on simply changing behaviour and learning skills (i.e. a CBT emphasis), then DBT is less convincing as relational therapy (except tangentially, given the focus on behaviour in relationships). Much would appear to depend on how the relationship is embraced.

In the case of Morgan's therapy, the relationship with Diana clearly played an important role in ensuring that Morgan engaged in the therapy and, despite her history, learnt to trust Diana. Diana's **relationality** was evident at the start, when she sought to interrupt Morgan's performance and bring her own presence into the room. Later, it was demonstrated when they shared their liking and appreciation of each other and when Diana disclosed feeling a bit 'used and abused' by Morgan's excessive phone calls/text messaging. Their extended preparation for the end of therapy, involving the explicit management of issues around attachment and dependency, further attests to the relational approach taken.

While DBT emphasises building a strong therapeutic relationship, some individuals become overly reliant on their therapist, particularly during crises or when struggling with intense emotions. This can hinder the development of self-confidence and coping skills while creating a sense of **dependency** that is unsustainable in the long-term (particularly in private practice, as contrasted with the application of DBT in a contained team setting). This was a clear and present danger in Morgan's therapy. What proved crucial was Diana's ability to 'wean' Morgan off the practice of seeking support via phone calls/texts and instead build her own resources.

Diana's focus on the therapeutic relationship aligns with research that supports its value in facilitating validation and acceptance, while providing a model for healthy relationships. Research confirms that more favourable therapeutic relationships are associated with better suicidality outcomes (Linehan et al., 2006). In their study on the impact of the therapeutic relationship on introjects, Bedics et al. (2012) found that individuals receiving DBT who perceived their therapist as loving, affirming and protective reported less self-harm and greater self-care and self-love.

Conclusion

This chapter has told the story of Morgan's therapy and her attachment to Diana. Their three-year journey proved to be a rollercoaster of emotions for both. With her history of trauma, abuse, self-harm and toxic relationships, Morgan had to find a way to learn to respond in a choiceful, thoughtful way rather than react impulsively, and to find more balance in her life.

Diana's contribution, in turn, involved considerable emotional labour. She worked hard to contain and set a boundary around Morgan's dysregulated process while being mindful of safeguarding responsibilities to protect Morgan from harm (or at least minimise her self-harming by helping her delay her urge to act or reduce the intensity of it). On top of this, Diana had to check her strong countertransferential reactions of feeling helpless and frustrated while her fondness for Morgan grew. Over time, Morgan internalised these loving/caring aspects as self-love/self-care.

The main lesson from this chapter is that even in situations involving the use of empirically-based manualised therapies, the relational component is crucial. Diana's *DBT* approach of offering calm validation and protective challenges was central to helping Morgan engage positively with the therapy process, gain self-awareness and learn new coping strategies. This approach promoted Morgan's self-reliance and wellbeing, ultimately helping her become more resourceful.

The chapter also underlines how challenging therapeutic work can be, particularly when we have to labour hard to contain both our client's emotions/acting out and our own responses. The emotional demands of therapy, particularly when it involves longer-term trauma work, can result in therapists feeling exhausted and depleted. For Diana, her supervision group was vital. With such support – from others and/or from one's own inner resources – the work can be meaningful and satisfying.

Discussion questions

1. Morgan reported that a therapist refused to see her because of her diagnosis of BPD. What is your view of the ethics of this?
2. Should Diana have left the therapy door explicitly open for Morgan to come back should she struggle again in the future? If not, why not?
3. Therapists should avoid recommending and using AI apps like ChatGPT. Discuss.

Chapter 7 – Liam: *Eros* enters the therapy room

At 47, **Liam** doesn't just walk into the therapy room – he owns it. With his good looks, tailored suit that somehow looks like it was made just for him, and crinkly blue-eyed smile dancing with charm, he's effortlessly magnetic. A successful CEO of a large company, he carries his cloak of power and privilege effortlessly.

Liam has sought therapy because he thinks it's time he settled down and got married. However, he struggles to maintain longer-term, intimate relationships, and he takes the step to have some therapy to explore what may be happening.

Chloe is an experienced *psychodynamically-orientated developmental-relational integrative* psychotherapist who has been highly recommended to Liam. Contracting with Chloe, Liam agrees to an initial batch of 10 sessions. This is then extended to a further 10 following the unearthing of trauma in Liam's past to do additional work with 'parts of self' plus three extra sessions of eye movement desensitisation and reprocessing (EMDR) therapy.

The reflective discussion at the end highlights various elements of their relational process, spotlighting the nature of **erotic cotransference** and the challenges of **working with privilege**.

Liam's story

Liam recognises a problematic relationship pattern he repeatedly falls into, where the women he becomes involved with tend to be beautiful but vulnerable. While that initially attracts him, he eventually becomes bored and irritated by their clingy dependency. He becomes bad-tempered and as the relationship unravels he seeks solace in pornography. Ultimately, the relationship ends.

Alliance-building with boundaries

Liam and Chloe swiftly form a therapeutic alliance, one marked by notable chemistry. There's a lively charge to their sessions, and they share a playful and sophisticated sense of humour. Chloe enjoys Liam's charismatic, if flirtatious, presence and his non-defensive preparedness to take responsibility for relational failures. While not unaffected by his good looks, she is careful to maintain her professionalism. She knows it would be too easy to succumb to his charming presence.

In their first session, Chloe asks what exactly happens in Liam's 'failed relationships'. Engagingly honest, Liam reveals how 'match-making mammas' make a play for him. Their daughters then might become 'eye candy' at some corporate gala event.

'Sorry.' Liam interrupts his narrative with an embarrassed, if engaging apology. 'It's demeaning to talk about women like that. They don't deserve it. They aren't just empty-headed bimbos – intelligent, well-travelled, socially skilled, all of them.'

'Sounds tough,' Chloe responds drily.

'It's just that there are lots of mothers out there with their gleaming smiles who orbit me. They try to convince me that *their* Samantha or Jemima could be "the one". Yeah, I know. I'm blessed and all those women are definitely too good for me.'

'That's a big statement, Liam. Do I hear a hint of shame or regret?'

'Yes. I've hurt them; they don't deserve what I've done to them. It starts well enough for the first couple of months; sex is often fantastic; we have a great time. But then I start feeling bored and, as I pull away, they fawn, cry, get clingy and I can't bear that. I pull away more.' While he shares this information factually, his tone is earnest. He then hesitates before deciding to share more deeply. 'And that's when I turn to pornography. I'm ashamed to admit, I like BDSM – domination, sadism, the hard stuff. Once that takes root, the relationship is lucky to last the month.'

Chloe sees Liam checking her response. Although she is careful to show no reaction and continues to listen compassionately, she finds herself torn. As a self-identified feminist, she supports the idea of being free to choose the type of sex you like. But she doesn't like the way pornography objectifies women, and BDSM troubles her. She remains suspicious of claims that these sexual practices have no connection to power dynamics outside of the bedroom. Despite her professional and life experience, she lacks confidence about working specifically with 'kink', beyond the need to respect diverse sexual expressions.

'I'm actually a gentle lover,' Liam adds with a rueful smile. Chloe has to dampen her response to this seductive announcement, though she can't help wondering how nice that gentle sex with him might be. Momentarily ungrounded, she is relieved when he carries on talking. 'And, while I can go with a bit of kink, I don't actually like BDSM. So why do I engage it? It seems to represent everything I'm not and don't want to be. It's gotta change. *I've* gotta change.'

'I can hear you're judging yourself and trying to do something about it.' Chloe's response is bland when compared with the direction of her thoughts. Liam nods, confirming Chloe's observation, and that helps her focus. 'I suspect there are different parts of you reacting to the pornography,' she continues. 'Some pro, some anti. And, by the way, I'd say that all our emotions are like that. You can have a lovely moment of joy, but lurking behind will be a part of you that is grieving because it won't last long. And that is what we explore in therapy: we try to understand our mixed-up feelings and how we act on them.'

'Yeah, you're right, I'm mixed. There's probably a part of me that likes the furtive taboo of it all; the world drops away when I reach into that space.'

'I think it's significant that it's less about the sex and more about having a secret life. I sense there is part of you that is split off – that's also often our focus in therapy.'

'Really interesting to think about therapy that way; it's not at all what I was expecting,' responds Liam, looking fascinated. '*You're* not what I was expecting, either.'

'What were you expecting?' Chloe hopes Liam doesn't hear her question as anything other than professional curiosity. She is aware, however, of feeling tempted to ask this gorgeous man in front of her the same question in a flirty way.

'I don't know,' Liam smiles. 'Maybe I expected to talk about my mother. Or that you'd be judgemental about pornography?'

His smiling mouth is disarming and devastatingly attractive. Chloe struggles with mortifying thoughts, and she reminds herself that she is a happily married woman with two gorgeous children. She can feel the seductive pull of Liam and firmly reminds herself once more that she has to batten down her professional hatches. Thankfully, she has a supervision session later this week.

'I'm not here to judge you, Liam,' she replies. 'It's about us working together to puzzle you out and look at what is happening in your relationships.'

When Chloe meets her supervisor, he appreciates her awareness of erotic transferences. He affirms her view that experiencing sexual attraction is not necessarily harmful, providing she is careful to maintain the boundary. Any sexual contact between client and therapist would, of course, be morally wrong and professionally unethical. He also reminds her that having kinky BDSM fantasies does not necessarily imply psychopathology. He agrees that her focus should be on what underlies Liam's failures in intimate relationships, embracing factors such as trust, attachment issues and perhaps some element of 'dissociative splitting'.

In Chloe's next session with Liam, their dialogue takes an unexpected turn. Liam acknowledges that his tendency to be attracted to vulnerable women is a 'mistake'. He says he would like to find an 'independent, intelligent, attractive woman' – like Chloe.

Glad that she has already discussed this client with her supervisor, she takes a sip of water, proffers a soft smile of acknowledgement but remains silent.

'I shouldn't have said that, should I? I'm sorry. I don't know what I'm doing. I don't mean to disrespect your professionalism.'

'It's alright, Liam. Therapy is a strange thing – we become close in unusual ways, and I too feel that we have some chemistry. The question is what we do with it. What is going to be most helpful *to you*?'

Silence.

When Liam doesn't respond, Chloe decides to be upfront about what's happening between them. 'Do you know, Liam, it's like we're having some sort of "honeymoon". I suspect you're enjoying my complete attention – and it's unusual for you to allow someone beneath your polished veneer. I wonder if the parts of you that aren't seen much in your everyday life are enjoying being more seen?'

'That's it! That's exactly right. You see, that's why I'm saying I wish I could find someone with your intelligence and insight, someone who really gets me.'

Chloe is aware that they are on dangerous ground and that they've got there incredibly quickly. The intimacy between them has grown like wildfire. Can she contain it? It's not just a case of stepping back coldly – that would be an avoidance of intimacy, perhaps matching Liam's pornography process. She needs to stay *in* this process, *Eros* and all. But how to keep it firmly therapeutic and safe? With a mentally encouraging nod from her 'internal supervisor' she decides to take the bull by the horns.

'I wonder, Liam, if I too will become "boring" once you feel like your needs aren't getting met?'

This provocative comment proves a breakthrough moment. From this point onwards, Chloe and Liam use their own relationship as a point of comparison with the way Liam engages in relationships outside therapy. As they do this, Chloe communicates her care about what is in *his* interests: an unusual experience for Liam, given how drained he feels by the instrumentality and dependence exhibited by so many women in his past.

Disclosing secrets

During their sixth session, Chloe shares her intuition that, below his 'polished professional self' and his 'magnetic social self', Liam has vulnerable parts he is not so proud of and wants to push away. She challenges him, suggesting that parts of him are 'intimacy junkies' that jump easily into deep connection and feeling 'high' until attachments get real, upon which he backs away.

'What's going on here, Liam? Is it like you crave the external validation that fuels your self-worth? Or is some part of you scared to be hurt by a relationship so you back off?'

Liam's internal struggle is apparent. He takes a breath before making an unexpected disclosure: that, as an adolescent on a camping trip, he had been sexually abused by a male scout leader. This is a shameful secret he has never shared with anyone, even his parents.

It's a painful disclosure, and Chloe encourages them both to stay with his words and give his 'adolescent self' compassionate space and time to 'speak his truth'. Liam acknowledges that however much he tries to block that night out, it continues to haunt him. Chloe explains that people who have suffered such horrific experiences often get flashbacks and feel they are reliving the event: the past becomes the present.

The two of them recognise that if they are to begin working through Liam's early sexual trauma, therapy will take longer than originally contracted. Chloe suggests the possibility of long-term work, but Liam says his business and travel commitments make it impossible for him to prioritise psychotherapy. They agree on an additional 10 sessions.

Chloe adapts her approach to accommodate this time limit. She proposes they also try three sessions of EMDR.

The following week, Liam's experience of being sexually abused becomes the focus of standalone sessions involving EMDR. At the start, Chloe explains what is involved.

'This technique is somewhat odd and involves you moving your eyes a specific way while processing traumatic memories. EMDR's goal is to change the way that the memory is stored in your brain, allowing you to heal from distressing life experiences. That saves you from having to bury a horrible memory so deep.'

'Okay, I'll try anything.'

Encouraging Liam to move his eyes repeatedly from right to left, Chloe begins rhythmic stimulation with tones and taps. While Liam focuses on the trauma memory of being abused, he simultaneously experiences this *bilateral stimulation* to reduce the vividness and emotion of the memory.

The week following these EMDR treatments, Liam says he feels different, although he is not sure how. Paradoxically, his intense focus on that bad abuse experience has helped him feel both closer to it and that it happened to someone else. Importantly, he may no longer be reliving it.

Exploring 'parts'

Over the next few sessions, Liam and Chloe explore the impact of the abuse. They look at how it may have caused or contributed to his need to 'prove' his heterosexuality at university by gaining a reputation as a 'stud' with women. Liam also acknowledges feelings of shame about being sexually 'needy' and turning so readily to pornography that compounds his shame about being sexually abused.

They begin to work with Liam's different sides, or parts of self: the 'sexually needy part', the 'abused adolescent', the 'charismatic flirt', the 'dynamic CEO', the 'protector' saving him from attachment, and so on…

When Chloe invites Liam to go deeper into other 'child parts', he explains that live-in nannies loomed large in his early years. These nannies were like 'foster parents', while his relationship with his parents was benign but distant. At the age of 7, he was sent away to boarding school. Without siblings, he was a lonely child who was driven to excel in sports and studies.

As their explorations deepen, the two of them begin to understand Liam's promiscuity and pornography as substitutes for deeper attachments and intimacy. They also see how he disowns these more vulnerable parts of himself. Questioning how Liam can sustain a relationship when only parts of himself are present, Chloe invites him to view his 'adolescent part' with compassion and respect, particularly given the resilience he has shown. They also recognise how his boredom in relationships masks his desire for something different, something *more*, which he has been unable to express, or feel he deserves, until now.

For her part, Chloe – aided by another much-needed session of supervision – begins to better understand the dynamics of what is happening in their erotic transference. In supervision, she acknowledges her own shame and confused cocktail of emotional needs while also recognising how her responses may be mirroring Liam's subjective world.

Both she and her supervisor are clear that she must protect Liam where earlier caregivers (particularly his parents and the scout leader) had failed. As her own thoughts turn in this direction, she tunes into how her own countertransference is morphing from sexual fantasies to being more 'maternal'. They note that this shift may be a result of attuning more to the young child who grew up with multiple losses and abandonments.

Chloe, who has working-class roots, also admits to struggling to attune sympathetically to Liam's upper-class, privileged background.

Familiar with the concept of 'boarding school syndrome', Chloe's supervisor explains how such children often become unable to soothe themselves and develop a defensive 'false self' (Winnicott's 1960 term for a psychological armour that hides and protects the vulnerable self from overwhelmingly un-processable feelings). Her supervisor also discusses research findings on the dissociative splitting of 'home selves' from 'school selves', which can occur when children feel abandoned. He wonders if Liam's secretive pornography life is another version of his splitting process. Chloe admits with embarrassment that she has not appreciated the dark layers of broken relationships that children born into privilege may suffer and thanks her supervisor for challenging her 'unthinking classism'.

Chloe brings her insights from supervision back to Liam. Together, they acknowledge the impact of the developmental wounds he has suffered: ones arising from both the sexual abuse incident and the more pervasive losses around nannies and being sent to boarding school so young.

Over time, Liam learns to be more aware of his relational needs (e.g. for security, to be seen, mirrored, appreciated, validated and be able to express love) (Erskine, 2011). He also learns to be more attentive to different parts of himself, including his 'shame-self', and he discovers the dangers of being stuck in replays of power dynamics. In his case, the pattern has been one of alternating between 'rescuing' vulnerable women and invoking his 'protector' self-part to prevent him from getting too attached, if landing up in a toxic relationship or (worse) being abandoned. He even recognises that his initial attraction to Chloe was a further instance of his tendency to pursue impossible/undesirable relationships.

Through understanding these patterns, Liam develops a new 'self-caring' part to hold all his parts together. He recognises that the potency he exerts so effortlessly in the corporate world needs to move beyond simple sexual power in his intimate relationships.

At the end of their 20+3 sessions, Liam expresses gratitude for all his new insights. He now feels clearer about what he needs in a new partner, and why he needs to communicate these needs before 'boredom' sets in. He is grateful for Chloe's perceptive honesty and her ability to read him better than anyone has ever done before.

Chloe herself is aware of feeling a sense of loss. She will miss their lively sessions, and Liam's charismatic presence. Part of her even feels abandoned. (Or is that coming from him?)

Reflecting on relational processes

The therapeutic relationship here can be viewed as a microcosm of Liam's life relationships, where the dialogic gestalt concept of '**enduring relational themes**' (Jacobs, 2017) is helpful. These are the clients' embodied patterns of relating derived from historical experiences, which become co-created in relationships. Therefore, a relational focus is recommended rather than working solely intrapsychically. Here, the therapeutic relationship was itself placed under the spotlight; it became the means by which Liam and Chloe could shine light on what was actually happening in Liam's relationships outside therapy. All of these elements testify to the committed relational approach taken.

Chloe's apparent **non-judgemental acceptance** of Liam's promiscuity and use of kinky pornography is also relationally significant. There is a place for therapists to share their personal/political views; however, doing so must be specifically in the client's interests. While such disclosures may help deepen therapeutic relationships, in this case, it seems that it was helpful that Chloe did not reveal her own viewpoint.

The focus on Liam's **internal relational world** as part of Chloe's *psychodynamically-orientated developmental-relational integrative approach* (Erskine et al., 1999) can be seen as another aspect of Chloe's relational work. Together, Liam and Chloe found and named different parts in an informal, spontaneously emergent way, a process that culminated in the fostering of Liam's 'self-caring part'. This could also have been done using particular theoretical frameworks. Applying *internal family systems* theory (IFS) (Schwartz, 1995), for example, Liam's care-taking of vulnerable women could be categorised as 'manager' or 'protector' parts trying to prevent his abused 'exile' part from coming into awareness. In the same way, his use of pornography could be seen as coming from his 'firefighter' part, whose role had been to divert attention away from 'exile's' shame (Finlay, 2025).

If Liam's therapy was distinctly relational at the beginning, the use of **EMDR** (Shapiro, 2001) was *not* relational per se. While standard EMDR doesn't explicitly focus on the therapeutic relationship, that relationship could be seen as a vital component in scaffolding the effectiveness of EMDR. Chloe's choice of three standalone sessions of EMDR as part of wider relational therapy is a less common, but still accepted, protocol. It would appear that her clinical judgement (from her specialist training) told her that this ring-fenced approach would be helpful, given the 'one-off' nature of the sexual abuse incident. That Liam's memories of the abuse were still intrusive, and were fuelling his difficulties with trust and attachment, shouted out the need for a therapeutic response.

Towards the end of therapy, their relationship came to the fore again as Liam showed his gratitude for Chloe's work and they celebrated his gains. That the therapy only lasted 20+3 sessions needs some comment. The likely depth of the developmental wounds Liam revealed warrants longer-term attachment work. However, for the time being, he did not seem ready to begin that exploration. He may return to therapy in future if he again struggles with relationships or uses pornography.

For her part, Chloe had to cope with her loss as their therapy ended. 'Termination is a jolting reminder of the built-in cruelty of the psychotherapeutic process' (Yalom, 1985, p. 373).

The discussion below considers their *erotic cotransference* and nature of *working with privilege* further.

Erotic cotransference

The **chemistry** between Liam and Chloe is noteworthy. We might interpret that Liam was struggling with feelings of sexual shame and that he was projecting those feelings onto Chloe, leading her to experience a sense of discomfort, sexual tension, or even attraction. Chloe, for her part, had to struggle against the seductive pull of the erotic process, which might involve being playful, alive and risky, rather than being directly sexual. She knew it was crucial to manage these feelings, rather than suppress them. The question at stake was whether her feelings of attraction arose from Liam's process or stemmed from her own unmet needs.

That Chloe's initial sexual attraction towards Liam morphed into **maternal countertransference** is unsurprising, given the revelations of hidden losses and traumas in his childhood. These long-term wounds resulted in broken relationships and dissociative splitting while encouraging him to develop a polished veneer. In interpretive psychoanalysis, where libidinal energy is viewed as enlivening, such *maternal eroticism* is seen as the vitality a mother can bring to enable a child's growth – a metaphor for the analytic process (Elise, 2019).

As Mann (1999) notes, erotic feelings experienced by both clients and therapists can be used to bring about positive transference. Professional ethics require that boundaries be firmly and safely held, while it could be considered unethical to avoid acknowledging the playful charge of *Eros*. Such feelings are a normal, if often unspoken, part of the therapeutic relationship; they stem from the intimacy and intensity of the therapeutic process, which must, of course, be managed ethically (Finlay, 2019). With **erotic countertransference**, a therapist's romantic, intimate, sensual or sexual feelings towards a client can be understood in different ways. Commonly, erotic countertransference is interpreted in psychoanalysis as *projective identification* where the therapist is seen to be a container of disavowed wishes. This might be understood as a client projecting unwanted or intolerable feelings onto the therapist who, in turn, experiences those feelings as their own, potentially leading to an erotic countertransference response. They could signal a 'repetition', an 'oedipal conquest', a 'need', a 'guilty pleasure' and so forth. An absence of erotic energy could even be seen as problematic, prompting therapists to explore whether the inhibition is in the client or themselves (Celenza, 2025).

Other authors argue that the intimacy created by working with the sexual dimension of the therapeutic relationship can initiate a co-created unconscious dance that presents opportunities for **relational insight and growth**. The 'dance' begins with therapists attending to, rather than avoiding, highly charged issues around sexuality. But the profession as a whole may prefer to deflect such difficult conversations. As Celenza (2025, p. 1) notes, 'The place of sexuality and eroticism in psychoanalysis is like the lost city of Atlantis, shrouded in mystery, fantastic, and ideal, yet uncannily disappeared and dismissed.'

While research suggests that erotic feelings in therapy are common, it finds the topic insufficiently addressed in therapists' training, where it remains an elephant in the room (Lans et al., 2024; Vesentini et al., 2022). If therapists are to handle (and not act out) such challenging transferences, they need the space in therapy, supervision *and* training to explore the processes.

Working with privilege

It took Liam time to reveal issues related to his privilege, specifically his experience at boarding school. As Schaverien (2011) underlines, the pain and dynamics around **boarding school trauma** (see Box 7.1) can stay well hidden, passing unnoticed in psychotherapy. Ex-boarders can be masters of 'emotional disguise', where their acquired 'veneer of confidence' hides deeper wounds that can be overlooked in therapy (2011, p. 147).

Box 7.1 Boarding school syndrome

Research (e.g. James, 2023) indicates the possibility of deep developmental wounds and long-term psychological harm in the case of children sent away at a young age to boarding school. Schaverien (2021), who first coined the term 'boarding school syndrome', highlights how going to boarding school so young may inflict long-term psychological damage by separating children from their primary attachments. Regular bullying and/or abuse experiences may then make it difficult for children to acquire new attachment figures, whether at school or in later life.

Schaverien summarises the developmental wounds that may result via the mnemonic ABC–D: Abandonment, Bereavement, Captivity and, for some, Dissociation. These initials refer to the multiple traumas suffered by the children, who may then be vulnerable to sexual advances from paedophile adults, school bullies and/or other confused, lonely children in school dormitories. These experiences can have long-term impact, damaging future relationships and sexuality, and may result in 'false self' veneers.

Through supervision, Chloe became aware of having blind spots regarding Liam's privileged background. Fors (2018) acknowledges how discovering such blind spots can be challenging and that there is no such thing as a completely unprejudiced therapist. Arguing against the fictive split between unprejudiced good therapists and prejudiced bad ones, she urges therapists not to think in terms of 'never doing wrong'. Instead, she dares them to explore their mistakes, where honest self-exploration brings rewarding 'vital curiosity' (2018, p. 4).

One significant potential blind spot is **class**. As Schaverien (2011, 2021) notes, this can go unmentioned both by clients (who may carry shame around their privilege) and by psychotherapists unfamiliar with the potential wounds that can result from being socially and economically advantaged (*wounds of privilege*). Where therapists and clients share a similar upper/middle-class background, both may be in denial about the implications. Alternatively, where therapists are not of the client's class, some 'unconscious deference' or hostile prejudices may enter the picture, and these may obstruct the process of attuning to and challenging defensive splitting presentations.

Conclusion

This therapy tale has centred on the simmering sexual chemistry between Liam and Chloe. Despite herself, Chloe found herself enjoying Liam's charismatic, charming, flirtatious presence and his readiness to take responsibility for his relational failures. But while their sessions carried a lively, erotic charge, Chloe was careful to maintain her professional ethical boundaries, supported through supervision. She used their relationship explicitly to compare/contrast how Liam engaged in relationships outside therapy.

Their therapy focus was on Liam's difficulties around sustaining long-term intimate relationships. As part of Chloe's *developmental-relational, psychodynamic integrative approach*, she shared her intuition that under his polished 'CEO armour', Liam might be an 'intimacy junkie': someone who swiftly dives deep into relationships, enjoys the 'high', and then retreats when attachments get real. Together they explored how Liam shied away from his insecure/vulnerable/shame child parts: those parts of self that carry traumatic feelings of abuse, abandonment, betrayal and grief.

Following the initial 10 sessions, Liam and Chloe agreed on a further 10 (plus three EMDR sessions) to provide space to explore traumas resulting from Liam's experience of sexual abuse and from events and losses during his childhood. While the developmental wounds holding Liam back from attachments probably required longer-term therapy, he was not yet ready for that degree of time and effort. Obliged to accept this constraint, Chloe adapted her interventions, offering the EMDR sessions to directly address his flashback memories of being sexually abused.

Over time, Liam learnt to attend to different parts of himself. He came to recognise his pattern of alternating between rescuing vulnerable women and rejecting them, given fears of loss, betrayal and abandonment. Working closely with Chloe, he began to develop a 'self-caring' part capable of recognising the choices open to him beyond the exertion of sexual power. The question of whether Liam will be able to follow through and find a nourishing long-term relationship remains open.

Discussion questions

1. To what extent do you think that Chloe's erotic countertransference was problematic?
2. It is an ethical imperative to adapt therapy depending on the length of time available. Explain this statement with examples.
3. How might therapeutic relationships where the client carries more privileged societal positions (e.g. in relation to class) be challenging?

Part 2

Layered meshing of worlds: Applying a socio-cultural lens

Introduction to Part 2

Relational therapy does not confine us to focusing on the therapeutic relationship alone. It also requires us to attend to those wider social relations played out in families, friendship networks and communities. It demands that we address the unique and shared culture and historical heritage that shapes our varied social identities and our sense of inclusion/exclusion, of belonging/isolation, of being valued/discounted (Finlay, 2025). The phrase 'the personal is political' (popularised by feminists, and the civil rights and black power movements from the 1960s) underscores the connections between personal experience and larger social structures (Orbach, 2003).

The six stories in this second part apply this lens. We hear about clients' and therapists' cultural, racial/ethnic, and intergenerational heritage, as well as their relationships in workplaces, schools and families. Different *systemic* therapies beyond one-to-one work are foregrounded, including constellations therapy, family therapy and groupwork.

The point stressed throughout is that, since therapists work with complex human beings with different backgrounds and intricate social histories, therapy involves more than changing individual behaviour or internal emotional states. Instead, therapy takes place in a *relational-cultural* context (Jordan, 2024) where the social worlds of both therapist and client are in play.

The chapters particularly highlight the role played by *power* (privilege and oppression) and *intersectionality* (interacting social factors such as gender, race and age) in the therapeutic relationship. See Burnham's (2012) account of the evolution of his 'Social Graces' – GGRRAAACCEEESSS – which he developed with Roper-Hall (1998):

- Gender; Gender identity; Geography
- Race; Religion
- Age; Ability; Appearance
- Class; Culture [also, Caste]
- Education; Ethnicity; Economics
- Spirituality; Sexuality; Sexual orientation.

Intersections of these social factors can create overlapping systems of discrimination and disadvantage. They position us all in certain ways that result in a kaleidoscope of potency, privilege and powerlessness (Finlay, 2025). Our job as therapists is to be responsive to each individual's unique constellation of social identities and how they are positioned within intergenerational relationships and social systems. Most of us would not intentionally discriminate, which makes it more challenging when we realise that our beliefs or actions may inadvertently contribute to further demeaning others.

Often, an apparently straightforward 'problem' turns out to have deeper elements and ambiguously complex, intergenerational or cultural richness. The intriguing question at stake with relational work is how the layered social worlds of therapist and client mesh.

Chapter 8 – Taigh: Murdered 'part of self'

Taigh is a 28-year-old neurodivergent (autistic) website designer who has embraced a non-binary gender identity. Usually buzzing with creative energy, Taigh is currently depressed following a traumatic loss and has been struggling to get out of bed and off to work in the morning. They decide to seek counselling.

Taigh deliberately seeks out a therapist who is familiar with, and accepting of, their alternative lifestyle as an 'autistic, non-binary Goth' and their hobby around LARPing (live action role-playing). The psychotherapeutic counsellor – Amanda – makes her openness and acceptance clear, reassuring Taigh that she can engage *LGBTQ+ affirmative therapy* – an approach that validates and advocates for the needs of sexual/gender minority individuals and acknowledges the stigma and social obstacles they can face.

Taigh and Amanda agree eight sessions of counselling focused on Taigh's grief. Amanda's approach is largely *existential* while drawing on *psychodramatic techniques*. Throughout, she is attentive to Taigh's sub-cultural/community identities. In particular, she acknowledges Taigh's preferred pronouns are they/them and mentally notes she needs to try to avoid thinking of Taigh as 'him'.

This therapy tale shows the vital importance of attuning to another's way of being through adapting one's approach and language to meet that individual in their preferred way. The reflective discussion at the end of the chapter engages socio political aspects, examining the nature of **affirmative therapy** and issues around **working relationally with neurodiversity**.

Taigh's story

Taigh embraces an alternative Goth style (piercings, long black hair, eyeliner and black nail polish) and has a large circle of friends centred on LARPing. Enthusiasts attend group fantasy game events involving more than 1,000 players who dress in character and act out roles within the creative community. Recently, 'Skyler', a powerful wizard character Taigh had played for several years, was 'assassinated' as part of the political manoeuvrings in the game. This character was a central part of Taigh's identity – within and outside the game – and the loss feels traumatic.

Taigh also reveals being autistic but they prefer the label 'neurospicy'. Amanda and Taigh talk about Taigh's experience of 'masking', where Taigh hides behind characters and imitates others to fit in. Asked what reasonable adjustments Amanda can make for the autism, Taigh requests that the lights be lowered slightly and that Amanda be straightforward in her responses.

While responsive and obliging, Amanda privately has some doubts and discomforts. She wonders if she can do justice to her self-professed affirmative therapy practice, given that she is neurotypical herself and has not previously worked with an autistic non-binary client.

Grief work

'My character, Skyler, was murdered,' announces Taigh somewhat melodramatically in their first session. 'They were out to get me.'

As she learns more about Taigh's grief, Amanda suggests it is an experience of 'traumatic, disenfranchised grief' because of the violence involved and the fact that others may not see grief over a fictional character as 'real' or 'legitimate'. She acknowledges this is just another facet of how Taigh's life does not conform to society's attitudes/norms/expectations and how that increases the risk of Taigh being and feeling isolated.

Amanda explains how grief is a process that takes time. The first tasks, she says, are about 'accepting the loss' and 'feeling its pain'. Then it's about 'adjusting to the world without the lost person' and 'finding ways to re-invest the emotional energy of grieving'. These four tasks offer a loose but explicit structure of clear goals that Taigh appreciates.

They talk about what Skyler had meant to Taigh. Amanda validates this grief as 'completely understandable'. As she notes, 'When we lose an attachment figure, it's common to feel lost, abandoned and even a little panicky'.

Acknowledging deeper layers of grief, Taigh shares a sense of feeling betrayed by friends. 'I think they murdered me because they were jealous. Sometimes, I hate all those petty political intrigues.' Amanda acknowledges that Taigh is expressing hurt feelings and dented trust in others. Taigh voices doubts about ever feeling at home again in the LARPing community – a particularly poignant comment given that 'Taigh' is a Scottish Gaelic word, meaning 'at home'. Amanda makes clear her compassion by noting that it is additionally hard for Taigh to lose that sense of trust and safety with the other players, given the importance of friendships in providing a sense of acceptance and belonging – something Taigh doesn't experience elsewhere. She checks to see whether Taigh is still active on social media forums, as such involvement will reduce the risk of feeling greater isolation, while possibly increasing the risk of feeling belittled by spiteful comments.

Looking ahead to their third session of therapy, Taigh and Amanda plan a re-enactment of a ritual funeral service for Skyler, with Amanda playing a key role as a witness representing a wider community. As Amanda suggests, this ritual should help honour Skyler while also reinforcing Amanda and Taigh's symbolic bond.

During the service, Taigh lights some candles and reads out a pre-written letter to Skyler, followed by a popular funeral verse: 'Those we love don't go away. They walk beside us every day. Unseen, unheard, but always near. Still loved, still missed, and very dear' (Alex MacLean, n.d.).

This was the relational closure that Taigh had been deprived of. The structure and formality of the ritual also gave Taigh a sense of taking control of the situation.

Working with parts of self

At the start of the next session, Taigh dives right in: 'That funeral was cool. I think Skyler needed that.'

'I think Taigh needed that, too,' Amanda smiles.

Taigh nods sadly. 'But I still feel him. He hasn't gone.'

'Of course, Taigh. And, you don't want him to disappear, do you? Skyler will always be with you, a part of you. Remember your funeral verse.' They move swiftly into a deeper discussion about Taigh finding solace in the idea that the wizard will remain a part of Taigh's own 'internal family community'.

'I'm a *Trill*!' Taigh exclaims in delight and Amanda nods vigorously with pleasure as she picks up the *Star Trek* reference about 'Trills' (a humanoid alien species who carry a symbiont within who holds the memories of other lives).

'You can't be a Trekkie! Truly?'

'You've outed me,' Amanda grins, and they both laugh. Following her intuition, Amanda pursues the metaphor. 'Do you remember that episode in DS9 where Jadzia Dax performs that *Trill* ritual?'

'The *zhian'tara*, which allows her to meet previous Dax hosts?'

'I wonder, could we do a version of that here?'

With Taigh's agreement, Amanda sets up two chairs – one for Taigh, one for Skyler. She invites Taigh to imagine talking with Skyler, moving between the chairs while embodying both Taigh and Skyler. In the dialogue, they talk about Taigh's loss and their shared anger at the 'sect' who had 'murdered' Skyler.

'But,' Skyler adds in a reassuring tone, 'I don't want you to feel all this resentment, Taigh. Many in the community are sorry to lose me.'

Together, Taigh and Skyler come up with a plan to introduce Skyler's 'nephew' as Taigh's new character for the LARPing community. Amanda affirms this idea, saying that this introduction will be helpful and healing because it will give Taigh a legitimate way to talk to others about the loss of Skyler.

Endings

As the end of therapy approaches, Amanda knows that she will miss Taigh, and she resolves to take their work to supervision. She feels some embarrassment that, thus far, she has avoided bringing Taigh to supervision. This is partly because she is unsure of her supervisor's attitude to affirmative therapy and partly because she fears some judgement about being a 'Trekkie'. Recognising this avoidance, Amanda sees a possible parallel process with Taigh around shame and acceptance.

When Amanda opens up to her supervisor, her fears (projections?) turn out to be unfounded, as the supervisor warmly applauds Amanda's creative approach. Amanda then feels able to acknowledge her tender attachment to this original, intelligent, fascinating individual. She notes that Taigh, too, has attached to her – surprisingly quickly – and trusts her.

'Taigh will stay with me for a long time after ending therapy,' Amanda acknowledges. 'Taigh carries me with them too, I'd say. Perhaps one day they will return with some new crisis?' Picking up on some lingering hope that this might prove to be the case, they discuss the importance of her not explicitly inviting Taigh back into future therapy, which might convey the message that she does not believe Taigh will cope. And, of course, she wants Taigh not to feel the need for therapy.

'For now, you need to let them go even if you'll never know how they will fare,' says the supervisor with a compassionate nod, acknowledging the pain of endings.

The supervisor then nudges Amanda to raise the issue of her being neurotypical. Might Taigh benefit from therapy with a specialist in neurodivergent therapy in the future (perhaps a therapist who is autistic themselves)? They discuss the importance for Taigh of taking control by knowing the options available.

Taigh's final therapy session arrives. In their review of the therapy, they talk about how Taigh carries many parts, while Taigh – like Trill hosts – retains control and takes care of all the parts. Taigh recognises that this is a helpful way of looking at their internal world, which ensures they don't get lost in any one character. Taigh admits to particularly valuing their talks with Skyler. 'Having that link and knowing I can always talk to Skyler; I will never feel lonely again.'

This opens the opportunity to discuss what support Taigh might find useful in the future. They acknowledge that short-term therapy has helped Taigh through this crisis, but what will happen if there are future crises, particularly given the vagaries of the politics of the LARPing community where Taigh can feel both supported and rejected? Taigh agrees that therapy may well be helpful in the future. Amanda reminds Taigh that, while she has an understanding of his LARPing, she is not an expert on neurodiversity and Taigh might want to consider a different therapist. Taigh checks matter-of-factly whether Amanda will be available to offer some advice when the time comes, if she isn't the best choice, and she agrees.

As Taigh and Amanda part, they have one last special moment of contact. Taigh gives Amanda a V-shaped Vulcan gesture from Star Trek, 'Live long and prosper'.

'Peace and long life', she responds promptly, giving her own practised hand gesture in return.

Reflecting on relational processes

Disenfranchised grief and **existential issues** were the focus of Taigh's therapy. The attention paid to Taigh's internal intrapsychic relationships, as well as their community involvements, makes this therapy explicitly relational.

Amanda's admission to being a Trekkie is an example of when it can be beneficial for therapists to offer personal **self-disclosure** that accentuates their human connection. It also allowed them to evolve a special shared language together, deepening their contact. Her reflections on the possible shame/avoidance parallel process she was recreating with her supervisor, which might have reflected Taigh's experience, added further relational dimensions.

Amanda invited Taigh to engage in various creative **psychodramatic re-enactments**, including a ritual funeral and two-chair work. Evidence affirms the potential for healing offered by such enactments – for example, Constien et al. (2024), Amonkar et al. (2021) and Wojtkowiak et al. (2021).

The discussion below addresses the application of *affirmative therapy* and issues related to *working relationally with neurodiversity*.

Affirmative therapy

Through offering explicit affirmative LGBTQ+ therapy, Amanda endorsed Taigh's gender identity and alternative lifestyle. [Note that the acronym of GSRD (gender, sexuality and relationship diversity) is gaining traction in the UK as an alternative to LGBTQ+ terminology.]

Amanda's **radical acceptance** was not simply about being non-judgemental. She respectfully tuned into Taigh's alternative lifestyle and was concerned to promote their wellbeing. This relational ethical approach (Finlay, 2019) was illustrated in several ways, as discussed below.

1. By validating Taigh's non-binary gender identity and *preferred pronouns*, Amanda recognised that overt or subtle forms of prejudice can creep into and compromise the therapeutic alliance (Rosati et al., 2022).
2. She recognised that Taigh's sense of isolation and wounded trust meant Taigh needed space to be *witnessed and accepted*. This need was all the more pressing given that insufficient support had been forthcoming from Taigh's friends and wider social world.
3. Amanda showed an appreciation of Taigh's long-term need for sustained acceptance by a specific LARPing *community*. She encouraged this bond, rather than fostering Taigh's dependence on therapy.
4. Amanda's interventions were both *creatively fluid and structured* as she endeavoured to respond to Taigh's neurodivergence.

A key question arising from this therapy tale relates to the extent to which a therapist's understandings, values and/or background need to match those of their client. While Amanda did not share Taigh's neurodivergence, gender identity or hobby/social network of LARPing, her openness was key in their therapy work. The happenstance of a shared interest in Star Trek helped cement mutual trust and understanding, strengthening the attachment (probably both ways).

Amanda's and Taigh's alliance with each other formed surprisingly quickly. Amanda felt Taigh's trust, and she owned her own tender attachment and emotional labour to let them go (a process supported in supervision). Had the therapeutic work continued longer, attachment-based psychotherapy might have been productive. This would have allowed for greater exploration of Taigh's early life, including experiences of feeling different or excluded, and how these may have shaped Taigh's adult life. However, recognising the time-limited nature of the therapy, Amanda appropriately kept the focus on the grief while touching on the potential for deeper integration through work with 'parts of self'.

Working relationally with neurodivergence

The movement around the needs of neurodivergent people opposes potentially dehumanising, traumatising and abusive therapeutic interventions focused on 'fixing' autistic individuals (Anderson, 2023).

Fuld and McKelvie (2024) highlight the paucity of research on relational therapy for neurodivergent individuals. They point to the need to challenge incorrect assumptions that autistic people invariably struggle with relational connection. Noting how relational therapy might tackle the limitations of more behaviourally orientated approaches, the authors discuss the value of addressing experiences of internalised stigma and invalidation, enhancing a cohesive sense of self, affirming intersectional identity, tuning into emotional experiences, and healing through connections.

In their exploration of the lived experiences of six neurodivergent clients, Bowers and Widdowson (2023) demonstrate how transactional analysis (TA) psychotherapy can be effectively applied to this group. As part of their findings, they recommend four specific client needs:

1. understanding and non-pathologising acceptance that they are not 'too much'
2. a therapeutic relationship where they feel safe
3. balance between structure and tolerable nurture
4. therapy that is different from previous shaming, unsafe or conditional relationships.

As Grace et al. (2022) explain, autistic individuals experience loneliness because their distinctive ways of interacting socially are not sensitively responded to by 'neurotypicals'. Applying these points to Taigh's therapy, the explicit adaptations for Taigh's autism early on, and the creative grief-work interventions later, were well chosen and responsive to Taigh's needs and way of being.

Beyond her efforts to cement their Star Trek connection, Amanda made **reasonable adjustments** accommodating to Taigh's particular needs (as per the Equalities Act 2010). Not only did she take practical steps (such as adjusting the lights), but she also respected their gender-neutral choices. She also made a point of cueing into Taigh's interests, evolving a metaphorical and contactful way of working that suited Taigh's world view.

Amanda's use of **psychodramatic techniques** is interesting as it is linked to Taigh's LARPing hobby. Research suggests the use of metaphors and creative forms of therapy can be helpful when working with autism. The value of the psychodrama here was its spontaneous as-if quality that 'gives newness and vivacity to feelings, acting, and verbal utterances… This form of spontaneity has apparently a great practical importance in energizing and unifying the self.' (Moreno, 1972, pp. 89–90, as cited in Giacomucci, 2021, p. 103).

Aside from Amanda's accommodations, we might question why Taigh did not specifically look to engage an **autistic therapist**, or at least an expert in working with neurodivergence. It was important that Amanda eventually discussed this with her supervisor, who nudged her to speak more openly with Taigh about what might be in Taigh's best future interests. While Taigh might well find an autistic therapist for the future as part of working on their wider social relationships (both intimate and within the LARPing community), it's the quality of the relationship with the person, rather than them having a particular attribute or label, that is more significant.

Conclusion

Taigh's short-term therapy was focused on *disenfranchised grief* where they had felt insufficiently supported. The profound pain of their loss was amplified by a sense of having been betrayed by the LARPing community – a relational home that had accepted (even celebrated) Taigh's neurospicy, non-binary identity and creative fantasy pastimes. For Taigh, the assassination of the Skyler character felt personal; it was as if a special part of them had been 'murdered'.

Affirmative therapy offered a radical acceptance of, and openness towards, Taigh's neurodiversity and gender identity. Through her approach and chosen interventions, Amanda consistently worked to respond to Taigh's interests and way of being.

The bond that was quickly formed was rooted in a shared interest in science fiction. The creative, psychodramatic interventions used (ritual re-enactments, two-chair work), chosen to appeal to Taigh, proved to be powerful tools for expressing, enacting and working through painful emotions, thereby garnering some insight and healing. Taigh found a way to reconnect with Skyler, offering an effective, longer-term means to begin to integrate multiple divergent parts of self.

While Taigh's therapy helped with a particular crisis, Taigh could well benefit from therapy in the future – perhaps taking a longer-term attachment-based approach or working more directly with relational issues arising due to Taigh's neurodivergence.

Discussion questions

1. Would you have been able to work effectively with Taigh? What factors might discourage you from taking them on?
2. To what extent do you think a therapist must share similar intersectional characteristics and values as their client?
3. What is your view of Amanda's reluctance to take her work with Taigh to supervision?

Chapter 9 – Wei: Cultural legacy?

This chapter presents Wei's therapeutic story – one that shows how he learns to appreciate the significance of his Chinese colonial heritage.

Wei seeks online therapy for his gambling addiction, but his sense of shame and social dislocation have been so strongly imprinted by his family dynamics and his cultural legacy that these become the focus of long-term therapy with Anne. She uses a *systemic pluralistic approach*, including therapeutic techniques from mindfulness to family constellations, over Zoom.

Research indicates that there are cultural-historical aspects of Chinese heritage that may contribute to developing gambling habits, given it is a favourite pastime in Chinese communities (Chan et al., 2019). However, beyond stereotypes of gambling Asians, studies such as Colby et al. (2022) highlight the need to delve more deeply into the root causes of problem gambling, including those stemming from poverty, racism and the social-cultural isolation of immigrants. While Wei's parents are financially privileged, the challenges of migration (both historical and current) remain.

The reflective discussion examines the nature of a systemic, relational-cultural approach (Jordan, 2024), and the **relational moves** the therapist makes around family dynamics and cultural history while considering the nature of **online therapy**.

Wei's story

Wei is a 29-year-old man who lives with his parents in the UK and works in IT, mostly from home. He has sought counselling because he feels lonely, depressed and deeply ashamed of his problematic gambling behaviour (online casino games). His parents have agreed to fund the online therapy with Anne, an experienced senior therapist who has come highly recommended.

Wei's intake assessment reveals that he is significantly preoccupied with gambling, a preoccupation that intensifies when he is feeling anxious or guilty (particularly when he has lost a lot of money). He admits to gambling in secret, and that his parents do not know that he has lost control of this habit, resulting in considerable debts. He is increasingly reclusive, preferring to stay at his computer rather than socialising, severely curtailing his social life.

Acknowledging his familiarity and expertise with online work, Wei is clear that he is comfortable with the technology and would feel less safe and in control if he saw Anne in person. So, he agrees to six sessions over Zoom to manage his depression and gambling.

Anne indicates her sense that Wei may benefit from longer-term work and asks if, after a few sessions, they might review his progress and their therapy contract before deciding how to proceed. As it unfolds, Wei's therapy lasts for a year.

Psychoeducation

In their first session, Wei furtively admits to being ashamed of his current situation. Through Anne's gently neutral line of questioning, he eventually discloses the extent of his secret gambling problem.

To decide whether he does or does not have an 'addiction', Anne introduces Wei to the four C's of addiction:

- Craving
- loss of Control of amount or frequency of use
- Compulsion to use
- despite Consequences.

Jointly, they agree that Wei has a 'significant problem'. Anne explains that it is not an uncommon one, particularly for people in his age group, given that online gambling is now so easily accessible and anonymous. She explains how the process of gambling activates reward centres in the brain, stimulating the release of dopamine, which makes the user want to repeat their 'high'. Her matter-of-fact approach normalises Wei's behaviour and the explanation that there are social and biological factors at play, rather than just 'personal weakness', is helpful.

Tackling his gambling habit square on, Wei agrees, formally, to gradually reduce the hours spent gambling to achieve several non-gambling days each week. Anne also suggests that Wei may benefit from organising more sociable evenings at a local casino.

For her part, Anne is acutely aware of how Wei's gambling has the potential to be triggering for her personally. Her own father had been a gambler and had lost a great deal of money on horse racing. She remembers moving frequently as a child when the family were forced to downsize to cheaper regions and houses. Aware that her 'inner child' feels angry with Wei's irresponsible gambling, she reflexively wonders if the psychoeducational approach she has taken so far might have the helpful function of keeping her detached and 'in her head', rather than in her angry heart.

Recognising the lurking negative countertransference, she works to contain her judgements, which she takes to supervision. Her supervisor wonders if she might be picking up critical introjected messages from Wei. Has he pulled her into embodying his parents' critical stance? The supervisor suggests focusing more generally on Wei's mental state and lived experience. Anne resolves to work more relationally with Wei to help her see him as a person rather than an 'irresponsible gambler'.

In the next session, Anne shifts their focus to Wei's sense of depression and isolation. She offers a formulation that Wei is using his addiction to push down and regulate his emotions (being self-soothing plus distracting from emotions), and that he might benefit from stepping back from negative ruminative thinking patterns that are often associated with depression. Anne nudges Wei towards owning and confronting anything he may be trying to avoid by teaching him some mindfulness techniques to enhance his awareness of inner thoughts and feelings. He begins to see how he is stuck in patterns of 'avoidance'.

Given his tech skills, Anne recommends that he try the meditation/mindfulness *Headspace* app to learn techniques he can apply daily, particularly when his cravings begin. She also encourages him to have space away from his computer and exercise outside each day, perhaps walking while engaging in mindfulness.

At their next session, Wei owns some emotions he has recognised. 'My life is rubbish,' he says. 'It's all pointless. My parents just keep driving at me to work harder.'

'Let's talk about your home life and relationships with your parents,' Anne suggests, nudging him to open up to her further. As deeper tensions are quickly revealed, Anne proposes longer-term work could be helpful.

'I don't want to waste your time,' Wei responds.

'You're not, and I want to be here for you. I can see how hopeless you feel at the moment – how you don't believe things can get better. But, if I hold onto that hope for you temporarily, would you try to keep working with me for a few more months?'

Wei knows his parents are 'more than keen' to keep paying for his therapy because he is trying to change his life. Touched by Anne's care, he agrees to having open-ended therapy.

Exploring home life

When Wei arrives onscreen at their next session, Anne notes a new brightness in his eyes.

'Yeah, it's strange. Last week was kinda helpful. I've gambled less and I'm surprisingly liking my regular walks in the park. Gingko, our dog, likes them too!'

'Wow. That's a shift and sounds amazing,' she responds. 'You say last week was helpful. What do you think *we* did to help that?'

'It's strange but, I dunno, I suppose, maybe you care, that you are interested,' says Wei, looking a little puzzled. 'I so wanted to tell you about my progress. I can't talk to my parents because we don't talk much and, it's like… you know more about what's going on with me than they do.'

'You're right, Wei. I am interested.' Anne smiles warmly, looking directly at the camera to show Wei her attentiveness. 'Are you saying you feel your parents aren't so interested in you?'

'I guess so.' Wei goes on to explain that he hardly ever sees them. Mostly, he avoids them. 'They are always finding fault with me. They are critical of me for not being married and giving them grandchildren. They call me their "useless son".'

'That's a tough label, Wei. Is that just a recent message about not getting married?'

'No – they've always said that stuff. All through my childhood I was regularly flogged for not being good enough.'

Anne can't help but physically react to his word 'flogged', but tries to restrain her heartfelt response and offer compassionate enquiry. 'Can you talk more about your experience growing up?'

Wei explains that most beatings occurred when he didn't get top marks at school. 'That's what they care about. Whatever I do isn't good enough. They're always saying how hard they had to work, and I'm lazy in comparison.'

Anne feels a sudden shift within her – a new anger bubbling up against Wei parents, rather than with Wei. Accessing her *internal supervisor*, she recognises how she may be tuning into different levels of angry, critical feelings introjected both by Wei and his parents. She also notes her discomfort about hearing of the potential childhood physical abuse. She makes a note to discuss safeguarding in supervision, while recognising she needs to avoid impulsively overreacting now.

In their next session, Anne invites Wei to draw a family tree, which he reproduces on his computer to send to her. His picture (see Figure 9.1) shows that his maternal grandparents severed ties with their homeland when they immigrated to the UK from Hong Kong in the late 1970s , fearing the spread of the policy of the Chinese mainland to only have one child.. Once in the UK, they had a daughter, Wei's mother.

Both of Wei's parents are highly educated. His father, a senior scientist-researcher, is the only son of a couple who had wanted more children. Wei's aunt Ling, his father's sister, has three children and is seen as having made an advantageous marriage that led to their family relocating to the USA.

Anne notes that Wei's picture shows something of a schism between his parents and the wider family. The relative isolation of Wei and his parents from their wider family and community seems important.

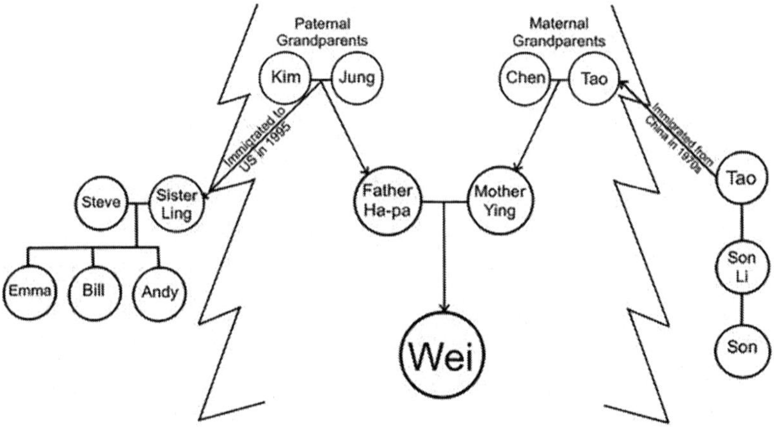

Figure 9.1 Wei's family tree

'Perhaps you are not alone in your isolation?' Anne says. She goes on to explain how issues in families can echo across, and down through, generations. She wonders whether Wei might in some way be carrying a family sense of isolation, stemming from the trauma of leaving their homeland.

Wei looks thoughtful. 'I never thought about it like that,' he says. They mutually agree that this should be the focus of their next few sessions.

Intergenerational pain?

Anne introduces Wei to *family constellations therapy* to help him embrace his wider cultural and family history. She gets Wei to put placemats on the floor around his room to represent different family members and their relationship to each other in terms of physical closeness/distance. They adjust Wei's computer camera so that Anne can see the mat placements. [Were this being done in a group setting, different group members would play each part.] Wei is told he can shift any placemat closer to, or away from, others until it all feels right.

When Wei is ready, Anne invites him to stand on each placemat in turn, imagining himself to be that person. 'What does it feel like to be in this position?' 'What does this person want to say?' and 'How might this person speak to this other family member?' Of course, he cannot be sure about the things each of his ancestors would have said, but the aim of the exercise, Anne points out, is to access what he may have picked up and be carrying unconsciously.

Over the course of the next few sessions, Wei begins to understand more about his family history and the relationships between individuals. He becomes alert to the possible trauma lurking in the experiences of his great-grandparents: for example, when they fled from mainland China to Hong Kong in the 1950s to escape political persecution. He also acknowledges the pressures on his grandparents when they avoided possible future restrictions around China's one child policy by moving to the UK. He recognises that his own experience of shame, isolation and avoidance – fuelled by critical injunctions – is a recurrent theme in his family's history.

Wei now grasps how his parents were likely subjected to physical and emotional pressure from their own parents to excel academically. Noting the way in which children are especially valued in their culture, he begins to appreciate the pressure and expectations laid on each generation of his family and how this might link to being seen as a 'success' or as 'thriving'. His parents' taunts about him being 'useless' begin to make sense. He sees how they have their own critical-shame voices in their heads, and, for the first time, he has compassion for his parents and recognises their critical aggressiveness and exhortations as a pattern beyond his life.

This newfound awareness enables Wei to return to his parents and engage in dialogue about the impact of their experiences on him. They jointly plan a trip to the US to see his American cousins. Over time, they are all enabled to have more compassion for themselves and each other.

Looking to the future

Over time, Wei and Anne explore how the risk-taking and cultural aspects of Wei's gambling offer him a way of expressing his masculinity and competitiveness. They examine the way his feelings of shame, inadequacy and impotence may be subverted through his gambling. Anne shares some research she has found showing how such psychological and social factors may contribute to men being more likely to develop problematic gambling habits than women. She suggests that this research might be something he can reflect on in the future, after their therapy ends.

Recognising that Wei's gambling isn't going to go away, Anne suggests other sources of continuing support, such as regularly attending the group meetings of a local branch of Gamblers' Anonymous. Wei agrees and also sees a possible opportunity to make some new friends.

Wei shares that he would eventually like to leave home, get married and have children. Together, he and Anne devise a plan to replace his focus on gambling, which consumes a significant portion of his time, with a new emphasis on finding alternative ways to socialise, including using dating apps. On his own initiative, Wei decides to change jobs and shift away from online work. He also resolves to start a new pattern of meeting up with friends at least once a week.

On his final ending session a year later, Wei's parting shot to Anne is: 'When I find my life partner, you're invited to the wedding!'

Reflecting on relational processes

The most commonly applied approaches when working with both depression and gambling/addictive behaviours are mindfulness, motivational interviewing and CBT (Menchon et al., 2018). While Wei's therapy touched on these elements, Anne's move to a **pluralistic** (Cooper & McLeod, 2011), **systemic, relational-cultural** (Jordan, 2024) approach through *family constellations therapy* (FCT) (Hellinger, 2003) proved apt and fruitful towards gaining deeper understandings of his cultural history and awareness of traumatic patterns of the family system (see Box 9.1).

Therapy could have also employed other interventions, such as compassion-focused therapy (CFT) (Gilbert & Simos, 2022), for example, by combining CBT with evolutionary and developmental psychology, Buddhism and neuroscience to cultivate mindfulness and compassion for oneself and others. Research (such as by Millard et al., 2023) has found CFT to be effective in reducing shame, self-criticism and mental health symptoms across a range of issues, though it is not entirely clear whether it is the CFT techniques or the relational caring that makes it effective.

Alternatively, it could have moved towards neuroscience and/or body approaches in focusing explicitly on Wei's childhood attachment and abuse (physical and emotional) experience and its links to his depression and addiction. The critical question for therapists is how to choose one's focus.

Box 9.1 Constellations therapy

Constellations (Hellinger, 2003) are traditionally applied in groups, where the client begins with a question or concern, then chooses representatives of different family members (or parts of themselves) and places them (constellating) in specific positions around the room. Through intuitive movements and dialogues, the facilitator enables the expression of messages, entanglements and/or unresolved trauma towards finding resolution (forgiveness, love, understanding…).

Beyond the readily available qualitative accounts of its impact, Konkolÿ Thege et al. (2021) provide a systematic review of research into the effectiveness of constellations. Results show significant post-intervention improvements in most outcome variables, including quality of life.

Research over the last half-century has confirmed strong links between mental distress and **wider social factors** such as inequalities, political unrest, poverty and/or lack of social support. As Kirkbride et al. (2024) note, addressing the social determinants of mental health is imperative for social justice. There is a need to acknowledge the role played by wider systemic/structural factors – be they *micro*-family dynamics or *macro*-sociopolitical realities – in all our therapeutic relationships (Finlay, 2025).

In Wei's case, trauma lurking in his family's history, along with parental abuse, emerges as a significant factor in his problematic gambling. The concept of **intergenerational trauma** (Yehuda & Lehrner, 2018) acknowledges how children can find themselves grappling with their parents' post-traumatic states; in turn, their own offspring may continue to feel the effects. With this understanding, there is a growing consensus that therapeutic interventions for psychological trauma – transgenerational trauma specifically –

need to embrace a broader approach.

The exploration below probes Anne's *relational moves* and the use of *online therapy* further.

Relational moves

Anne's warm relational approach of **invited contact** (within himself and with her) was significant. This approach was evident in the first session, where Anne's non-judgemental, matter-of-fact and compassionate enquiry encouraged Wei to open up about his gambling, despite his shame. But the relational element kicked in explicitly with her question: 'You're saying you found last week helpful. What were *we* doing to help that?' She then invited Wei to contrast his openness with her with how he was with his parents. Such interventions are designed to check into the here-and-now of the therapy relationship, emphasising the collaborative nature of the therapy.

Another key element of Anne's relational approach was her **reflexive attention** around her own complicated responses to Wei's gambling because of her personal family history. That she made an active decision not to reveal her angry responses is an important aspect of relational ethics (Finlay, 2019). However, her reflexive awareness of her feelings would have helped her tune into layers of anger bubbling beneath the surface of both Wei and his parents. Transferentially speaking, we might hypothesise that the anger sensed in the room could have risen from Wei's unexpressed anger–resentment, his parents' anger–frustration, Anne's anger–bitterness towards her own father, and/or the anger experienced intergenerationally by various family members fleeing from political conflicts.

Anne made constructive use of **supervision** to contain both the nascent negative countertransference, her archaic anger and her growing anger towards Wei's critical parents. This ensured she was present with Wei in their relational space. She needed to acknowledge her own process, even if it was not explicitly disclosed in sessions. She also recognised the need to slow down to understand more, rather than react impulsively, about Wei's disclosure that he had been 'flogged' and what this might mean (Rouf & Waites, 2023).

Anne also tried to equalise **power differentials**. 'Issues of power imbalance and oppression are central to any therapeutic understanding and intervention', says Jordan (2024, p. 11). She goes on to say: 'Unacknowledged privilege and the subtle or blatant use of power over others inevitably create division, anger, disempowerment, depression, shame, and disconnection.' While most therapists would not intentionally discriminate, it is challenging to realise that our belief systems and actions may sometimes have a demeaning impact on others (Sue et al., 2022). This can happen in obvious ways, such as when unintentional racism or sexism creeps in. More subtly, it can happen if therapists pathologise their clients by using reductionist labels or lose a holistic sense of their being.

Anne was careful from the start to adopt a neutral, **matter-of-fact approach** that recognised how wider social factors were fuelling Wei's behaviour. While her use of psychoeducation might have risked making Wei feel small or silenced in the face of expert authority (Proctor, 2018), she avoided this trap by engaging a collaborative approach. Furthermore, the way Anne adapted therapy to leverage Wei's technical expertise and agency in exploring apps at his own pace, rather than simply employing CBT (or MBCT) protocols in a top-down manner, is also significant.

Online therapy

That Wei's therapy took place over Zoom needs comment. It is interesting that, with minor modifications, Anne was still able to apply the same interventions she would have done had they been in-person. Wei's ease with being online and Anne's awareness of her online presentation (e.g. ensuring she looked at the camera) were significant factors ensuring their online contact worked.

T. Brown (2025) recognises that some clients (and Wei would appear to be one of these) find it safer, familiar and more containing to be in their own space. Importantly, online work potentially gives the client more control over what can be seen, allowing them to titrate levels of contact and manage any sense of intrusion directly. However, some clients find online work unsatisfactory. They can struggle to hold boundaries with their family/home life (for instance, children suddenly joining the session), while others find it too distancing or the technology alienating.

Since the pandemic, when lockdown forced online work, many

therapists have stayed online and/or manage hybrid practices, finding it a cost-effective, convenient, accessible way of working. BACP (2025), drawing on findings from its annual Public Perceptions Survey, suggests that twice as many people are having therapy via video conferencing (e.g. Zoom) compared to five years ago (13% in 2025).

Research (e.g. Full et al., 2024) suggests that online therapy can be as effective as in-person therapy and that therapists can still be attentive to embodied communications and nurture a therapeutic relationship. Studies have even shown that online work can be a protective factor in reducing psychotherapists' burnout (Cavarretta et al., 2025). As it can also be problematic, extra training is recommended to promote best practice, while special care is needed to ensure confidentiality and online security (Aafjes-van Doorn et al., 2020).

Conclusion

Wei's therapy story highlights the importance of actively acknowledging the complex tapestry of social, cultural and historical relationships we all carry (McKenzie-Mavinga, 2016). Recognising this helped Wei to understand the gambling, the isolation and his parents' critical harshness, in terms of the insidious 'cultural scripts' he had absorbed. Through therapy, he learnt how messages internalised from his family and wider Chinese community/culture may have influenced them all (Shivanath & Hiremath, 2003). Wei's cultural legacy – including punitive exhortations to work hard and produce a family – proved a burden.

While Anne could, equally, have used more cognitive behavioural techniques to work with both Wei's depression and addictive gambling behaviour, her *systemic, pluralistic, relational-cultural approach* applying *constellations therapy* seemed to bring dividends. Rather than the gambling, Anne chose to focus on Wei's relational history as fuelling his need to feel more potent and to self-soothe (through isolating secretive habits). That their work took place online, a familiar and safe space for Wei, probably helped promote his ease and their relationship-building.

Therapy has enabled Wei to step onto a new life path. Will he be able to stay on it…?

Discussion questions

1. Compare and contrast the pros and cons of offering CBT versus systemic approaches for Wei's therapy.
2. What enables online therapy to be as effective as in-person?
3. Critically explain how your values (deeply held ideals) and belief systems (ideas and assumptions about the world) influence your choice of therapeutic approach.

Chapter 10 – Khalid: Finding a 'voice' through decolonising therapy

Khalid, a 35-year-old Syrian refugee newly settled in the UK, has been referred to The Therapy Centre for Refugees following his GP's diagnosis of 'clinical depression' (major depressive disorder). The Centre provides culturally/linguistically appropriate individual and group therapy for those who have experienced torture and/or trauma, and organises social events and English classes.

Khalid's allocated therapist is Asha, a middle-aged woman with several years' experience working with refugees as a counselling psychologist. Her parents migrated to London from Sri Lanka in the 1960s. Married to a white British man, she retains roots in her Sri Lankan Hindu Tamil community.

As Asha does not speak Arabic, an interpreter (Ali) has been allocated for her work with Khalid. Ali is a gently spoken older man who has worked closely with Asha for a year or two and they enjoy a mutually supportive professional relationship.

After six one-to-one therapy sessions, Asha's formulation of Khalid's mental state extends – and possibly refutes – Khalid's official medical diagnosis of depression. She believes Khalid to be experiencing 'complex post-traumatic stress disorder' (C-PTSD) and profound loneliness due to the losses and trauma he has suffered and continues to suffer. So that Khalid can continue to find his 'voice' and access a wider support network, Asha recommends long-term groupwork (without interpreters) at the Centre's weekly forum.

The precarious delicacy of the *individual therapy* emerges from their verbatim dialogue, presented below, while Khalid's *group therapy* is only sketchily indicated. The subsequent academic discussion explores the value of cultural openness through **decolonising therapy** and the use of **interpreter-assisted therapy**.

Khalid's story

During his intake assessment with Asha, Khalid appears to be in partial shutdown as he describes feeling that his life is empty and that he has no interest in doing anything other than lying in his bed. He understands that his doctor has referred him for therapy for depression.

Aided by Ali (an Arabic interpreter), Asha explains that the Centre offers different types of therapies and support. She asks if Khalid would agree to see her for six one-to-one sessions to help her understand his needs and the support he may require. He admits to hopeless feelings about his 'worthless' life and prospects but agrees to her proposal.

Khalid also accepts Ali as a translator, despite initial reservations about Ali's background and concerns that he might not be neutral. Ali explains that he arrived in the UK over 10 years ago to flee the civil war, and he appreciates Khalid has done the same. Khalid accepts this but says he is reluctant to have someone 'take' his words: 'I try to speak English,' he says. 'I want to speak English. I must be learning.'

Sensing the importance Khalid attaches to owning his voice, Asha thinks carefully. Although she wants to respect his request, she is aware that the language barrier may make it harder for her to connect with Khalid as therapy progresses. She offers a way forward: Ali's role will mainly be to translate Asha's words, only helping Asha's understanding when asked. All three of them agree to this. Khalid describes how his translation app on his phone is his usual interpreter, and they all smilingly agree that Ali is a 'real-life therapy app'.

Intake assessment

Asha asks Khalid to share a little of his story since he arrived in the UK a year or so ago and about his daily routines. He talks in a halting, painful way about the challenges of living in the squalor of a crowded refugee hotel while emphasising that he has no wish to complain. Except for a daily walk, he explains, he mainly hangs out in a small bedroom that he shares with his elderly, infirm father.

Asha invites Khalid to describe, if possible, his deeper feelings about being a refugee. She acknowledges his relative isolation despite living in the same room as his father.

Khalid: I can't speak anything what is happening to me. No one here is understanding. They see something different.

Asha: And does that include not being able to speak with your father?

Khalid: [tearing up] My father very sick. He lie in bed; I care for him. Too much troubles before. He no wants speaking; just praying.

Asha recognises the need to tread sensitively around his father's history, and decides, for now, to stay focused on Khalid's experience.

Asha: So, there's nobody you meet who knows you and you can't tell strangers about yourself, so you can't explain who you are?

Khalid: [nods] Yes, too much feeling is difficult to speak.

Asha: Is it difficult here now for you because I'm asking you about those feelings? You don't know me; I'm a woman; do these things make it all too difficult?

Khalid: It's okay, you doctor, you are kind, so I try to speak. I know is better I speak. But, men don't speak together about feelings.

Asha: Do you have to be strong with other men? [Khalid and Ali share a nod.]

Khalid: Yes, men must be strong or we not men. My friend is calling me, he saying, 'Are you ok, bro?' and I say, 'Yes bro, I fine'. Men can't say more together.

Asha: How is it speaking here with Ali in the room? [Khalid motions to Ali that he doesn't need translation.]

Khalid: Is okay. Ali good, kind man. He tell me he speaking with many refugees from Syria, so he understanding.

Asha: [She smiles at Ali and gives Khalid an affirming nod.] Yes, Ali is a good, kind man, and he understands much about the difficulties for refugees.

Asha is aware of Ali's own traumatic immigration experiences, but they both know neither will speak of it out of respect for Ali and because they need to keep their focus on the client.

After a brief silence, Asha acknowledges that Khalid's difficulties with English can make it challenging to communicate and connect with non-Syrians. She explains that there is an English class running at the Centre with a teacher who speaks Arabic. Would he like to attend? As Khalid is interested, they arrange for Ali to register Khalid for the class when they finish the session.

Towards the end of the intake assessment, Asha explains that she is not surprised that Khalid is feeling low and empty. He has suffered, and continues to suffer, extensive trauma (both physical and emotional). She explains a little about the impact of trauma and gives Khalid the Centre's standard Arabic handout about the nature of PTSD and C-PTSD, which describes options for help and support.

Asha and Ali meet up afterwards for a formal debrief, a practice the Centre encourages following each session. Asha tells Ali of the darkness she senses surrounding Khalid (not surprising given his refugee status). But as that there are just five more agreed sessions, she suggests that it might be best to avoid delving too deeply into Khalid's past trauma at this stage. Instead, she proposes a more pragmatic focus on his wellbeing. The English classes will be helpful, they acknowledge, as will the connection Ali and Khalid are forming.

Exploring loneliness

In the next session, when reviewing the week before, Asha offers an interpretation: 'I think that you are saying that you are feeling lonely, Khalid. One Arabic word for feeling lonely is "*ghurba*", I believe?' She glances at Ali, who nods. 'I think this translates as "feeling alone and separated as a foreigner in a foreign land, away from home".'

Khalid: Yes. [He breathes in deeply.] Coming deep from my heart, my broken heart, no longer with my life in my country. [Khalid checks the word he is looking for with Ali.] I not connected to my life, to my country. And is very hard because I am lost everything, my history, my future. I not know Khalid now.

Asha: You have had a lot of loss. And it sounds like you are confused about who you are and what this means . [Khalid nods, tearing up.] And is it difficult to speak about that?

Khalid: Yes, of course. I am no talking about being refugee with anybody, my family, my friends, no. Shame I am feeling, it's bad.

Asha: I think the shame is made worse when you feel people look down on you. Is that right?

Khalid: I am nothing, weak. I have nothing. I not man anymore. I am refugee.

Asha: [After a moment's silence] I think it must be even harder when you don't have family and a community around you, as they would have been the ones to respect you and show you that you were strong and a man.

Khalid: Yes, there is no one now to speak like this. In our hotel I think some people are from Syria, but I must be not talking because you don't know who he is.

Asha: Do you mean that it is difficult to trust people here as you don't know them and that there might be danger around speaking with them?

Khalid: Yes, is problem. No trust.

Asha: So you have to be careful with strangers because you cannot tell what stories they may tell about you and who they might tell them to. It must be difficult to trust anyone. I am thinking that your need to be silent makes the loneliness worse. [Khalid nods again.] But you need connection; we all need connection.

Khalid: [after conferring with Ali] My silence is my pain. Is lonely pain.

Asha: I think this 'lonely pain' of yours is important and we need to speak more about it. [Khalid nods] What comes to your mind if you think about this lonely pain? [After a pause, where it seems Khalid is struggling to answer, Asha prompts him.] Perhaps it will help to think of what picture or image comes to mind. Or is there a colour or texture that comes forward?

Khalid: Difficult to say. Grey, I think, like the sky here. [He suggests tentatively after conferring with Ali.] I also seeing old tree alone in the middle of a desert. It is big but dead, no green. Some is broken [again conferring with Ali]. Some branches are on the ground, broken off.

Asha: That is a powerful image, Khalid. A broken tree all alone with no other trees. Trees like to be with other trees. [Asha leaves a pause to respect the powerful message.] I hear you also say the tree is dead. I'm thinking it is dead from the lack of water and nutrients in the ground. I wonder if that is a bit like how it is for you being in Britain. You feel alone in the desert but also parched without water to sustain you.

Khalid: The *Qur'an* describes that 'Allah made from water every living thing.' Without water, we all die.

Khalid then hesitantly shares some memories of the hardships of travelling across the Syrian desert as he was fleeing the country. The lack of clean water was a particular problem. He still remembers his parched throat: he says that he thinks he will be thirsty for the rest of his life.

Asha acknowledges the poignancy of his words by allowing Khalid to see some tears in her eyes. 'You really are like this lone tree that has died of thirst.' Khalid tears up in response.

Touching the trauma

It takes another couple of sessions for Khalid to share more about how the political situation in Syria pushed him to flee. Asha is mindful of the need to contain his disclosures and minimise the impact of retelling the story. She gently states that she does not need to hear all the details of his imprisonment and torture, so he should just share as much as is comfortable.

Khalid describes how each sunrise of his challenging journey to the UK had brought a renewed sense of desperation, a relentless struggle for survival against the elements and against the crippling fear that plagued his every waking moment. He then shares how the regime had imprisoned him with his father and that they had both been regularly tortured until their release (an uncle had paid a hefty bribe). The hardest thing for him about this, he admits, was being forced to watch his father being tortured naked, and he carries guilt about this.

Asha and Ali listen in respectful silence, indicating how deeply touched they are by Khalid's harrowing account. '*Allah ma'ak*' [God be with you], offers Ali eventually and the two of them share a male-bonding moment.

When Khalid admits to having disturbing flashbacks, the discussion turns to his experience of 'survivor's guilt' and the nature of C-PTSD. Asha teaches him the 5 senses grounding technique (inviting him to name 5 things he can see, 4 things he can touch, 3 things he can hear, 2 things he can smell and 1 thing he can taste). She recommends applying this technique when he is struggling with his guilt or feeling disturbed by memories.

During the *team debrief* that follows each session, Asha and Ali acknowledge how tough it has been for them to hear – and to stay with – Khalid's pain-fuelled words. Asha checks that Ali is okay, and they discuss how to proceed in the next session or two. Asha's strategy is to aim for a future-orientated focus, one that encourages Khalid to move away from repeating the details of past trauma and torture. Six sessions, she explains, are too few for her to help him into and through that process. Instead, it seems they are already having an impact towards enabling Khalid's self-expression, and that needs to be nurtured. They wonder if additional therapy with an EMDR specialist might be useful, but Asha decides to leave that option open for now.

At the start of their sixth (and final) session, Khalid begins by expressing his appreciation of Asha's time with him. He says that their talks have helped him see that he has stories he could share with others. Asha, in turn, thanks Khalid for sharing his experiences. Ali also expresses gratitude for the trust Khalid has shown. Together, they celebrate how Khalid is slowly finding his voice.

Reviewing their work together, Asha recommends that Khalid consider attending the Centre's weekly men's group. She explains that this includes around eight men and is run by a therapist who speaks Arabic. 'There, I think you will find it easier to find the space to talk more freely with others, because their struggles are something like yours.' Khalid is interested and agrees to try it.

Asha then explains that she needs to write a report to Khalid's referring GP and would like his input on what she is going to say. Khalid is surprised to be asked to be involved but agrees. The eventual report states Asha's formulation that Khalid is experiencing C-PTSD compounded by the loneliness of his current situation and his lack of structured, meaningful activity. It concludes that further longer-term groupwork at the Centre is recommended.

Groupwork

The group Khalid joins three weeks later is a psychosocial support group for Syrian refugees, conducted mostly in Arabic by Louay, together with a male counselling psychology trainee. The group meets weekly for two hours, with the aim of providing practical and emotional support to promote increased mental health and resilience. Supporting the values underpinning the decolonisation of therapy, Louay invites group members to bring their past histories and 'ancestral wisdom' along with their current sanctuary-seeker selves into their sessions while cautioning against undue political references. Their contracting process acknowledges that holding conflicting political positions is a significant problem and an ethical concern for sanctuary seekers, so mutual respect and support are encouraged.

Each session follows a set structure. The first hour is devoted to a mutually supportive 'check in', where participants discuss events and share their experiences of the preceding week. The second hour is dedicated to a more structured group discussion on key topics agreed in advance. Participants might also engage in some creative or practical activity such as pottery or writing a CV. Or they might focus on something explicit: health promotion, for example, or working with stress, distress and emotion management. At the end of the session, everyone gathers to drink tea (traditional mint or cardamom).

Khalid feels shy initially, but he soon feels comfortable with the group and its sense of community.

At his fourth session, participants have been asked to bring along meaningful objects, pictures or artefacts to share. Khalid explains that he has been unable to bring any special belongings from Syria – a significant disclosure. He remembers some beautiful Damascene jewellery and brocade shawls that his mother had owned, but all are now lost, stolen or sold. But, with his father's permission, he brings a small wooden box inlaid with mother-of-pearl that he had smuggled in his backpack when escaping. Khalid reverently unwraps it to show the others. This sparks a heart-rending discussion about the beautiful belongings they each have lost.

In another session, Louay discusses the management of C-PTSD, including the use of mindfulness and grounding exercises to manage overwhelming emotions or flashbacks. Khalid recognises how flashbacks and PTSD will probably stalk him for ever; this damaged – and damaging – part of himself will never disappear.

A few sessions on, discussion focuses on 'what *home* means'. Louay encourages members to express the 'biggest emotions' they feel when they think of home.

'My "home" will always be Syria,' admits Khalid, 'but I am in the UK now. I know I can never go back.' They all share how home means lively family meals and hospitality: these are their 'happy' times. They recognise how important it is to organise communal events in their new lives. Another member says that home is where he can feel safe with people and not fear betrayal at any minute. This sparks a deeper discussion about the extent to which they can feel secure in Britain. Khalid surprises himself when he says that he thinks people can help to make him feel safe and he has hopes of 'finding good people in Britain', including his new Syrian friends.

Some months later, Khalid applies for a full-time job as an Arabic-speaking refugee resettlement support worker with the local council. Louay helps him write his application and CV, while the group helps him prepare for his job interview by doing some role plays where members share their advice and experiences. To everyone's delight, Khalid secures the job.

Reflecting on relational processes

Khalid's therapy involved both individual work and groupwork (see Box 10.1), both of which recognised his profound loneliness related to multiple losses and trauma (Finlay & Charura, 2026).

Box 10.1 Groupwork

Groupwork encompasses a broad spectrum, ranging from practical, activity-based groups focused on skills training and psychoeducation at one end, to explicitly psychotherapeutic ones involving emotional exploration and support (Finlay, 1993).

The value of groupwork over individual work is that groups provide opportunities for people to (re-)discover shared humanity, connection, community and a sense of belonging. Ideally, the group becomes a safe 'holding container' and supportive 'haven' for learning and connecting with a sense of self and others towards recovery. Members have opportunities to explore their experiences, similarities and differences while offering peer support to counteract feelings of isolation. In this way, the therapist serves as a holder–facilitator while the participants offer therapy.

Research shows the potential beneficial effects of groupwork, particularly when working with sanctuary seekers (Boyles et al., 2023). Across many studies, group therapy has been found to successfully support those with complex trauma (see Kirsch et al., 2024; Mahoney et al., 2019).

The **multimodal therapy provided a combination** of activities and support. The relational component was highlighted in the ways that the individual work emphasised cultural sensitivity, while group discussion topics were collaboratively negotiated.

Research highlights how the impact of refugee trauma extends beyond individuals' symptoms and involves families and communities (Karatzias et al., 2019). Supportive programmes need to be both trauma-informed and built around cultural competency. Findings also affirm the need for more **community-based support programmes** targeting the mental health and wellbeing of sanctuary seekers (Siddiq et al., 2023).

Asha seemed mindful that they only had a handful of sessions. Aware of lurking trauma (regarding both past and present), she had to maintain a tricky balance between enabling Khalid to voice his needs in the moment while not eliciting too many triggering and painful details.

Two relationally focused practices particularly relevant to Khalid's therapy are discussed below: *decolonising therapy* and the use of culturally informed *interpreter-assisted therapy.*

Decolonising therapy

Highlighting the need to explore the impact of systemic inequities, oppression, and institutional violence on mental health, Mullan (2023) called for a global 'decolonizing psychology' movement that reimagines therapy and mental health to promote liberation, joy and healing for all. She invited her Instagram followers to create spaces to 'call mental health professions IN' (rather than call people out). She recommended therapists stay curious about every individual's social history and recognise any alienation from their homelands and healing practices.

The concept of decolonising therapy (Turner, 2025; George, 2025) lies at the intersection of mental health and social justice, and is underscored by a relational intent. Recognising that systems of colonisation are continually reconstituted within our profession, decolonising involves an ongoing process of challenging the legacy of colonialism and associated inherited oppressions while deconstructing lurking Western colonial ideologies of superiority. It questions the 'colonial gaze': the tendency to look down upon and dehumanise the colonised – or formerly colonised – 'inferior other' (Fanon, 1952). At the same time, it strives for an attitude of openness towards the indigenous knowledge and cultural practices of the client's community of origin.

Abundant research testifies to the damaging impact of **systemic racism** and smug, arrogant colonial superiority on people's mental wellbeing (Liu et al., 2023). However, the degree to which such damage (inherited from the past as well as suffered in the present) can be rectified is debatable. Even where attempts are made to infuse therapy with a decolonising spirit, not all alienating practices will be eliminated.

At its heart, decolonising therapy invites us to be aware of **power dynamics** and oppression while being reflexively aware of how our own positionality and prejudices can be involved (Proctor, 2018). It starts by acknowledging – and challenging – how colonial bias and deeply embedded notions of cultural superiority can shape research and therapy practice, and how power structures can pathologise particular communities.

Beyond 'cultural competence', an attitude of **cultural humility** that recognises diverse knowledge systems and therapy, is more relational. The goal is to develop collaborative partnerships that are *horizontal* rather than hierarchical, being alert to intersectional interests and nuances, and wary of favouring Euro-centric and culturally inappropriate treatments (Schiavo, 2023).

It can be helpful to view historical trauma and colonisation as core **attachment wounds** that can be passed down generations. At the same time, it's essential to avoid making assumptions that intergenerational wounds are inevitably carried. Familial heritage can be a source of strength and nourishment. We need to remain open to whatever an individual brings.

At the heart of the therapy offered to Khalid was a decolonising spirit that underpinned the **values** fostered by the refugee organisation. Asha attempted to respect and act on such values by:

- questioning/problematising the *Western model* of diagnosing clinical depression
- ensuring a *collaborative* approach involving consent and regular checking that Khalid was okay to proceed
- taking a *flexible* approach that respected Khalid's preference to try to speak in English, despite the problems associated with this (less precise language spoken by Khalid; lack of clarity for Asha)

- valuing Khalid's language and *cultural understandings* (e.g. acknowledging '*ghurba*')
- being creative with *language use*: for example, inviting Khalid to express his subjectivity in metaphorical images
- being aware of the *trauma histories* of refugees
- referring Khalid for longer-term groupwork and to other agencies to build his resources and social network (which also implicitly acknowledged, with appropriate *professional humility*, that what she could offer one-to-one was not enough).

We do not learn about Khalid's work and family history back in Syria. However, we might assume that such meaningful identity-affirming discussions took place in the group. This valuing of family–social connections is a key feature of decolonising therapy. These social networks can be categorised as 'bonding' (the connections made within the ethnic group), 'bridging' (connections made with the host society) and 'linking' (connections made with instances) ties (Ager & Strang, 2008). Studies (e.g. Nakeyar & Frewen, 2016; Nwosu, 2024) highlight how robust social relations have a significant impact on each refugee's health and wellbeing during resettlement.

At the same time, the decolonising spirit of Khalid's therapy had its limits. For one thing, Khalid's respect for Asha's doctor status interjected a subtle, if unintended, power relationship. While Asha made attempts to equalise the relationship (e.g. by asking for his input with her report), this may have struck Khalid as out of step with his own cultural background and assumptions.

Furthermore, the decolonising spirit does not mean unconditionally and uncritically accepting all traditional practices; rather, it promotes awareness of their meaning, and values their contributions. This recognises the limits of 'cultural humility' and acceptance while promoting '**cultural openness**'.

Interpreter-assisted therapy

When an interpreter is introduced, the therapeutic relationship shifts from dyad to triad, creating a more **complex relational dynamic**. This point is stressed in research by Schweitzer et al. (2013), who discuss a case study on the challenges and dynamics of conducting psychodynamic therapy in an interpreter-assisted setting. They highlight the complexities of transference and countertransference in such contexts.

The use of Ali, the interpreter, in a flexible and supplementary way in Khalid's therapy warrants some comment, although we lack sufficient information to explore any of the transferences/countertransferences that may have been involved. The fact that Asha respected Khalid's desire to try to talk in English in the first instance was important relationally, as it valued his 'voice' directly. At the same time, Ali was available to support Khalid's self-expression and clarify cultural references, his sensitivity undoubtedly aiding communication. This highlights the importance of having an interpreter who is idiomatically fluent in both languages. That Ali was an experienced team member well-acquainted with the therapy process was also important. The presence of an older Arabic-speaking male may also have been stabilising for both Khalid and Asha.

Some studies show that psychotherapy mediated by qualified interpreters can be as effective as psychotherapy conducted without them (e.g. Brune et al., 2011). However, others suggest that using interpreters can be problematic and can result in less effective therapy. Sander et al. (2019), for instance, found that the effectiveness of CBT with trauma-affected refugees was occasionally compromised. For some, the use of interpreters is problematic given their past role as colonial tools or facilitators. For others, translation can act as a vehicle of decolonisation – if it is used to enable clients to be seen and have a voice (Chambers & Denir, 2024).

The literature affirms that while interpreters may be necessary, even greatly appreciated, they can potentially interfere with nurturing the therapeutic alliance. There is a need for caution, as a third person in the room can change the dynamics. Beyond the interruption experienced when an intervening voice is present, language/meanings can be inadvertently altered, adding to the challenge.

Interpreters must negotiate a precarious **balancing act** to perform their job effectively. Specifically, they must balance closeness and distance, being emotionally attuned without being overly involved, and present themselves as human beings while remaining unobtrusive. The interpreter needs to maintain a certain neutrality and self-control to avoid drawing attention away from the therapy (for example, by overreacting).

When working relationally, interpreters are part of the relational matrix – and not just a translation machine (BPS, 2026). This might be emphasised in a **three-way contractual agreement** involving the client-therapist-interpreter, as shown in Khalid's therapy. It helps if the interpreter has relational skills (e.g. empathy, compassion, intuition and the ability to communicate) not dissimilar to those of the therapist (Costa, 2022).

Specific challenges arise when working with clients who are sanctuary seekers. Given their insecure immigration status, they may worry about the confidentiality of any shared information. If interpreter and client share the same country of origin, the client may fear the interpreter's judgements. Interpreters need to be sensitive here.

Further, considering the context of working with trauma, interpreters may find themselves experiencing **vicarious traumatisation** along with the therapist (Charura, 2024). Interpreters run the risk of becoming overly involved and pulled in. Alternatively, they can become distanced, even dissociated. In both instances, translation can be compromised. In Khalid's story, the *debriefing* meetings that followed each therapy session likely provided vital support for both the therapist and the interpreter.

Conclusion

Khalid's therapy story of finding his 'voice' involved exploring his being a refugee, his survivor's guilt, and his experience of profound loneliness related to multiple losses and trauma. It shows how survival and recovery from traumatic violence is a personal story rooted in significant social, cultural and political contexts.

Research demonstrates that the impact of refugee trauma extends beyond the symptoms of individuals to families and communities. The therapy offered needs to be both *trauma-informed* and built around *cultural competency* and *openness*. Findings affirm the need to provide more *community-based psychosocial support* programmes targeting the mental health and wellbeing of sanctuary seekers. If healing and resilience are to be fostered, culturally sensitive group/community approaches are valuable, perhaps even necessary, towards combating refugees' alienation, disconnection and isolation.

Khalid benefitted from the multi-pronged approach available at his community-based refugee centre. He accessed time-limited individual therapy using an interpreter, English classes, and longer-term groupwork (specifically, a men's group, with Louay). Throughout, the values of *decolonised therapy* were emphasised.

Asha's care as a therapist was shown in her sensitive and supportive use of an interpreter, as well as in her containing acknowledgements of the horrific and harrowing nature of Khalid's journey as a refugee. Significantly, she also humbly recognised the limitations of what she could offer in their brief therapy.

Discussion questions

1. Attempts to equalise the therapeutic relationship by minimising power differentials are themselves evidence of Western bias and should be avoided. Discuss.
2. How might therapists develop greater cultural competence, humility and openness towards clients from other countries and cultures?
3. To what extent is it important for therapists to have similar backgrounds to their clients, to empathise and relate?

Chapter 11 – Ivy (and Karen): Re-tuning relationships at home and school

Two separate-but-connected therapy tales unfold in this chapter. One is the story of the therapy offered to **Ivy**, a 15-year-old girl with diagnoses of ADHD and dyslexia who has been acting up at school and creating difficulties at home. The second is the more complex story of Karen, Ivy's person-centred counsellor, and her struggle to cope with despair, impotence and anger prompted by her work with dysfunctional families and austerity-hit schools.

Karen, aged 38, is married but childless (her choice) and has been working with children in various settings for the last 10 years. She has seen a steady decline of services and systems, including an ever-growing waiting list for treatment at her Child and Adolescent Mental Health Services (CAMHS) unit. In this story, Karen's struggle with despair and anger at the dysfunctional NHS, family and school systems that she works with is foregrounded. Near burnout, she turns to her supervisor and team members for support.

The reflective discussion considers how Ivy's therapy engaged different **layers of relationality** before addressing **therapist burnout**.

Ivy's story

At the story's opening, the school's inclusion team have struggled to help Ivy. She has had an increasing number of absences over the last couple of years (post-Covid lockdown) and, when in school, an excessive number of detentions for poor behaviour, leading the school to consider suspension. At home, she is sullen and aggressive with her mother, stepfather and 6-year-old stepsibling. Aware of Ivy's poor school performance and problematic behaviour, her parents have tried punishing her, but so far, their interventions have been ineffectual.

Ivy is referred to the NHS-run CAMHS and their local multidisciplinary team (including mental health nurses, social workers, psychiatrists, educational psychologist, occupational therapist and other support staff). After assessment, the psychiatrist prescribes some medication, which will be monitored, and recommends that Ivy have weekly individual counselling with Karen. As family therapy is no longer offered at the unit, the family agree to pay privately for six family therapy sessions with Otto, a family therapist. Karen will also work with the school to create an individualised education plan for Ivy as part of her role in promoting 'emotionally regulated classrooms'; however, this aspect of the story is not included here.

Building trust

Karen starts the first counselling session by asking Ivy to put her phone away, which Ivy does, resentfully.

'Thank you.' Karen acknowledges Ivy's action with a perfunctory smile to cover the irritation she feels. She looks at Ivy, slouched in a chair with a hoodie hiding her face, and feels the urge to slap her, as she does with almost all the young people she meets. She pushes her unprofessional response away and works to attune more to Ivy's experience.

'I'm guessing you don't want to be here, and I'm sorry about that. However, we're here now, and I want us to try to work together.' Ruefully, Karen recognises inwardly that she doesn't want to be there, either. Nevertheless, she offers her standard encouraging line, hoping her weariness isn't leaking out.

'Whatever,' Ivy responds sulkily.

Taking care not to react by showing impatience at this teenage sullenness, Karen falls back on her contracting script. 'This is a place where you may say whatever you want to say – anything is fine. Know that it will be kept in confidence within the team. We won't share it with your parents or teachers without your prior agreement.

The only exception would be if we were concerned for your safety or that of others.'

Ivy reacts with some surprise. 'You mean I can say stuff and I won't get into trouble?'

It takes a couple more sessions for trust to start growing, but slowly Ivy opens up. Initially, Ivy and Karen talk about Ivy's difficulties at school, which are amplified by her dyslexia and ADHD. Ivy talks about 'boring' schoolwork and how she is increasingly behind. 'I hate school,' she declares. 'They keep giving me detentions. It's not fair! The teachers say I'm a "troublemaker" and they blame me, and most of the time I didn't even do it.'

Karen acknowledges how tough such school experiences can be and asks what Ivy thinks would help her cope better there. Ivy makes some sensible observations and Karen checks with her that she can pass this information on to the school. She also explains that the CAMHS treatment team includes a psychologist who will work directly with her school and teachers to create a specific education plan for Ivy. What she doesn't say is that the psychologist's role is also to help the school develop 'emotionally regulated classrooms' by teaching emotional resilience and de-escalation skills to the teachers, but Karen doubts they will get anywhere.

Karen is aware of feeling angry with the school and its teachers. This is often her response when she hears just how inadequate the schools in the area can be and how the whole system seems 'broken' due to the withdrawal of government funding over the last few years. Just what are they doing? Didn't they see the warning signs? Why haven't they been giving Ivy resources for her dyslexia? How can one psychologist hope to have any impact on a whole school? She swallows her bubbling resentment and impotence, aware that she may also be absorbing some of Ivy's anger and helplessness. Trying to be more positive, she makes a mental note to talk with the team and Ivy's family to recommend Ivy's parents pay for a few sessions of tutoring by a dyslexia specialist.

The recognition of her own emotional reactions prompts Karen to work more directly with Ivy's emotional issues. Together, they note how Ivy struggles to regulate her emotions. They take a couple of sessions to discuss strategies that might help. Karen explains that if Ivy can mindfully accept that she can't control what happens to her, she can control how she responds.

Karen also recommends some supportive apps, which she suggests Ivy try out at home, including *WhatsUp* (promoting positive mental wellbeing) and *Wysa* (a supportive chatbot that tracks moods and offers CBT-type advice). Karen pushes herself to talk positively about the 'new really cool' AR/VR (augmented and virtual reality) gamified meditation tool being developed called *FloatMind* (Luo, 2025), and suggests Ivy might like to check it out.

Karen is encouraged seeing Ivy brighten on hearing about the apps and gaming tools. But she also knows that in most cases, the young people she works with don't follow through with the exercises. Aware of a lurking part within her that believes her interventions are pointless, her *internal supervisor* urges her to stay engaged.

Probing family history

A couple of sessions later, Ivy shares more about her difficulties at home. She describes how she gets frustrated and how her angry behaviour often covers painful feelings of inadequacy and hurt. Younger sister Poppy is the 'perfect' child apparently, while Ivy is routinely seen as the 'failure', the 'bad' one, particularly when she hits out at Poppy or causes her to cry.

'Do you hit Poppy often?' Karen enquires in as casual a tone as she can manage.

'No. She lies.'

'You don't hit her?'

'Well, err, yes sorta. But I'm just hitting her back; she hits me first. They never see, of course. It's not fair!'

Karen subdues her initial irritated reaction to Ivy's victim-playing. She wonders if there is an unconscious *parallel process* in play where she may be experiencing something of what Ivy's parents feel.

Karen is aware that this is a key moment in their alliance. If she reacts like a critical parent, Ivy is likely to see her as yet another problematic authority figure and withdraw. Karen urges herself to return to her person-centred values of respect and empathy. She also supports herself by running through some psychodynamic interpretations her supervisor would likely suggest, among them the idea that bullies tend to act out their own pain or jealousy. She wonders if Ivy may be projecting her own feelings of 'badness' onto Poppy. Different interpretations swirl around, helping her to stay in her thinking and away from her negative emotions.

Karen temporises by finding a non-judgemental, if bland, response. 'I can see the situation feels emotionally loaded and really unfair.' These words seem to have a calming impact on Ivy and encourage Karen to take a risk: 'I'm thinking that both you and Poppy contribute to this unhappiness. In fact, I'd see the issue here is as much to do with your family issues, and it's not just about your problematic behaviour.'

'Yeah, my parents don't see that. They just see Poppy's side. Perfect Poppy gets me into trouble all the time.'

Ivy remains silent, seemingly reflective, and Karen is satisfied to let her dwell on these ideas for a few moments. Karen is aware that Ivy's family is due to start their family therapy this week, and she wonders if it is perhaps needed more than whatever she can offer.

'Try this if you can, Ivy.' Karen pauses briefly before continuing. 'Say we call it 50:50 responsibility – you're both in this, acting and reacting – would you agree?' Ivy nods reluctantly, and this encourages Karen to explain how the dynamic plays out in practice. 'You know, you're going to be having some family therapy and this thing with Poppy is something that you might explore. But maybe we could also talk more about your family here, which might help you when your whole family is in therapy. Would you be up for that?'

In further preparation for family therapy, Karen invites Ivy to create a '*life story timeline*'. They discover significant life events that seem to have contributed to Ivy's struggles with schoolwork and to her aggression towards her sister:

1. Ivy's biological father left home when she was 3 and he has had no contact with her since.
2. Her mother found it difficult to be a single mother and was depressed for several years.
3. Ivy vaguely remembers her mother having a couple of problematic relationships before meeting Paul, the man Ivy now calls 'father'. Ivy was 8 years old when they married.

4. Her stepsister, Poppy, was born when Ivy was 10.
5. Covid lockdown occurred during Ivy's transition to secondary school, and for a year, she was home-schooled. Her sister was born shortly before the Covid outbreak, meaning that her parents had little time or energy for Ivy. They had struggles of their own and were effectively preoccupied with those and their toddler. Ivy's schoolwork suffered.
6. Ivy never settled at secondary school. As the months passed, she fell further and further behind in her work and her behaviour deteriorated.
7. Ivy's change of school also meant a loss of her friends from her primary school, and she has not been able to make others, leading to her being lonely. Poppy, on the other hand, has many friends.

Karen helps Ivy understand the pain she experiences resulting from feeling 'abandoned' by her parents, and the roots of the jealousy she feels towards her sister. Such jealousy, Karen says, is 'understandable' given that Poppy has received lots of love and attention, which Ivy didn't experience. It is these emotional reactions that have led Ivy to hit out in whatever ways she could. 'But,' says Karen, 'you have the chance to decide what kind of person you want to become. What future do you want?'

What Karen doesn't say is how she shares Ivy's sense of being overlooked in her family, though Karen's circumstances were different. Her mother had had a psychotic breakdown after Karen's birth and had been in and out of institutions until her eventual suicide when Karen was 5. Her father remarried a woman with two of her own children. Karen felt bullied by this stepmother, who came between her and her beloved but passive father. Karen's fear of passing on 'faulty genes' were part of what fuelled her decision to remain childless.

Taking matters to supervision

At this point, Karen decides to take her complicated responses to supervision. She admits, sheepishly, to her continuing irritation with Ivy and how she often wants to slap her despite Ivy's evident engagement in therapy and the progress they've made. She hangs her head in shame, muttering that she calls herself 'person-centred' but is falling a long way from its values of unconditional positive regard and congruence. Her supervisor is understanding and invites her to 'process with curiosity'.

Karen admits to feeling angry at the managers at CAMHS for closing the family therapy facilities, which means only a few privileged families can now access such therapy. She also admits to feeling emotionally drained, impotent and despairing about the schools and pupils in her area. It seems to her that all the fine talk about 'emotionally healthy schools' is just that: talk. The local schools seem to be 'war zones', while budgetary and curriculum constraints incessantly work against young people's wellbeing. She wonders if it might be time for her to quit CAMHS, because the work has begun to feel impossible, overwhelming and pointless.

As Karen continues to explore her anger at Ivy's school and parents for their neglect – even rejection – of Ivy, she discovers new and unexpected dimensions of her own process to work through. Her supervisor is compassionately sensitive to her sharing bits around how her own childhood is in the mix and how she too had been a lonely, emotionally unnourished child who had been pushed out. Karen sees, not for the first time, the clear link between her childhood trauma, her decision to remain childless, and her motivation to work with children.

Supervision helps her separate her own historical issues from Ivy's. While she notes similarities around being overlooked in her family, she also notes key differences, including Ivy's parents' apparently positive response to engaging therapy.

Karen's supervisor recognises the compassion fatigue in Karen and voices concerns about 'therapist burnout' seeming imminent. He suggests that she focus on the small gains that can be achieved and take this same discussion to team meetings in the hope of receiving further support. They also consider other possibilities, such as working part-time, engaging more supervision and CPD, and even returning to therapy for a few sessions.

Family therapy

Ivy and her family begin their (privately funded) work with Otto. Otto starts by assuming a neutral voice and invites each family member in turn to describe what they believe is the primary 'problem issue'. Ivy expresses the view that her parents 'hate' her and 'love' Poppy. Ivy's mother, June, describes how exhausted they all feel because of Ivy's incessant acting up. Stepfather Paul describes his frustration with Ivy's aggressive and disrespectful behaviour and his concern about the bad example she is setting for Poppy. Poppy says she doesn't like Ivy hitting her 'all the time'.

The issue of Ivy's excessive phone use is then put under the microscope. When June and Paul express their irritation that she is 'always on the phone', Ivy says they are 'not being fair'. When invited by Otto to talk about what 'fairness' would look like to everyone, Ivy disingenuously claims Karen told her to use her phone apps. Paul fires back an irritated comment: 'Don't lie, Ivy – your phone use was happening before you ever saw that therapist.' Otto intervenes to prevent the conflict from escalating. He asks Ivy what else about the phone use criticism feels unfair. Ivy says that it calms her down, and this starts a more constructive discussion about other things she could do. June and Paul speak with sadness about how they 'miss' Ivy and want more contact with her.

In the next session, Otto meets with June and Paul only. He invites them to talk about their own relationship. In what ways do they agree and disagree about their attitudes towards Ivy? June admits to feeling resentful that she is expected to do most of the childcare, and Paul shares how he feels obliged to act as the family disciplinarian. Prompted by Otto, they recognise the importance of speaking to Ivy in more unified ways and being mutually supportive of each other.

Discussing new, potentially more constructive ways to handle parental boundaries, Otto emphasises the importance of remaining calm and avoiding hostility where possible. He stresses the value of consistency in the way they treat Ivy: for example, when setting rules, conveying expectations, encouraging good behaviour, and imposing consequences for misbehaviour. He suggests the 'two free requests approach': 'The first time you ask Ivy to do something, give her two minutes to respond. If she doesn't do as you have asked, calmly tell her, for example, "Now I'm asking you for a second time to xxx. Do you understand what I'm asking you to do and what the consequences are if you refuse?"'

Over their six sessions, the family members begin to recognise and understand how they all contribute to Ivy's 'bad' behaviour. Through Otto's 'circular questioning' and suggestions, each learns to frame their views of others' behaviour more constructively. In particular, Ivy begins to recognise that her parents' reactions stem from protectiveness and worry about *both* Poppy and herself; they aren't just rejecting her. She also recognises the importance of discussing her upsets rather than just hitting out. Similarly, her parents begin to recognise how Ivy has felt 'pushed out' by Poppy. They begin to discuss these things at home and try to foster positive interactions with Ivy. These include playing board games where all family members can play equally. Paul agrees to take on more of Poppy's day-to-day care, creating more nourishing 'mother–daughter time' for June and Ivy.

The family also addresses the eternal issue of screen time. Otto urges a 'carrot and stick' approach to phone use, making it a privilege rather than a right. This proves effective. In an effort to embrace Ivy within the home more, her parents give her extra pocket money in exchange for her helping with household chores (a by-product of which is to give Ivy time alone with her mother). This also helps the general family dynamics, with Ivy's positive contributions to the family now being acknowledged by everyone.

During their final session, the family give permission for Otto to be involved in a review meeting of Ivy's treatment organised by CAMHS. Although this is not common practice, the CAMHS team is trying to cultivate more joined-up services.

Reflecting on relational processes

Different levels of relationships within the family, school and the therapy itself are central to understanding how Ivy's therapy was relational. In this therapy tale, the **systemic** focus (Savenije et al., 2022) of the family therapy was not on Ivy as the 'problem'. Rather, it was on interactions between family members and how everyone had a part to play.

The following explorations focus specifically on the *layers of intervention* and *managing therapist burnout*.

Layers of relationality

The therapeutic focus on **family dynamics**, rather than on school issues and learning new behaviours (e.g. through using CBT), needs comment. All therapy is selective in the sense that priority is given to what are identified as the key issues, given available resources, and this inevitably results in the downplaying of other aspects. Differences of approach and physical resources also come into play: a different therapist (or CAMHS team), drawing on more ample local resources, might prioritise different therapies. Arguably, improvements in one area have a positive impact on others; perhaps it doesn't matter how or where we intervene initially.

On the other hand, critical questions are raised when therapists recommend extra privately-funded therapy, which potentially exacerbates inequalities in care. Considering the 'ethics of financial accessibility', principles of justice, beneficence, non-maleficence and autonomy are highlighted. Here, it might be argued that healthcare should be equitably distributed. In an ideal world, recommendations for therapy/care would be based on clinical need, not the perceived ability to pay. Therapists need to be mindful of potential biases and assumptions about clients' financial situations and choices.

Karen's **person-centred** counselling approach emphasised the importance of individualised care, empathy and therapeutic relationship. At the same time, relationship patterns in the family were addressed through the **systemic** approach taken by the team, which also encompassed family and school interventions. This multi-pronged (private–public) multidisciplinary, *multi-agency* approach recognised Ivy's position within broader social systems.

Much research over the last 50 years around the effectiveness of working with families and couples attests to the need to go beyond the individual. Stratton's (2016) comprehensive report on family-systemic work and other research, including reviews of multisystemic therapy (Henggeler & Schaeffer, 2016), provides a powerful evidence base.

However, a critical question remains around the extent to which family-orientated work is necessarily 'relational'. Some would argue that unless the therapeutic relationship is itself seen as a vehicle for change, it remains 'light-touch relational' (Finlay, 2025). In

Otto's case, his neutral approach could be seen as deliberately less relational despite his focus on family interactions.

Karen's decision to focus on Ivy's emotional world and apply a relational lens offers a contrast. Ivy's therapy with Karen offered her a vital **haven** to express and explore her emotions openly.

A further relational dimension was revealed in Karen's own responses, including feelings of resentment towards her own family and a despairing attitude towards the local school system. Such responses raised the possibility of **parallel processes** in action. Karen felt fed-up. Do we understand Karen's responses as intersubjective and countertransferential, or more about the impact of the realities of the social context?

Karen's focus on Ivy's intrapsychic emotional being was appropriate, given the strong link between **adverse childhood experiences** (ACEs) and ADHD and how the cumulative quantity of ACEs contribute to ADHD severity (Wojtara et al., 2023). Ivy's history suggests numerous potential ACEs, including the disappearance of her father and the possibility of her mother's depression and involvement in problematic relationships. The Covid-19 pandemic's disruption of Ivy's schooling and its impact on family relationships could also be factored in as an ACE (McManus & Ball, 2020).

Karen could have engaged **CBT** to help change Ivy's negative thought patterns and modify her behaviour towards improving self-management skills (impulse control, de-escalation techniques, time-management, organisation of study techniques and so on). Accumulated evidence shows that ADHD symptoms can be improved with individualised combinations of psychological therapy and medication, though the picture is mixed and inconsistent (Ostinelli et al., 2025).

That said, we do not hear how Ivy's challenges around dyslexia and ADHD were managed beyond medication, and knowing that a psychologist was liaising with the school and a private tutor was recommended. Further therapeutic input here would have been helpful *if* the resources were made available, either within the school or organised privately by the parents. In particular, further exploration would have been needed to establish whether there was agreement on what the actual problem was and for whom it was a problem, given that schools, children and parents often hold very different views, which can result in each group pulling in a different direction. Might the ADHD have been a symptom rather than a fixed disorder?

Managing therapist burnout

Karen's frustrations, anger, detachment and sense of hopelessness suggest she was at risk of burning out. She had to manage her irritability and **compassion fatigue**, and possibly even some vicarious trauma. Karen's supervisory and team relationships – further circles within circles – offered crucial bulwarks against potential burnout. Her decision to seek the support of supervision (internal and external) helped her cope while also ensuring the ethical efficacy of her work (Finlay, 2019).

Karen's experience underlines the potential costs and **emotional labour** of being a therapist. Constant exposure to clients' emotional pain and trauma can take its toll on our wellbeing. At times, all of us are likely to experience stress and empathy fatigue and be affected by challenging clients and their complex histories, to say nothing of the challenge of facing our own demons. All this is made worse if therapists are underpaid, have overloaded caseloads, and/or have unsupportive colleagues (E.M. Brown, 2025).

We also all find ourselves up against budgetary and **organisational constraints**, particularly in the current Western political/economic climate, where ongoing austerity and government cut-backs are steadily depleting public resources. Referrals for children and young people's mental health services in England, for instance, have been rising steadily over the last 10 years. It seems that there is now a postcode lottery for therapy, with waiting lists stretching years in many areas. As the *Good Childhood Report 2024* states, there is a worrying decline in children's wellbeing, accompanied by an increase in the challenges they face (Chollet et al., 2024).

Therapist burnout can significantly affect the relational aspects of therapy, given increased levels of irritability, frustration, fatigue, boredom and stress, decreased empathy, and/or a sense of hopelessness or detachment from clients (Sutton, 2023). These can negatively affect the therapeutic alliance and the care provided. Therapist self-care then becomes a critical priority in order to anticipate and manage these layers of disturbance and find appropriate ways of responding to them. Bush (2015), for instance, recommends numerous helpful restorative practices for *grounding*, *energising* and/or *relaxing* as antidotes to compassion fatigue and burnout.

Conclusion

As a lonely teenager diagnosed with ADHD and dyslexia, Ivy found life challenging, and reacted with behavioural disruption at school and sullen aggressiveness at home. Her CAMHS team pursued a *multi-pronged therapeutic approach*, including medication, individual counselling, family therapy and work with Ivy's school, while recommending privately-funded family therapy and private tutoring.

Ivy's therapy tackled how she felt overlooked. Karen's person-centred approach invited her to express herself and better understand her emotional pain. The family therapy with Otto, at the same time, encouraged all family members to recognise their contribution to Ivy's difficulties and to engage in more positive interactions.

Ivy's therapy tale raises questions about how best to work with complex systemic problems and financial pressures, the impact of which is felt throughout society. For therapists, crucial decisions must be made about which issues are best targeted for intervention and how to apply the available resources effectively. Is it enough to work therapeutically with individuals and/or their families? Or should therapists also be engaged at the community level – for example, in schools, towards the promotion of 'emotionally regulated classrooms', or in youth/activity centres? Was it okay for this team to encourage the family to pay privately for tutoring and family therapy sessions, given that these are no longer offered in the service?

Alongside the relatively straightforward story of the effective therapy offered to Ivy and her family, we followed Karen's attempt to manage her emotions and cope with incipient burnout: the result of her slow-burning despair at the dysfunctional family and school systems within which both she and Ivy had somehow to survive. At the same time, Karen had to manage the impacts of her own problematic childhood. Therapists' work involves routine confrontation with stressful and distressing situations, almost all of which require significant 'emotional labour' that takes its toll on therapists' emotional wellbeing. Such situations highlight the scarcity of vital, health-promoting resources, adding to the pressures therapists face daily. More than ever, therapists need nourishing supervision and to undertake replenishing self-care activities.

Discussion questions

1. Do you agree with Karen's approach to working with Ivy? Why do you support – or not support – it?
2. Is it unethical and unprofessional for therapists to feel irritation at, and/or a lack of compassion for, their clients?
3. What role could/should therapists play in the wider community to promote mental health and resilience in young people?

Chapter 12 – Kaleisha: Raging at racism

Kaleisha, a 35-year-old Black British woman of African Caribbean heritage, is the only woman on her company's PR team, and recently she has been experiencing racist, bullying behaviour by her male colleagues, all of whom are white. In addition to providing extra staff training on bullying, her employers have referred her for eight sessions of counselling as part of an Employee Assistance Programme (EAP).

Kaleisha's therapist is Sarah, a British Jewish woman in her 60s. An experienced *integrative-pluralist* psychotherapist, Sarah works both in private practice and as an independent contractor with the EAP. Sarah prizes a collaborative approach with her clients.

Kaleisha's therapy begins with eight EAP-funded sessions, which focus on short-term solutions to workplace issues around bullying, anger and possible racism. As their therapeutic relationship develops, Kaleisha and Sarah agree to embark on further privately funded, longer-term therapy to work with rage and intergenerational trauma.

The story of their therapeutic relationship foregrounds significant questions, including whether white therapists can work effectively with racially minoritised clients. In this story, it's even more complicated, as Sarah is herself part of a racialised minority. So, the key question then, is – to what extent might differences in therapists' and clients' ethnic heritage constitute barriers in therapy?

This chapter argues that therapy around racial and ethnic tensions can be healing, provided the therapist works sensitively with racial trauma and is committed to anti-racist practice. This issue is explored in the reflections section on **selective therapist self-disclosure** and the nature of **therapy to counter racism**.

Kaleisha's story

Kaleisha describes herself as a 'bright, strong-willed, capable woman, full of ideas and energy'. She is frustrated and angry that her white, male colleagues don't seem to appreciate her. She feels bullied and marginalised by them and views this as evidence of their racism. Aware that her health and wellbeing are being impacted, she complies with her employer's referral for therapy.

Contracting and building trust

In their initial contracting session, Kaleisha starts by saying that she had been hoping to see a Black therapist.

'It sounds like racial background is important to you,' Sarah responds neutrally.

'Well, I just thought they might know more about what I am going through; that would save me having to explain everything.'

'Well, as you'll probably know, few Black therapists practise around here; you have more choice if you go online.'

Kaleisha nods. 'I realise, but I spend much of my working day online, working social media. I would like to see a human.'

'I appreciate that, Kaleisha. I also appreciate that you don't want to feel you have to educate me about racism. Would it help if I said that I am committed to being a culturally-sensitive therapist? I value cultural humility and respect others' experience.'

'That's a good start,' Kaleisha says. All the same, she breaks eye contact and looks uncomfortable.

'I'm sensing there is more you want to ask. Is me not being Black going to be an issue for you?'

Kaleisha hesitates before replying. 'I guess you're not responsible for your origins. I grew up in a poor, rough area; I had to fight for the smallest advance.' Kaleisha's tone and body language bristles.

Sarah swallows her defensive reaction and acknowledges the truth in what Kaleisha has just said. 'Yes, and I come from a privileged white middle-class background,' she replies. 'I'm ready to acknowledge that my capacity to truly understand your experience has limits. But if we work together, I will try to really hear *your* experience and your frustrations.' (She says nothing about her Jewish heritage or the fact that she, too, has experienced racist bullying and abuse. She makes a mental note to reflect on why this non-disclosure feels right.)

'Thank you,' Kaleisha replies. 'A woman in your profession, I bet you also have struggles with male colleagues, if nothing else.'

'You'd be correct, Kaleisha!' Sarah smiles, underlining a point of positive contact. 'Though there's less sexism around now than there was when I started practising back in the 1980s.'

'Yeah, that's what my mum says – and she would add that I need to respect your age. Okay, let's talk about what your brand of therapy involves.'

Sarah is relieved to have cleared the initial hurdles, allowing contracting to begin. However, she knows that building trust takes time, and it soon becomes apparent that trust is an ongoing issue for Kaleisha.

The rest of the session is taken up with Kaleisha's understandable concerns about confidentiality and what information will be shared with the company.

Sarah strives to reassure Kaleisha by emphasising her professionalism and ethical boundaries, including the confidentiality of their sessions, except for information that Kaleisha approves can be shared. They agree that their remaining seven sessions will focus on the experience of being 'bullied at work by racist colleagues', and how to cope with it.

Feeling bullied

Over the next couple of sessions, Kaleisha describes the numerous bruising microaggressions she has experienced at work. She tells of moments where colleagues fall into stereotyping, exclude her from conversations or opportunities, and in other ways treat her like a 'foreigner'. She describes how she is pushed into handing around refreshments in meetings or being the note-taker 'like a slave'. After one conversation where a colleague made a troubling remark, Kaleisha directly accused him of racism. He dismissed her concerns by declaring: 'I'm not a racist; I have Black friends.'

Sarah validates the microaggressions as offensive and humiliating. At the same time, she wonders to herself if all these tensions at work derive from racism. But when she suggests the possibility of other motives, Kaleisha's response is dismissive and disparaging.

Holding back her own defensive reactions, Sarah apologises to Kaleisha for her clumsiness. She also takes the opportunity to reflect more deeply. Has she herself got blind spots when it comes to issues of race, ethnicity, religion and other differences?

As she works with Kaleisha and mulls things over with her supervisor, Sarah begins to see how the microaggressions that torment Kaleisha at work may indeed spring from unacknowledged racism and how the cumulative impact of this may be creating a toxic work environment where Kaleisha feels marginalised and undervalued.

Writing up her notes following the sessions, Sarah confronts her own (and her family's) experience of being at the receiving end of microaggressions related to their Jewish heritage. She also recognises that her reasons for not disclosing her Jewish roots to Kaleisha was to protect herself. After all, she admits to herself, she hasn't even talked about this to her supervisor either. Might this have something to do with toxic shame and silencing reaching back to her childhood: issues she has never really worked through, even in therapy?

Sarah is on stronger ground when it comes to Kaleisha's experience of being bullied and she compassionately acknowledges how painful and power-sapping this must be. She suggests that it would be beneficial to examine the process more closely, and Kaleisha agrees to keep a personal diary for a couple of weeks, recording the details of microaggressions she experiences, and her responses. This becomes the basis for identifying strategic ways to address them. That her company is invested in equality, diversity and inclusion (EDI) and has tried to be supportive by sending her to therapy, helps.

Kaleisha accepts that she cannot do much to change the injustice and institutionalised racism embedded in her workplace. She and Sarah instead work on ways to disrupt and disarm Kaleisha's colleagues' microaggressions. She could, for example, try the option of talking calmly but firmly to the person doing the bullying and explain how it makes her feel. Alternatively, she could approach her manager and ask for support. Together, they also wonder if the firm itself might do something more as part of their EDI policies, and maybe Kaleisha could discuss having some role here.

Kaleisha begins to appreciate both the value of expressing herself freely and the exercise of finding strategic responses that she might engage in future. The two of them play around with phrases such as, 'I know you really care about representing everyone on the team, but acting in this way undermines your wish to be inclusive,' and 'I'm sure you mean well but that's quite hurtful.' And the next time she is asked to serve the refreshments, she could say, 'How about a different division of labour for a change? Maybe it's a man's turn?'

Sarah suggests asking the bully if they 'intend to bully' or if Kaleisha has 'misunderstood'. As Sarah explains, this means the bully either has to back down or admit the bullying and take responsibility. Kaleisha appreciates the elegance of this move, and they share a chuckle, imagining what she might do to reclaim some power.

In their sixth contracted session, Kaleisha starts by announcing she has filed an official complaint against one of her bullying colleagues. In a meeting, he had held up her work as an example of what not to do. 'Even though it is done in this way in other countries, it's not what we do,' he had said.

Sarah responds, momentarily off-track, by wondering if Kaleisha is in danger of getting mired in a toxic 'drama triangle dynamic' (one where Kaleisha feels herself to be a 'victim' while simultaneously adopting the 'persecutor' position). She asks Kaleisha if putting in a complaint could work against her.

'I might have expected you to support them,' Kaleisha retorts scathingly. 'I thought you were encouraging me to voice my truth. I see that I was mistaken. You're as racist as they are. It's worse because you think you're not! Don't you have rules against this in your professional body?'

Sarah is horrified by the rupture her clumsy response has created. She tries a repair by apologising and congratulating Kaleisha for standing up for herself – both at work and now here in their therapy session. Somewhat mollified, Kaleisha makes it clear that she is still angry with Sarah and that some trust has been broken.

Following the session, Sarah immediately arranges an extra supervision. Here, she expresses her anxiety that Kaleisha may now file an official complaint against her with her professional organisation. Sarah has already been through one damaging experience of this. Although the earlier complaint against her had not been upheld, the year-long stress and struggle of waiting for the adjudication from her professional body had been traumatic. She tells her supervisor how she feels 'triggered' and unable to think clearly as she has 'rubber-banded' back to that previous complaint.

Seeking to soothe, Sarah's supervisor emphasises that she has 'not done anything wrong'. He raises the possibility of using this 'parallel process' where Sarah herself now feels bullied. To encourage Sarah to analyse what may be happening, the supervisor wonders if Kaleisha is evoking the threat and fear she feels in Sarah as a kind of 'projective identification'. Perhaps Kaleisha's expression of anger is a helpful and necessary event if the therapy is going to be both relational and congruent? Maybe she is trying to make sense of her bullying and control reality by adopting the dominator's position? Might her decision to file an official complaint represent an attempt to transform her helplessness into action to help her feel more powerful?

The supervisor advises Sarah to own her 'clumsiness' and, with compassion to the fore, to continue to validate Kaleisha's choices while developing a deeper understanding of her process.

To Sarah's relief, Kaleisha comes back for her penultimate session and apologises for giving Sarah 'a hard time'. After taking time to reflect on the previous week's flare-up, she now understands that Sarah was expressing concern for her welfare.

This opens up a space to talk about how angry Kaleisha feels and how helpful it is to have a safe enough space to vent her rage. Together, they begin to unpack layers of rage that reach far deeper than Kaleisha's immediate anger with her colleagues. This more diffuse and generalised anger seems targeted at institutionalised racism. Could this be the real source of her rage?

In their last contracted session, Kaleisha starts by unexpectedly announcing, 'I don't want this therapy to end. We're just beginning.'

They renegotiate and agree a long-term private therapy contract, with a more pronounced focus on Kaleisha's 'historical and cultural rage'.

They use their remaining time to plan positive ways for her to move forward with her team. Together, they formulate the official three-sentence report that Sarah will submit to the EAP to account for their sessions.

Working with rage and intergenerational trauma

Meeting weekly over the following year, Kaleisha and Sarah continue to process Kaleisha's rage, recognising its power to trap her in self-destructive cycles of pain and paranoia. Kaleisha begins to see more clearly how her anger bubbles up as a protective response to the injustices she experiences daily. She learns how her experiences of bullying have triggered an ever-present sense of threat. At the same time, she learns to distinguish between 'functional, healthy, assertive anger' and 'explosive, corrosive, paranoid lashing out anger' that damages both herself and her relationships with others.

Their attention slowly moves on to intergenerational trauma relating to historical shame and rage. As Kaleisha learns how unprocessed trauma may perpetuate cycles of abuse, she resolves to dig deeper. She tells Sarah about her grandparents, who were part of the Windrush generation (the African Caribbeans who migrated to Britain in the immediate aftermath of World War II). She weeps for their struggle and the enduring impact of how badly they were treated. Despite legal entitlement to stay, many were denied benefits and work, and some faced deportation. 'Why did they never complain?' Kaleisha rails. Why did her grandparents always talk about being 'grateful' when they were the ones who made great sacrifices for their 'Mother country'? Why did they never feel entitled to citizenship rights when they were the ones who were helping to remake a country shattered by war?

Kaleisha also recalls her early childhood, when she and her family (parents, grandparents and brother) lived in a rundown three-bedroomed terraced house. She tells Sarah that her parents both worked in low-paying jobs; her mother sometimes took two jobs to support the family.

When reliving these childhood memories, Kaleisha becomes aware of some unfamiliar emotions involving elements of guilt and shame: feelings beyond her anger. Might she be 'carrying' some of the emotions that her parents/grandparents never let themselves express, asks Sarah?

As Kaleisha delves further into her ancestral history, she also begins to appreciate the tenacity, courage and spirit of her parents and the Windrush generation. She and Sarah learn that most Caribbean people are descended from Africans who were enslaved and brought to work on the plantations in the 17th and 18th centuries.

As part of their exploration, Sarah helps Kaleisha find affirming links to her ancestors. Kaleisha embarks on a detailed study of her African roots. She learns about the ancient African concept of *Ubuntu*, meaning humanity to others, communality, oneness and sharing.

Prompted by Sarah, Kaleisha enacts a psychodrama: one that will play a pivotal role in her healing. She recreates her own version of an 'ancestral circle', using different cushions placed around a circle to represent her parents, grandparents and African forebears. Evoking their presence, Kaleisha then sits on each cushion to talk for and with that person.

Over the next two months, the 'cushion ancestors' continue to play their part in the therapy. Kaleisha becomes fascinated with this approach and starts exploring the possibility of doing community work using these techniques. Researching further, she discovers a suitable training course, but it will require relocating to a different part of the country and finding another job.

Together, they decide that their therapy has run its course. Kaleisha thanks Sarah for changing her life and gracefully turns down the possibility of continuing work online.

Sarah, for her part, shares that she is thrilled for Kaleisha's newfound mission, even though it means the end of their work together. What she doesn't reveal is how much healing she had been vicariously gaining from Kaleisha's therapy journey.

Reflecting on relational processes

The relational component is strikingly demonstrated by the open dialogue between Kaleisha and Sarah about the role that intersectionality (the ways in which key social factors such as race, class and sex interact to affect our individual lives) played in their relationship. Intersectionality was acknowledged from the start, and in relation to the specific power dynamics of the therapy room (Proctor, 2018). More specifically, their explicit focus on race was relationally significant. It gave Kaleisha space to be angry while they both became open to learning more. As many authors underline (e.g. Turner, 2025), racism is an omnipresent, never-ending, everyday occurrence for people of colour and more needs to be done to 'meet black women at the intersection of the trauma(s) they experience' (George, 2025, p. 7).

Further elements of relationality were added as Kaleisha and Sarah moved into working with the transmission of historical, intergenerational trauma, including the 'survival messages' passed on to subsequent generations. Here, the use of the 'ancestral circle' helped nurture Kaleisha's resilience while adding a profound spiritual, soul-full **transpersonal** (i.e. beyond personal) layer of interconnectivity (Kaklauskas et al., 2016). The Ancestral Constellations therapy of Welch-Moring (2025) offers a version of this where Welch-Moring takes a brief, solution-focused approach to transgenerational diaspora.

The exploration below considers *selective therapist self-disclosure* and the nature of *therapy to counter racism.*

Selective therapist self-disclosure

Intergenerational trauma also seemed to stalk Sarah's history and process. The fact that she chose not to reveal her personal experience of anti-Semitism or her own shame history is noteworthy. That she also withheld this information from her supervisor raises questions about levels of mutual trust and respect in their relationship. A safe supervisory (or therapy) environment is, of course, a necessary precondition for disclosure of vulnerability. The supervisor carries particular responsibility to probe the impact of power dynamics and self-disclosures, and to notice supervisee silences around intersectionality.

Much research acknowledges that practitioners (particularly trainees) withhold self-disclosures in supervision due to shame, fear of negative evaluation, and impression management (Apostol et al., 2025). Studies also highlight how supervisor rigidity and a lack of relational attunement may contribute to non-disclosure (Žvelc & Žvelc, 2020).

While Sarah did not disclose her ethnic background, she revealed much in their dialogue, including her experiences as an older woman and her immediate, in-the-moment responsiveness, such as when she acknowledged her 'clumsiness' over their 'rupture'. She also demonstrated empathic appreciation of Kaleisha's experience – an attuned responsiveness that deepened her relationality.

Following Henretty and Levitt (2010), Monticelli et al. (2025) distinguished between therapist 'self-disclosure' of personal information and 'self-involving interventions' of here-and-now reactions (others call this 'immediacy'). They examined 57 interventions performed during 17 psychotherapy sessions with six patients. Results showed that self-involving interventions, compared to self-disclosure, were associated with higher metacognitive functioning in patients and more cooperative responses, promoting joint reflection and emotional regulation.

Other research similarly supports the importance of therapist responsiveness in the moment. Eubanks et al. (2021), for instance, explored how therapist–patient/client mutually influence each other throughout therapy. Highlighting rupture-repair cycles, they argued that therapist responsiveness is essential to maintaining a positive working alliance, while therapist attunement can successfully repair ruptures.

Therapy to counter racism

> Given the immense harm inflicted on individuals and groups of color via prejudice and discrimination, it becomes imperative for our nation to begin the process of disrupting, dismantling, and disarming the constant onslaught of micro- and macroaggressions. (Sue et al., 2019, p. 128)

Research underlines the damaging impact and pervasive consequences of racism, documenting how certain ethnic groups are disproportionately affected by historical and systemic inequalities. It flags up the need to address this throughout therapists' training, equipping practitioners with the lifelong ability to challenge their own prejudices, recognise unhelpful stereotypes, and engage with, rather than avoid, issues around race (Turner, 2025; George, 2025).

Charura and Lago (2021) argue that the profession has failed to adequately prepare trainees to meet the needs of today's multiracial, multicultural society. The starting point for working to heal racial harm is recognising that we all (clients, therapists, supervisors and trainers) have a role to play. Inaction may be problematic in itself, as it suggests some degree of complicity in the process (Sue et al., 2019).

Results of an online qualitative survey of the experiences of racially minoritised clients in the UK by Samuel and Simonds (2025) underline the healing capabilities of therapy in situations where practitioners work sensitively with racial trauma. They also dispute the idea that only therapists who themselves come from racial minority backgrounds can prove effective here. What matters is the degree to which therapists, irrespective of their ethnic origins, commit to anti-racist practice, education and self-reflection.

Beyond self-reflection and explicitly engaging with this topic in our training and professional development, what specifically can be done in therapy *with clients*? Research offers some practical suggestions around working with racism and racial justice including:

- talking about race
- being validating
- learning how to deal with microaggressions
- applying a trauma-informed lens
- engaging racial self-care.

These suggestions are explored in more detail in the following pages.

Kaleisha's therapy drew on elements of each of these strategies. Sarah strove to validate Kaleisha's experience as they worked together to develop creative strategies to handle the microaggressions. During their longer-term work with intergenerational trauma, they found additional ways for Kaleisha to move forward, drawing on ancestral wisdom, strengths and resilience (Welch-Moring, 2025).

Talking about race

Applying a *social justice* lens, Davis and Brien (2022) argue that we need to be comfortable engaging in conversations about race, racism and racial justice if we are to eliminate health disparities. Similar conclusions are drawn by Madre de Deus de Sousa et al. (2024) in their discourse-analytical research, which shows that being attuned and open to discussing race-related difficulties supports positive outcomes.

In her writings and podcasts, integrative, transcultural psychotherapist McKenzie-Mavinga (2016) notes the tendency of white therapists to 'swerve' when their Black clients raise issues around racism and oppression. She argues that this stems from a toxic mix of shame and fear: shame around feeling complicit in the enslavement of Black people, and fear of clients' potential rage. Both therapist and client are then psychologically 'gagged'. She urges therapists not to remain silent and to invite clients to *voice their truth*.

It's also worth striking a more cautionary note about how 'giving space' for racial dialogue can itself carry a whiff of misguided white liberalism: the very act of 'giving permission to speak' has a patronising ring. There is also a *reductive* quality to this, a tendency to reduce people to their race in a way that strips away diversity and complexity.

Being validating

Research underlines the importance of validating the experiences of clients suffering from racial stress/trauma. Endorsing clients' accounts rather than dismissing or questioning them enables clients to feel seen and heard. Therapists also need to confront preconceptions and assumptions that hinder listening.

Miller and colleagues (2018) recommend directly exploring *racist experiences* and racism-related stress, *normalising* clients' reactions, recognising the *strategies* they use to navigate racism, and celebrating clients' *strengths and resilience*. They also recommend that therapists directly express their support when a client first lays out their reasons for seeking therapy and describes how much racism has harmed them: for example, a compassionate response along the lines of, 'Nobody should have to put up with that'. In cases where a client expresses hostility to the therapist's race/ethnicity or flags up mistrust (as Kaleisha did at the start of her therapy with Sarah), therapists should avoid becoming defensive or taking it personally.

Learning how to deal with microaggressions

Microaggressions are those everyday demeaning put-downs that people of colour experience routinely, even from those who are well-intentioned. Harned (2022) identifies nine types of *traumatic invalidation*: ignoring, emotional neglect, criticising, blaming, misinterpreting, denying reality, controlling, excluding, and unequal treatment.

Sue (2023) offers numerous helpful strategies for dealing with racist microaggressions, such as the 'Ouch!' tactic in response to a potentially racist action to alert the perpetrator to its offensive character and encourage them to consider its impact.

Applying a trauma-informed lens

Much research highlights the damaging psychological impact of racism and discrimination, focusing on how these experiences can lead to trauma, particularly *PTSD*. The concept of complex racial trauma (CoRT) (Cénat, 2023), which is gaining traction in the literature, points to the cumulative psychological impact of ongoing exposure to racism.

In the story above, while Sarah applied an integrative/pluralist approach (Cooper & McLeod, 2011), other approaches could also work. Taking a cognitive behavioural perspective, Williams et al. (2023) draw on empirical evidence to offer guidelines for working with racial stress and trauma (they call this *The Healing Racial Trauma Protocol*). In essence, they suggest three phases of work:

1. *Stabilisation* – reducing shame by, for example, drawing attention to the social (as distinct from the personal/individual) origins of racism, and to cultivate positive self-care and support networks.
2. *Healing* – dismantling internalised racism messages through cognitive restructuring, cultural exploration and psychoeducation. Clients are encouraged to work through difficult experiences and learn strategies to cope.
3. *Empowerment* – enacting strategies to combat racial stress while recognising growth, meaning-making and successes. A move into social activism may also offer a positive route.

As part of their EDI practices, Azer et al. (2023) promote trauma-informed anti-racist strategy and actions to cultivate broader community learning and systemic change. They offer a range of training programmes, including ones geared towards aspiring and current trainees from racialised minority backgrounds.

Engaging radical self-care

Wyatt and Ampadu (2022) take issue with current individually centred self-care discourses that insufficiently recognise social justice and how individuals are intertwined with their communities. In pursuit of this justice, clients, therapists and supervisors alike may benefit from working with people of similar ethnic backgrounds. Hamilton's (2023) review of the literature suggests that Black clients benefit from working with Black therapists because their shared lived experiences more readily promote therapeutic connection. Other research (e.g. Cabral & Smith, 2011) points to more variable effects, suggesting that although ethnic matching may be preferred, there may not be particular benefit to therapeutic outcomes.

If ethnic matching is followed, however, it is essential not to assume cultural commonality and to avoid narrowly focusing on race/ethnicity, as this can be problematic and insensitive to individuals' broader needs (Olaniyan & Hayes, 2022). Connections can also be formed around other shared characteristics: in Kaleisha's therapy with Sarah, the fact that they were both women seeking to make their way in a male-dominated world helped forge a bond.

Conclusion

Kaleisha's therapy and her deepening relationship with Sarah involved a profound dive into Kaleisha's experiences of racism and its pernicious effects. While the therapy started with a short-term intervention around workplace bullying, the shift to long-term work enabled a deeper exploration of intergenerational trauma. Sarah offered Kaleisha a measure of healing by compassionately validating her experiences and providing a safe space for her to explore her rage. Kaleisha could then engage the history of her family and community, drawing strength, courage and resilience from connecting with her ancestry.

The value of explicitly confronting the complex dynamics around intersectionality within the therapeutic relationship has been emphasised as a key component of a *relational-cultural* approach (Jordan, 2024). The focus on intergenerational trauma and transformative resilience through connecting with 'ancestors' added further soulful, *transpersonal* (Kaklauskas et al., 2016) layers of relational connection.

A key lesson from this chapter is that therapists and clients from different ethnic backgrounds *can* work together effectively – and to mutual benefit. For healing to occur for those contending with racism, therapists need to work sensitively with racial trauma and invalidation; they need to reject reductive race-related tendencies and see their client as a person. They should also engage in honest reflection to identify their own blind spots and confront lurking prejudice (George, 2025).

Destructive cycles of pernicious power, shame and silencing undermine both therapy and supervision and can only be eased through dialogue and connection.

Discussion questions

1. Was Sarah right not to disclose her Jewish heritage to Kaleisha and her supervisor? Explain your position.
2. It is better to ethnically match clients and therapists. Discuss.
3. How might you helpfully challenge lurking prejudices in yourself and others?

Chapter 13 – Neela: Internalised oppressors?

Neela, 25, has sought therapy for 'fear of flying' in preparation for her marriage in six months, when she and her fiancé, Govind, plan to fly to India for their honeymoon. She commits earnestly to 16 therapy sessions with Phil, an experienced *integrative psychotherapist* with over 30 years of practice.

This story recounts how Neela's initial presentation (aviophobia) opens up into a deeper exploration of complex intersectional elements embracing her ethnicity, religion, gender and class. The evolving therapy exposes lurking tensions with her fiancé and cultural issues rooted in intergenerational, historical and colonial legacies. She soon learns that her seemingly straightforward presenting issues mask deeper issues.

The final reflective discussion raises questions about how therapists choose their focus and approach, while acknowledging professional and ethical limitations on what is realistic and/or feasible for any particular client. Critical questions are raised about how therapists select which parts of clients' invariably complicated lives to focus on. The issues at stake in this chapter concern Phil's **relational commitments** and his dilemmas around **choosing between approaches**. Another therapist could well have gone in a totally different direction.

Neela's story

Neela has never flown before, and social media posts about a major airline crash have made her terrified of the very thought of flying. However, more than managing this phobia, Neela is starting to worry about her relationship with Govind. While he listens to her flying fears, he is not sympathetic. This has left Neela wondering if, and how, she might cancel the honeymoon entirely. A feeling of scared confusion is suffusing her life.

Negotiating the therapeutic focus

Neela and Phil are at the beginning of a 16-session therapy contract. Phil is upfront about the strategic choice confronting them: would Neela prefer a relatively straightforward course of CBT to tackle her phobia? Or might she consider a deeper-going form of therapy that might broaden her understanding of what is fuelling the phobia, and on that basis, hopefully make her better able to cope with it?

'Can't we do both in these four months?' Neela enquires.

'Okay, let's see how we go; we can review what's needed as we go along,' Phil says. 'I can anyway recommend some basic fear-of-flying apps that you can use independently alongside our work. For now, I'd like to hear about what is important to you, what your life is like and what your hopes and fears might be. Maybe you could begin by telling me more about you and your background?'

Neela pauses a moment. Then her words spill out. 'I'm a British-Punjabi woman, a Christian; I have a law degree and I'm currently training to become a solicitor; I'd like to specialise in family law.'

'How are you finding your training and work life?'

'It's great, I love it, I'm doing well. I'm ambitious – it's a family trait but I also know how to work hard.'

'I can hear that,' says Phil with a smile. 'I'm imagining you've always done well at school and university, cheered on by your parents, is that right?'

'Spot on. It's our work ethic and I'm proud of that. I feel strong professionally and I'm basically a happy person. It's what makes what is happening to me now so confusing. I don't know what to do with myself; I've become a quivering wreck. I'm scared of flying… actually, scared of marriage, even of Govind himself. You don't want to be in my head just now – it's all over the place. I'm not me.'

'Let's just pause there, Neela, as I think this is key. It sounds like you have these two different parts of you: the strong, happy professional part and then this more unfamiliar scared part that has appeared?' What he doesn't say is that he already feels two different counter-transferential responses in himself – a sure sign that a splitting process is at work. Part of him feels admiring of this young woman – she's beautiful, articulate, intelligent, ambitious and clearly destined for big things. And then he feels protective, even fatherly, of that young woman who is anxious about flying and probably also about her impending marriage.

'Yes, I hadn't thought about it in that way.'

'I'm thinking one important focus for us in these therapy sessions is to look at what's going on with this split and try and help you come back more as a whole. Does that feel right?' When she nods her acceptance, he shares a little about his slightly strange experience of feeling both admiring and protective in response to her, even though they have just met.

Phil then invites Neela to express what is going on with each of these two sides of her. The professional part is 'satisfied' with her progress in her course and how she is being 'fast-tracked' with her placements, which bodes well for her future. The 'vulnerable, anxious part' of her is nervous about her impending marriage and feels 'called out' as, up until now, she has managed to avoid flying all her life.

'I'm supposed to be marrying Govind in six months. I was excited about that until that recent Air India crash. Now I'm obsessed with air crashes and am doom-scrolling, and now…' She pauses before plunging on. 'Now I want to cancel our planned honeymoon in India.'

'Tell me about you and Govind.' Aware of the diversity of practices within the British Indian community, Phil avoids making assumptions about whether theirs is an arranged marriage or a love match.

'We met a year ago. I was on placement with a law firm that was working with Govind's industrial company – he's one of the senior managers. We got together and have been dating for eight months.' Receiving an interested nod from Phil, she continues talking about their relationship. 'He's British, third-generation Sikh, but he has an extended family in the Punjab. Thankfully, Govind isn't particularly religious; he's a clean-shaven Sikh, and his community accepts non-Sikh liaisons, so we match pretty well. My parents really like him too; it helps he's well off.'

Phil, who has worked with many clients from diverse family backgrounds, respectfully acknowledges the complexity of Neela and Govind's ethnic and religious mix. 'You sound a good fit,' he says. 'But I can hear that it's also complicated.' When Neela offers no further comment, he continues: 'What's happening between you about your fear of flying? Is Govind aware of what you're going through?'

'He's irritated with me and becoming impatient with my "stupid craziness", as he calls it. He tells me to stop watching trashy online stories that, for him, are "all lies". He wants me to sort myself out in therapy.'

'Are you having lots of arguments?'

'Yes. The worst was last weekend; he shouted at me and accused me of being "pathetic" and not the strong, capable, calm, intelligent woman he thought he was marrying. He just stopped himself from slapping me, which shocked us both. It was almost like he was gaslighting me, saying he didn't know I was so neurotic. But, yes, I'm also a quivering, inadequate wreck. If I don't sort myself out soon, we won't be getting married anyway, and my flying issue will be irrelevant.' Neela shakes her head in confusion and continues. 'To be honest, I'm not sure I even know him now. Do I even want to marry him? It's like he's changed with the marriage thing. Does he expect me to be the traditional subservient Punjabi wife?'

The direction of Neela's reflections gives Phil pause for thought and he is momentarily ungrounded. Hearing the potential for domestic violence, he is instantly alert. Is there a risk of physical abuse? Is Govind inclined to be controlling? As it is, Phil is concerned to hear that some psychological violence is occurring. He makes a mental note to stay alert to any escalation and to call it out. For now, Neela's reference to 'gaslighting' suggests that she is aware of potentially problematic dynamics.

'Neela, I'm sorry you're having these relationship tensions. It seems like that is a separate, but perhaps priority, issue, and quite apart from anything you might do for your anxieties about flying.

There is a case, you know, for you to have some therapy as a couple now, before your marriage. You might benefit from mixing individual and couples therapy.'

'I'm up for doing both. With you?'

'I'm sorry. While some therapists offer both, I don't do couples work, I'm afraid.' Phil wonders if he should back off now as the couples work seems a priority. On the other hand, she is here now, presenting with turmoil suited to individual therapy. He lays out two options. 'You could see a couples therapist alongside our individual work; I could recommend one or two. Or we could just start with this therapy and decide later.'

'I think I need this therapy for me now, anyway, so shall we carry on?' 'Professional Neela' appears to have taken over with this decisiveness. 'I will talk with Govind about doing the other. I don't know what he'll say.'

'Okay, Neela. Concentrating on what is going on for you should help you understand yourself better, so you're clearer about what you want. Later, we can explore different possibilities, such as downloading fear-of-flying apps and working on your relationship as a couple. For now, you're hurting internally, which must be confusing and that's what we'll explore, okay?'

Neela nods her agreement, looking interested.

Exploring deeper underlying anxieties

Over their next few sessions, they explore Neela's fears and turmoil more directly. Phil offers a possible psychodynamic interpretation, wondering if her anxieties about flying are a kind of defence, a 'symbolic way' for her to avoid the bigger anxiety about getting married. He can feel a pull to work more deeply, but reins himself in, given their time-limited contract.

Neela is stunned by this interpretation and nods her head slowly.

'A few months ago, totally in love, being married to Govind sounded perfect,' she says. But as soon as we started talking about this India trip, I heard about his family and their traditions. It was like Govind became more Indian somehow and we started to grow apart. I wondered if his family were going to put pressure on for me to be a more traditional Indian wife.'

'Have you talked to him about this?'

'I've tried to, but he gets a bit resentful that somehow I am not excited for him to join all his cousins and to get to know more about their Sikh culture where celebrating marriages is a big thing.'

'Have you got a clash of religions?'

'It's never really been a problem as he is not really religious. Anyway, Sikhism supports the idea of one God so there are links to my Christian beliefs. It's more the idea of being an Indian wife that I'm not keen on if it means letting go of being a strong, professional woman.'

'But didn't you say, he loved your independent side?'

'He does. It's confusing.'

'Hmmm… Perhaps, he also has different parts within him, and while his main part is British, where he appreciates your independence, there is another part linked to his ancestors back in India that wants you to be more a part of his clan. In other words, both of you have different parts inside you and your challenge is to find a way for them *all* to be together.'

Amazed by this new insight, Neela says with a big smile that she looks forward to discussing this with Govind.

Following his intuition that both of their family backgrounds are playing a part, he asks her to say more. 'Tell me more about your family background.'

'I was really close to my grandmother, growing up. I called her *Nani-ji*. She lived with us, looked after me when my parents were working all hours and she told me all sorts of stories. My great-grandparents first came to this country through fleeing Partition, just after World War II. My grandmother was just a baby, and she didn't remember anything except the difficulties of them trying to settle in England. It can't have been easy for them.'

'Because they were fleeing their war-torn country?'

'I remember she talked of her mother suffering racist abuse both in India and when she came to the UK because she was a "half-caste", "*chee-chee*" in Hindi-Urdu. Literally, it means "dirt".' Neela goes on to describe her fascination with learning that her great-great-great-grandfather was actually a white British officer in India – a '*burra sahib*' ['big master']. 'That was the start of my Indian family becoming staunch Anglicans, apparently, and other ancestors had Anglo-Indian blood.'

'The 19th and 20th centuries were turbulent times for Anglo-Indians, I believe', interjects Phil. 'Weren't they shunned by Indians and British alike – looked at with suspicion and despised by both sides?' Phil starts to feel out of his depth and wonders if he should not be engaging in this work, given its attendant transgenerational trauma, and their time-limited contract. Still, he reasons, they have almost four months, and given her level of engagement and insight, it could work.

'Yeah, I mean it all feels like something out of a movie – not really my life. Me, I'm just British. With my slightly lighter skin – something I've always been grateful for – I guess I fit in more easily here. People often take me for a Spanish or Mediterranean person. Govind, on the other hand, has experienced more overt racism, perhaps because his skin is darker. Sometimes I worry that our children may inherit Govind's colour, rather than mine.'

'That is tough for him to be forced to face such racism. But it sounds like there is a shadow surrounding you both and it's something you may be forced to confront together.' Phil experiences a further twinge of inadequacy. As a white European who has never needed to justify (or disguise) his origins, how can he possibly get to grips with the everyday impact of racism in British society?

He starts to dither. Should he draw Neela's attention to exploring the possibility of *internalised oppression*? Would that be useful? Would it be pertinent to invite her to recognise how individuals from marginalised categories (racial minorities or married women in conservative cultures) can unconsciously adopt negative stereotypes? Might dominant cultural attitudes – white British ones in this case – have caused some feelings of shame and inferiority to enter Neela and Govind's relationship? Neela may have absorbed some prejudices against darker skin, internalising prejudices that have been passed down through generations. Phil's intuition tells him that Neela's family's Partition history could be an interesting area to explore, but again, he is cautious and holds back. He is aware that he could push this and, in being controlling, could be mirroring Govind or others in her life.

He decides to make an interpretive link without necessarily inviting Neela to go deeper.

'I believe that, somewhere inside us all, we carry messages and history from previous generations. More than that, I believe we may embody some of the trauma from previous generations, without knowing it, of course.'

They begin to acknowledge how, out of her awareness, Neela may be carrying some passed down emotional turmoil – including the grief of leaving one's home country, the trauma of the violence of Partition and her marginalisation in Britain.

'I wonder if some of your anxieties actually belong back there in history and perhaps were even really your great-grandmother's.'

'Wow, is that even possible? I think you could be right. I always assumed I got this flying fear from my parents as both of them tended to avoid flying too.'

'From *both* parents? No wonder you've avoided flying! It would be surprising if you didn't have fears.' As Phil normalises her responses, he feels an easing in her. It makes him more convinced that her deeper family history is important, while he intuits the grandmother holds a key. He follows his 'gut' instincts. Aware that Neela has robust Adult and healthy Child parts, he decides it might be safe enough to go deeper and perhaps work more creatively. He would be more cautious were she more vulnerable.

'How about we do something different and have an imaginary conversation with the version of Nani-ji that you carry inside of you, with you taking on being Nani-ji?' Seeing Neelas's intrigued smile and nod, he goes on to explain the process and how this is a special technique that requires going slowly and taking care. He proposes that they make their next session a double one, so they have time to follow this intergenerational dialogue wherever it may lead.

Meeting 'Nani-ji'

When the day comes, they set a special chair for Nani-ji, and Phil invites Neela to sit in it, just as Nani-ji would sit, trying to adopt something of her way of being and facial expression. Neela's task is then to respond to Phil's questions as if she were her grandmother. The aim is to allow the 'part' of Neela that experienced and vaguely remembers old family conversations, to speak. Phil emphasises that this will be a compassionate, safe, hospitable space and Neela can stop the exercise at any point if she feels uncomfortable.

When Neela is ready, Phil welcomes Nani-ji into the room. 'Thank you for being here. I wanted a chance to get to know you a bit. Can I also call you Nani-ji? [Neela/Nani-ji nods]. Mostly, you're here to help Neela and for her to understand how important you are to her and she is to you.' [Neela/Nani-ji nods again.] 'So, if you're happy to proceed, please can you tell me a bit about your childhood?'

'Nani-ji' begins to talk about how her mother had immigrated to Britain as a child with her family. They had suffered much with the terror, chaos and riots of Partition and leaving India; fleeing all that was safe and familiar, was hugely painful. 'But,' she says, 'while my parents always struggled, I learnt to love England. I then got married to a good man and eventually our son produced our beloved granddaughter Neela, who grew up a happy baby.'

After spending some time discussing particularly fond memories of times when Nani-ji took care of Neela, Phil brings her attention to the present and how Neela is soon to be married. 'Nani-ji' expresses her happiness about Neela finding love, and she gives them her blessing.

It proves a pivotal and powerful session as Neela becomes aware of a history that she has only been vaguely aware of. At the end of this emotional dialogue, Neela flops back in her original chair. 'Oh my God! That was bizarre; it was like I was channelling her! For a moment, it felt real, and I thought I was getting her blessing! I did so love her, and her death 10 years ago was a huge loss to many of us.'

Recognising her palpable grief, Phil gently invites Neela to continue imagining her grandmother still seated in her chair. 'Take your time. What would you like to say to her?'

With tears in her eyes, Neela reminds her beloved 'Nani-ji' that she was much loved and that she had created a good life for their family. From the bottom of her heart, Neela thanks her.

'Do you know, it's odd,' Neela smilingly tells Phil as they prepare to end. 'A little part of me wants to go to India now to learn more about my roots.'

'That seems like important progress, Neela. Committing to the flight is the first step to not avoiding it.' Phil then introduces her to a fear-of-flying app based on CBT and mindfulness so that she can start doing the exercises on her own.

Exploring couples work

Returning home that day, Neela excitedly shares her therapy experiences with Govind. He is pleased that she is connecting with her Indian heritage and no longer doom-scrolling. Together they enjoy her new app and start to feel hopeful about their planned trip.

In therapy a couple of weeks later, Neela reports that she and Govind have been watching TV programmes about colonial India, including the film *Gandhi*, to learn more about their colonial history and prepare for their trip. They are growing their awareness of how Partition created immense violence and social displacement while traumatising hundreds of millions of people. Neela finds it all harrowing yet engrossing. Perhaps something of that trauma lives on in the contemporary experiences of people from South Asia whose ancestors were caught up in the bloodshed, fear and trauma.

Interestingly, their shared TV viewing seems to be creating fresh bonds between Neela and Govind, while also fuelling new tensions. Govind's Punjabi family, who are still living with the shadow of Partition, resent Britain's role in the loss of the family's ancestral land in what became Pakistani Punjab. In contrast, the fact that Neela has British ancestors has given her a sense of pride in her perceived strain of Britishness.

As Neela continues processing her Anglo-Indian heritage with Phil, she experiences odd but powerful feelings of guilt and shame, along with pride in her Anglo-Indian identity. She recognises for the first time how her family's Anglican Christianity constitutes a direct link back to upper-class British ancestors. She now acknowledges the significant differences between Govind and herself in terms of their family histories and relationship with colonialism.

Phil invites her to answer the question she is skirting around: does it matter that Govind's background is Sikh, not Christian, and that his roots are *Dalit* (Neela has explained that this term is now preferred by Indians who would once have been labelled 'untouchable' or 'scheduled caste')? She shakes her head; of course it doesn't matter! All the same, she admits that it is odd and confusing to see Govind, her successful business manager fiancé, as a Dalit.

With the focus more on her and Govind as a couple, Neela again wonders if she is right to marry him. She remembers that incident when Govind all but hit her. Although she has forgiven him, is he seeking a subservient wife? She has assumed he had fallen in love with her independence and was supportive of her career. Might these assumptions be wrong?

'This is the kind of thing to explore in couples therapy. I'd strongly recommend some sessions before your marriage,' suggests Phil.

'Can't you do the couples work?' Neela implores. 'I feel safe with you.'

Phil gently explains that professional ethics typically discourage dual relationships. 'And, I'm afraid that I don't do couples work. Anyway, if I did, it wouldn't be fair to Govind, as I'd be more on your side than his,' he explains. 'I think we've done what we can now, and – given your impending marriage – this is the more urgent issue. You need someone who specialises in couples and can work impartially with both of you.'

Giving Neela the names of two respected, culturally-informed couples therapists in the area, he emphasises that Govind and she need to decide together if this is what they want and who will suit them best.

In their final contracted session, Neela thanks Phil for opening up a 'rich new world' for her and for recommending the couples therapy that she and Govind have started.

Phil regrets that he will never know if Neela and Govind benefit from their couples therapy. Will they get married? Will they fly and honeymoon in India? Ruefully, he acknowledges to himself that he longs to ask her to drop him a line. But he knows he has to let go. He hopes fervently that they can find a positive way forward and that India will bring healing for both.

Reflecting on relational processes

Phil's integrative psychotherapy embraced a *relational-systemic* approach drawing on *psychodynamic* ideas while touching some *transpersonal*, intergenerational elements towards Neela's healing integration.

His imaginal technique of talking with Neela's grandmother needs further comment. This could be seen as a '**Parent Interview**' in *transactional analytic* terms. McNeil (1976) first developed this technique, referring to work with the internalised 'Parent ego-state'. Erskine (2015) and colleagues (Erskine & Trautmann, 2003; Moursund & Erskine, 2004) have developed this intervention to provide in-depth therapy for this introjected part.

In their brief use of this powerful technique, Phil took **care** to ensure Neela felt safe as he enabled her to reconnect with her internalised grandmother and feel lovingly held. It seems that he also sought to raise Neela's awareness that she might be carrying something of her family's legacy, including experiences, attitudes, relational needs and defensive patterns. Although there wasn't space to fully explore these transgenerational processes, given their time-limited contract, a seed was planted.

Questions are raised about Phil's approach around how he demonstrates his *relational commitments* and goes about *choosing between approaches.*

Relational commitments

Phil showed his relational leanings through his:

1. **cultural sensitivity and openness** – he did not assume Neela's marriage would be an arranged one; he recognised, more than she did, that her mixed-race ancestral colonial history may have been playing out in her current life somehow as she navigated the space between her Indianness and Britishness (Acquah, 2025)
2. awareness of **intersectionality** – he respected Neela's self-identification as a middle-class Christian Punjabi woman, while guiding her to explore her previously unreflective 'Britishness' and 'light skin privilege' (Acquah, 2025)
3. explicit acknowledgement that he felt a **split in his response** to her (feeling both admiring and protective), corresponding to her own split self. Here, Phil might be seen as unconsciously embodying Neela's projected self-state that gave him potential insight into her internal world (Ogden, 1992)
4. awareness of **transgenerational trauma** addressed in part through the Parent Interview (Erskine, 2015)
5. recommending couples therapy and letting Neela go, which prioritised her needs while **ethically boundarying** their own relationship.

There were also limits to how relational Phil could be. In some ways, this therapy was only 'light-touch relational' (Finlay, 2025) in that it focused on relationships, but their therapeutic one was less foregrounded. It was significant that Phil did not encourage Neela to continue their therapy longer-term, leaving this choice with her.

Choosing between approaches

Beyond his relational stance, Phil committed to an approach towards helping Neela's **integration**. Faced with her layered history and needs, he had choices about what they focused on and what therapy to engage while ensuring her safety. Interestingly, Phil chose not to work with the initial presenting problem of the phobia and only tangentially worked with what he suggested might be the 'priority' of looking at their couple relationship. It seems he followed his intuition in the moment. Other therapists might have taken different approaches.

Phil's professional uncertainty about which therapeutic route to follow is something many therapists experience, particularly for integrative therapists, who, when faced with the complexity of an individual in front of them, have diverse options and tools in their kit bag. Three key questions arise:

1. How do therapists establish the problem issue or **point of focus**? In this therapy, a CBT-orientated therapist might have chosen to focus on the phobia; a humanistic one might have looked more existentially at how her identity would change from being single to being married; a more psychodynamic one would look at processes underlying her phobia and perhaps internalised oppression; a transpersonal one might well focus on her generational history; and a systemic one might commit to couples work. The client also plays a role in guiding the agenda, and much depends on their motivation to work on particular areas, as well as the practicalities of time available. Therapists need to take an individualised approach (Norcross & Goldfried, 2005).
2. How do therapists choose which **approach** to use? This is an important question, as a therapist's theoretical framework influences how a client's problems/issues are understood and

what interventions are suggested. The choice is also guided by the therapist's preferred style, the therapeutic relationship, the client's motivations and the practical context regarding what is possible (Finlay, 2016a). For Neela and Phil, their options were limited by the time frame. Phil rightly curtailed the intergenerational trauma work, while it made sense to delegate the work on her phobia to CBT-based fear-of-flying apps. However, should he have pushed the couples work from the beginning?

3. How might therapists **combine theoretical approaches**? In a survey of over 1,000 psychotherapists, only 15% focused on one theoretical orientation; the median number of theoretical orientations adopted in practice was four (Tasca et al., 2015). Phil chose to blend psychodynamic, systemic and transpersonal aspects.

Had Neela's therapy been longer term, they might have deepened their focus on transpersonal intergenerational trauma and/or the psychodynamic formulation of 'internalised oppression' (Orbach, 2003). But within time constraints, the focus remained on enabling greater self-awareness and understanding. When it became clearer that couples therapy might be more useful – even necessary – Phil took steps to let go and respect Neela's choices.

More than combining theoretical perspectives, integrative psychotherapists aim to bring together different aspects of the client's self, inviting renewed ways of being. Here, therapists work with clients in integrative ways, helping them hold polarities and connect with previously disowned parts (Erskine, 2015; Finlay, 2016a).

Perhaps it doesn't especially matter which route is taken, provided attention is paid to collaborative relational elements of the therapy relationship and to integrative aspects in clients' healing (Finlay, 2016b). This idea underpins the **common factors** approach (Wampold & Imel, 2015) that is built on a large pool of empirical evidence demonstrating that competing approaches get roughly similar results, with the therapeutic relationship acting as the glue. Healing integration occurs through the therapeutic relationship, which fosters positive expectations that encourage clients to engage in their therapy and grow.

Conclusion

This story has explored the way therapy responded to Neela's deep fear of flying. More than simply focusing on the phobia, Phil adopted an *integrative* approach aimed at raising her emotional awareness and building a sense of integration around Neela's being. Their work touched on Neela's intrapsychic splits, her relationship with her fiancé and her intergenerational cultural heritage – all different relational facets.

Given the limits of a 16-week course of therapy, Phil faced a not uncommon professional dilemma about his choice of therapeutic approach. It raises critical questions about how therapists select which parts of clients' complicated lives to focus on. Phil could have used CBT to work straightforwardly on Neela's flying phobia and avoidant behaviour, though he chose to recommend an app instead. Alternatively, he might have taken a psychodynamic view of phobic avoidance: one that sees it as a defence mechanism against anxiety and/or unacceptable impulses. He could also have focused more on the aspect of internalised oppression, perhaps related to both gender and ethnicity. Or he might have just suggested couples therapy from the outset to help Neela and Govind prepare for their marriage. *But he couldn't do it all.*

Given the many routes available, therapists are typically guided by the client's motivations and capacities. However, what they perceive as 'the problem' (i.e. their formulation) also guides the approach, along with their interests, informed by their experience, intuition, training and skills. The eventual choice may need to be tweaked or retuned as the client's understanding evolves, or new pressing issues arise. The therapist is presumed to be knowledgeable and ethically grounded, capable of continuously evolving strategies while focusing on their clients' best interests and wellbeing.

In this story, Phil chose to work with Neela on a one-to-one exploratory basis, where she came to understand that her fear of flying was a cover for deeper tensions and confusing emotions. They worked to merge two contradictory aspects, namely her being both 'strong' and 'vulnerable'. Then she came to appreciate something more of her heritage, discovering a mixture of guilt, shame and pride about her Indian roots, in particular its inclusion, in the remote past, of her upper-class British *burra sahib* ancestor. Other elements surfaced during the course of the therapy: among them was Neela's awareness of being able to 'pass as' white, in contrast to her darker-skinned fiancé, whose low caste family roots may also have been unconsciously generating tension between them. Another therapist, applying a different approach, might have paid more attention to these aspects.

The hope is that additional couples therapy will help Neela and Govind with their relationship tensions. Like Phil, we never find out what happens next.

Discussion questions

1. Could Phil's work with intergenerational aspects be seen as risky, given they only had 16 sessions?
2. CBT-type apps that focus on particular behaviours and fears (such as a fear of flying) usefully free up therapists to do deeper work. Discuss.
3. What therapeutic approach would you have favoured to work with Neela, and why?

Epilogue

As you come to the end of *Therapy Tales*, can I invite you to reflect on your journey of reading the stories? What was your favourite therapy tale, and why? Were there moments where you felt especially affected? Did you empathise with particular individuals? Were you surprised by anything? How did you react when you read about a therapist's vulnerability when they got overwhelmed with shame, compassion, sadness, frustration, tears, fears, and so on…?

What have you learnt about relational work? I've tried to show that relational therapy involves *both* embodied dialogical encounters and an appreciation of the meshing of social worlds. The intimate journey that can unfold is filled with mysterious, messy ambiguity, turmoil and confusion, as well as layered moments of mutually satisfying contact, profound insight, and poignant transformation.

While all therapists engage relationships (at intrapsychic, interpersonal and social levels), that doesn't necessarily make them relational. The term relational should, at least in my view, be reserved for those therapies that engage the intersubjective dynamics between therapist and client, *prioritising the therapeutic relationship as the source of healing.*

Every therapy is, of course, different, spontaneously following 'unanticipated riverbeds', as Yalom (2001, p. 34) puts it, where we need to '*create a new therapy for each patient*' [italics in original]. Relational therapy, at its best, is a dynamic, co-creative, compassionate process – beyond theoretical partialities – shaped moment-to-moment by the specific relationship between client and therapist, set in their social/cultural contexts.

Relational therapists use themselves therapeutically when they are present and invite clients to be present (Finlay, 2022). They offer openness and hospitality as they connect with their clients, enabling them to feel witnessed, affirmed, resourced, empathised with, and held. As Goldstein (2025) has so wisely said: 'The breakthrough happens when therapists finally understand:

- You're not here to take away pain – you're here to help it be held.
- You're not the expert on their life – you're the witness to their wisdom.
- You're not the parent they needed – you're the space they need now.'

As therapists challenge their clients to grow, so too are they challenged. Therapists are taxed with having to stay *present* to clients' stress and torment while being asked to play versions of mother/father/nursemaid, friend, witness, confidant, coach, or be an object to be adored or used, even battered… And there are those special, inspiring moments of connection that are as nourishing for the therapist as they are for the client.

As therapists, we are often left muddling through, going with our intuition, exercising our curiosity and professional judgement as best we can, even when the process is mystifying and the outcome unpredictable. There is a trust in the relational process as we surrender to what might be emerging in the *between*. The emotional labour can be intense and sometimes costly. But it's also a privilege and an honour to do this work. We invariably learn from our clients: about mysterious intersubjective processes but also about how to be better therapists and, ultimately, better people.

For myself, having now reached the end, I'm aware of several emotions simmering, and I can see a parallel process with what happens in therapy. I feel some satisfaction finishing the book; but I mostly feel sad, reluctant to let go. I have become strangely attached to the individuals in each story. Even though they are fictional characters, they have become entirely real to me in my imagination. I've even come to love some of them, and I mourn their loss.

References

Aafjes-van Doorn, K., Békés, V. & Prout, T.A. (2020). Grappling with our therapeutic relationship and professional self-doubt during COVID-19: Will we use video therapy again? *Counselling Psychology Quarterly*, *34*(3–4), 473–484. https://www.tandfonline.com/doi/full/10.1080/09515070.2020.1773404

Acquah, J. (2025). How we are made 'mixed-race': Multiplicity of mind; multiplicity of experience. In H.P. George (Ed.), *Black women, trauma and therapy: Revolutionising therapeutic thought and practice* (pp. 49–66). PCCS Books.

Adams, M. (2023). *The myth of the untroubled therapist: Private life, professional practice* (2nd ed.). Routledge/Taylor & Francis Group.

Adshead, G. & Horne, E. (2021). *The devil you know: Stories of human cruelty and compassion*. Faber and Faber.

Ager, A. & Strang, A. (2008). Understanding integration: A conceptual framework. *Journal of Refugee Studies*, *21*(2), 166–191.

Amonkar, N., Su, W.C., Bhat, A.N. & Srinivasan, S.M. (2021). Effects of creative movement therapies on social communication, behavioral-affective, sensorimotor, cognitive, and functional participation skills of individuals with autism spectrum disorder: A systematic review. *Frontiers in Psychiatry*, *12*, 722874. https://doi.org/10.3389/fpsyt.2021.722874

Anderson, L.K. (2023). Autistic experiences of applied behavior analysis. *Autism*, *27*(3), 737–750. https://doi.org/10.1177/13623613221118216

Apostol, A.E., Turner, K., Hoshi, R. & Pudduck, A. (2025). Contributory factors to self-disclosure in clinical supervision: A meta-ethnography. *Clinical Psychology and Psychotherapy*, *32*(2), e70068-n/a. https://doi.org/10.1002/cpp.70068

Arnd-Caddigan, M. & Stickle, M. (2017). A psychotherapist's exploration of clinical intuition: A review of the literature and discussion. *International Journal of Integrative Psychotherapy*, *8*, 79–102. https://integrative-journal.com/index.php/ijip/article/view/129

Avasthi, A., Grover, S. & Nischal, A. (2022). Ethical and legal issues in psychotherapy. *Indian Journal of Psychiatry*, *64* (Suppl 1), S47–S61. https://doi.org/10.4103/indianjpsychiatry.indianjpsychiatry_50_21

Azer, S., Butler, C., Janally, S. & Clarke, A. (2023). Adopting a trauma-informed anti-racist strategy and actions to cultivate community learning and systemic change. *Clinical Psychology Forum, 1*, 30–35. https://doi.org/10.53841/bpscpf.2023.1.371.30

BACP. (2025). *UK counselling and therapy trends and attitudes revealed.* News from BACP. https://www.bacp.co.uk/about-us/about-bacp/bacp-public-perceptions-survey/

Barat, S., Yazdani, S., Faramarzi, M., Khafri, S., Darvish, M., Rad, M.N. & Asnafi, N. (2020). The effect of brief supportive psychotherapy on prevention of psychiatric morbidity in women with miscarriage: A randomized controlled trial about the first 24-hours of hospitalization. *Oman Medical Journal, 35*(3), e130. https://doi.org/10.5001/omj.2020.48

Bateman, A. & Fonagy, P. (2013). Mentalization-based treatment. *Psychoanalytic Inquiry, 33*(6), 595–613. https://doi.org/10.1080/07351690.2013.835170

Bedics, J.D., Atkins, D.C., Comtois, K.A. & Linehan, M.M. (2012). Treatment differences in the therapeutic relationship and introject during a 2-year randomized controlled trial of dialectical behavior therapy versus nonbehavioral psychotherapy experts for borderline personality disorder. *Journal of Consulting and Clinical Psychology, 80*(1), 66–77. https://doi.org/10.1037/a0026113

Bernstein, D.P., Clercx, M. & Keulen-De Vos, M. (2019). Schema therapy in forensic settings. In D.L.L. Polaschek, A. Day & C.R. Hollin (Eds.), *The Wiley international handbook of correctional psychology* (pp. 654–668). Wiley Blackwell. https://doi.org/10.1002/9781119139980.ch41

Bian, C., Zhao, W.W., Yan, S.R., Chen, S.Y., Cheng, Y. & Zhang, Y.H. (2023). Effect of interpersonal psychotherapy on social functioning, overall functioning and negative emotions for depression: A meta-analysis. *Journal of Affective Disorders, 320*, 230–240. https://doi.org/10.1016/j.jad.2022.09.119

Bowers, C. & Widdowson, M. (2023). Transactional analysis psychotherapy with clients who are neurodivergent: Experiences and practice recommendations. *International Journal of Transactional Analysis Research, 14*(1), 32–54. https://doi.org/10.29044/v14i1p32

Bowlby, J. (1988). *A secure base: Parent-child attachment and healthy human development.* Basic Books.

Boyles, J., Ewart-Biggs, R., Horn, R. & Lamb, K. (2023). *Groupwork with refugees and survivors of human rights abuses: The power of togetherness.* Routledge.

BPS. (2026) *Working with interpreters in mental health.* https://doi.org/10.53841/bpsrep.2026.rep187

Bradshaw, J. (1988). *Healing the shame that binds you.* Health Communications.

Brown, B. (2021). *Atlas of the heart.* Vermilion.

Brown, E.M. (2025). Which therapists are more likely to burn out? *Psychology Today.* https://www.psychologytoday.com/gb/blog/healing-from-within/202503/which-therapists-are-more-likely-to-burn-out?eml

Brown, T. (2025). *Bodylistening: A practical approach to body psychotherapy.* PCCS Books.

Brune, M., Eiroa-Orosa, F.J., Fischer-Ortman, J., Delijaj, B. & Haasen, C. (2011). Intermediated communication by interpreters in psychotherapy with traumatized refugees. *International Journal of Culture and Mental Health, 4*(2), 144–151. https://doi.org/10.1080/17542863.2010.537821

Burnham, J. (2012). Developments in social GRRRAAACCEEESSS: Visible-invisible and voiced-unvoiced. In I.-B. Krause (Ed.), *Culture and reflexivity in systemic psychotherapy: Mutual perspectives* (pp. 139–160). Karnac Books.

Bush, A.D. (2015). *Simple self-care for therapists: Restorative practices to weave through your workday.* W.W. Norton & Company.

Byford, A. (2015). Lost and gained in translation: The impact of bilingual clients' choice of language in psychotherapy. *British Journal of Psychotherapy, 31*(3), 333–347. https://doi.org/10.1111/bjp.12148.

Cabral, R.R. & Smith, T.B. (2011). Racial/ethnic matching of clients and therapists in mental health services: A meta-analytic review of preferences, perceptions, and outcomes. *Journal of Counseling Psychology, 58*(4), 537–554. https://doi.org/10.1037/a0025266

Capone, G., Schroder, T., Clarke, S. & Braham, L. (2016). Outcomes of therapeutic community treatment for personality disorder. *Therapeutic Communities, 37*(2). https://doi.org/10.1108/TC-12-2015-0025

Carel, H. (2016). *Phenomenology of illness.* Oxford University Press.

Cavarretta, M.V., Pellerin, H., Maurel, E., Ansalone, S.M., Truck, I., Cohen, D. & Ingoglia, S. (2025). The effectiveness of online therapy in promoting wellbeing and reducing burnout among psychotherapists. *Frontiers in Psychology, 16.* https://doi.org/10.3389/fpsyg.2025.1510383

Caviglia G. (2021). Working on dreams, from neuroscience to psychotherapy. *Research in Psychotherapy, 24*(2), 540. https://doi.org/10.4081/ripppo.2021.540

Celenza, A. (2025). *Erotic transferences: A contemporary introduction.* Routledge.

Cénat, J.M. (2023). Complex racial trauma: Evidence, theory, assessment, and treatment. *Perspectives on Psychological Science: A Journal of the Association for Psychological Science, 18*(3), 675–687. https://doi.org/10.1177/17456916221120428

Chambers, C. & Denir, I. (Eds.). (2024). *Translation and decolonialization: Interdisciplinary approaches.* Routledge.

Chan, C.C., Li, W.W.L. & Chiu, A.S.L. (2019). *The psychology of Chinese gambling.* Springer.

Charura, D. (2024). Therapists' experience of working with refugees and asylum seekers who have been tortured: An interpretative phenomenological analysis. *Psychological Trauma: Theory, Research, Practice and Policy, 16*(3), 521–531. https://doi.org/10.1037/tra0001709

Charura, D. & Lago, C. (2021). *Black identities and white therapies: Race, respect and diversity*. PCCS Books.

Chollet, D., Turner, A., Marquez, J., O'Neill, J. & Moore, L. (2024). *The good childhood report 2024*. The Children's Society.

Colby, M.H., Hires, B., Le, L., Sauma, D., Yau, M.Y., Chu, M.T. & Rubin, H.L. (2022). Unpacking the root causes of gambling in the Asian community: Contesting the myth of the Asian gambling culture. *Frontiers in Public Health, 10*, 956956. https://doi.org/10.3389/fpubh.2022.956956

Constien, T., Khanna, A. & Wiberg, A. (2024). Client experiences of drama therapy: A systematic review and qualitative meta-analysis. *Qualitative Psychology 12*(3), 311-377. https://doi.org/10.1037/qup0000300

Cook, S.R. (2019). *Exploring the role of multilingualism in the therapeutic journey of survivors of torture and human trafficking* [Unpublished PhD dissertation]. University of London.

Cooper, M. (2008). *Essential research findings in counselling and psychotherapy: The facts are friendly*. Sage.

Cooper, M. & McLeod, J. (2011). *Pluralistic counselling and psychotherapy*. Sage.

Costa, B. (2022). Interpreter-mediated CBT: A practical implementation guide for working with spoken language interpreters. *The Cognitive Behaviour Therapist, 15*(8). https://doi.org/10.1017/S1754470X2200006X

Dana, D. (2018). *The polyvagal theory in therapy: Engaging the rhythm of regulation*. W. W. Norton & Company.

Davis, S. & Brien, A.-M. (2022). *Fast facts about diversity, equity, and inclusion in nursing: Building competencies for an antiracism practice*. Springer Publishing Company.

DeYoung, P.A. (2015). *Relational psychotherapy: A primer* (2nd ed.). Routledge.

DeYoung, P.A. (2022). *Understanding and treating chronic shame: A relational/neurobiological approach* (2nd ed.). Routledge.

Elise, D. (2019). *Creativity and the erotic dimensions of the analytic field*. Routledge.

Erskine, R.G. (2011). Attachment, relational-needs, and psychotherapeutic presence. *International Journal of Integrative Psychotherapy*, 2. https://www.researchgate.net/publication/277067258_Attachment_Relational-Needs_and_Psychotherapeutic_Presence

Erskine, R.G. (2015). *Relational patterns, therapeutic presence: Concepts and practice of integrative psychotherapy*. Karnac.

Erskine, R.G., Moursund, J.P. & Trautmann, R.L. (1999). *Beyond empathy: A therapy of contact-in-relationship*. Brunner/Mazel.

Erskine, R.G. & Trautmann, R.L. (2003). Resolving intrapsychic conflict: Psychotherapy of Parent Ego states. In C. Sills & H. Hargaden (Eds.), *Ego states: Key concepts in transactional analysis, contemporary views* (pp. 109–134). Worth Publishing.

Espeland, K., Hjelmeland, H. & Knizek, B.L. (2021). A call for change from impersonal risk assessment to a relational approach: Professionals' reflections on the national guidelines for suicide prevention in mental health care in Norway. *International Journal of Qualitative Studies on Health and Wellbeing, 16*(1), 1–11. https://doi.org/10.1080/17482631.2020.1868737

Eubanks, C.F., Sergi, J. & Muran, J.C. (2021). Responsiveness to ruptures and repairs in psychotherapy. In J.C. Watson & H. Wiseman (Eds.), *The responsive psychotherapist: Attuning to clients in the moment* (pp. 83–103). American Psychological Association. https://doi.org/10.1037/0000240-005

Fanon, F. (1952). *Black skin, white masks*. Grove Press.

Fernandes, C., Maguire, T., Berthollier, N., Cheung, J. & Sivyer, K. (2025). A qualitative review and thematic synthesis of resident experiences in prison-based democratic therapeutic communities. *The Journal of Forensic Psychiatry & Psychology, 36*(4), 550–581. https://doi.org/10.1080/14789949.2025.2485122

Finlay, L. (1993). *Groupwork in occupational therapy*. Wiley.

Finlay, L. (2011). *Phenomenology for therapists: Researching the lived world.* Wiley-Blackwell.

Finlay, L. (2016a). *Relational integrative psychotherapy: Engaging process and theory in practice*. Wiley.

Finlay, L. (2016b). Nurturing an Integrating 'Adult' in integrative psychotherapy. *International Journal of Integrative Psychotherapy, 7*. https://www.integrative-journal.com/index.php/ijip/article/view/114/81

Finlay, L. (2019). *Practical ethics in counselling and psychotherapy.* Sage.

Finlay, L. (2020). COVID-19 took my breath away: A personal narrative. *The Humanistic Psychologist, 48*(4), 321–339. https://doi.org/10.1037/hum0000200

Finlay, L. (2022). *The therapeutic use of self in counselling and psychotherapy.* Sage.

Finlay, L. (2025). *Relational counselling and psychotherapy.* Sage.

Finlay, L. & Charura, D. (2026). Refugees' experience of loneliness as disrupting '*be-ing-becoming*'. In A. Seemann, E. Hughes, J. Krueger & T. Roberts (Eds.), *Loneliness in our time.* Bloomsbury.

Finlay, L. & Hewitt Evans, J. (2022). The transformative experience of finding a relational home with a psychotherapist. *European Journal for Qualitative Research in Psychotherapy, 12*, 29–46. https://doi.org/10.24377/EJQRP.article3034

Fors, M. (2018). *A grammar of power in psychotherapy: Exploring the dynamics of privilege.* American Psychological Association. https://doi.org/10.1037/0000086-001

Fowlie, H. & Sills, C. (Eds.). (2011). *Relational transactional analysis: Principles in practice.* Routledge.

Frank, R. (2023). *The bodily roots of experience in psychotherapy.* Routledge.

Fuld, S. & McKelvie, M.R. (2024). A perspective on neurodivergent-affirming relational practice: Exploration of identity and the healing process. *Counselling and Psychotherapy Research*, *24*(4), 1141–1144. https://doi.org/10.1002/capr.12792

Full, W., Vossler, A., Moller, N., Pybis, J. & Roddy, J. (2024). Therapists' and counsellors' perceptions and experiences of offering online therapy during COVID-19: A qualitative survey. *Counselling and Psychotherapy Research*, 703–718. https://doi.org/10.1002/capr.12707

Gallagher, O., Regan, E.E. & O'Reilly, G. (2024). The power threat meaning framework 5 years on – A scoping review of the emergent empirical literature. *British Journal of Psychology*, *115*(3), 555–576. https://doi.org/10.1111/bjop.12702

Gendlin, E.T. (1981). *Focusing* (2nd ed.). Bantam Books.

George, H.P. (Ed.). (2025). *Black women, trauma and therapy: Revolutionising therapeutic thought and practice*. PCCS Books.

Giacomucci, S.A. (2021). Psychodrama and social work theory. *Social Work, Sociometry, and Psychodrama, 1*, 101–124. https://doi.org/10.1007/978-981-33-6342-7_6

Giannelli, E., Gold, C., Bieleninik, L., Ghetti, C. & Gelo, O.C.G. (2019). Dialectical behaviour therapy and 12-step programmes for substance use disorder: A systematic review and meta-analysis. *Counselling and Psychotherapy Research*, *9*, 274–285.

Gilbert, M.C. & Evans, K. (2000). *Psychotherapy supervision: An integrative relational approach to psychotherapy supervision*. Open University Press.

Gilbert, P. & Simos, G. (Eds.). (2022). *Compassion focused therapy: Clinical practice and applications*. Routledge.

Gillespie, C., Murphy, M., Kells, M. & Flynn, D. (2022). Individuals who report having benefitted from dialectical behaviour therapy (DBT): A qualitative exploration of processes and experiences at long-term follow-up. *Borderline Personality Disorder and Emotion Dysregulation*, *9*(1), 8. https://doi.org/10.1186/s40479-022-00179-9

Gilling McIntosh, L., Janes, S., O'Rourke, S. & Thomson, L.D.G. (2021). Effectiveness of psychological and psychosocial interventions for forensic mental health inpatients: A meta-analysis. *Aggression and Violent Behavior*, 58(101551). https://doi.org/10.1016/j.avb.2021.101551

Goldstein, E. (2025, November). Re: *I've supervised hundreds of trauma therapists. The ones who break through all discover the same truth*. [Comment]. LinkedIn. https://www.linkedin.com/posts/esthergoldsteinlcsw_ive-supervised-hundreds-of-trauma-therapists-activity-7390763702003867648-_xT2/?utm_source=share&utm_medium=member_desktop&rcm=ACoAAAJx2YcBXi4yJjQnm9GC7e8e533Ac4kNDyI

Grace, K., Remington, A., Lloyd-Evans, B., Davies, J. & Crane, L. (2022). Loneliness in autistic adults: A systematic review. *Autism*, *26 (8)*, 2117–2135. https://doi.org/10.1177/13623613221077721

Hamilton, A. (2023). Black therapists' experiences with their Black clients: A systematic review. *Journal of Marital and Family Therapy, 50*(1), 150–174. https://doi.org/10.1111/jmft.12678

Harned, M.S. (2022). *Treating trauma in dialectical behavior therapy: The DBT prolonged exposure protocol*. Guilford Press.

Hauser, C.T. (2016). *Shame and resilience among mental health trainees: A scale construction study* (Unpublished doctoral dissertation). University of Nebraska-Lincoln.

Hawkins, P. & Shohet, R. (2012). *Supervision in the helping professions*. (Updated edition). Open University Press.

Hayes, S.C. & Hofmann, S.G. (Eds.). (2017). *Process-based CBT: The science and core clinical competencies of cognitive behavioral therapy*. New Harbinger.

Heinonen, E. & Nissen-Lie, H.A. (2020). The professional and personal characteristics of effective psychotherapists: A systematic review. *Psychotherapy Research: Journal of the Society for Psychotherapy Research, 30*(4), 417–432. https://doi.org/10.1080/10503307.2019.1620366

Hellinger, B. (2003). *To the heart of the matter: Brief therapies*. Carl-Auer Verlag.

Henggeler, S.W. & Schaeffer, C.M. (2016). Multisystemic Therapy®: Clinical overview, outcomes, and implementation research. *Family Process, 55*(3), 514–528. https://doi.org/10.1111/famp.12232

Henretty, J.R. & Levitt, H.M. (2010). The role of therapist self-disclosure in psychotherapy: A qualitative review. *Clinical Psychology Review, 30*(1), 63–77. https://doi.org/10.1016/j.cpr.2009.09.004

Hernandez-Bustamante, M., Cjuno, J., Hernández, R.M. & Ponce-Meza, J.C. (2024). Efficacy of dialectical behavior therapy in the treatment of borderline personality disorder: A systematic review of randomized controlled trials. *Iranian Journal of Psychiatry, 19*(1), 119–129. https://doi.org/10.18502/ijps.v19i1.14347

Hill, C.E., Knox, S. & Pinto-Coelho, K.G. (2019). Self-disclosure and immediacy. In J.C. Norcross & M.J. Lambert (Eds.), *Psychotherapy relationships that work: Evidence-based therapist contributions* (Vol. 1, 3rd ed., pp. 379–420). Oxford University Press.

Horowitz, L.M., Alden, L.E., Wiggins, J.S. & Pincus, A.L. (2000). Inventory of interpersonal problems. *Mind Garden*. https://www.mindgarden.com

Jacobs, L. (2017). Hopes, fears, and enduring relational themes. *British Gestalt Journal, 26*(1), 7–16.

Jacobs, L. & Hycner, R. (Eds.). (2009). *Relational approaches in Gestalt therapy*. Gestalt Press.

James, G. (2023). The psychological impact of sending children away to boarding schools in Britain: Is there cause for concern? *British Journal of Psychotherapy, 39*, 592–610. https://doi.org/10.1111/bjp.12854

Johnstone, L. & Boyle, M. with Cromby, J., Dillon, J., Harper, D., Kinderman, P., Longden, E., Pilgrim, D. & Read, J. (2018). *The Power Threat Meaning Framework: Towards the identification of patterns in emotional distress, unusual experiences and troubled or troubling behaviour, as an alternative to functional psychiatric diagnosis*. British Psychological Society.

Jordan, J.V. (2024). *Relational–cultural therapy* (3rd ed.). American Psychological Association.

Jørgensen, M.S., Storebø, O.J., Bo, S., Poulsen, S., Gondan, M., Beck, E., Chanen, A.M., Bateman, A., Pedersen, J. & Simonsen, E. (2021). Mentalization-based treatment in groups for adolescents with Borderline Personality Disorder: 3- and 12-month follow-up of a randomized controlled trial. *European Child & Adolescent Psychiatry, 30*(5), 699–710. https://doi.org/10.1007/s00787-020-01551-2

Kaklauskas, F., Clements, C., Hocoy, D. & Hoffman, L. (2016). *Shadows and light: Theory, research, and practice in transpersonal psychology*. University Professors Press.

Kapitan, L. (2003). *Re-enchanting art therapy: Transformational practices for restoring creative vitality*. Charles C. Thomas.

Karatzias, T., Murphy, P., Cloitre, M., Bisson, J., Roberts, N., Shevlin, M., Hyland, P., Maercker, A., Ben-Ezra, M., Coventry, P., Mason-Roberts, S., Bradley, A. & Hutton, P. (2019). Psychological interventions for ICD-11 complex PTSD symptoms: Systematic review and meta-analysis. *Psychological Medicine, 49*(11), 1761–1775. https://doi.org/10.1017/S0033291719000436

Karpman, S. (2014). *A game free life: The new transactional analysis of intimacy, openness, and happiness*. Drama Triangle Publications.

Karris, M. & Kim, A.B. (2022). MFT trainee experiences of shame, self-criticism, and self-compassion in their first practicum. *Counseling and Family Therapy Scholarship Review, (4)*2.

Kirkbride, J.B., Anglin, D.M., Colman, I., Dykxhoorn, J., Jones, P.B., Patalay, P., Pitman, A., Soneson, E., Steare, T., Wright, T. & Griffiths, S.L. (2024). The social determinants of mental health and disorder: Evidence, prevention and recommendations. *World Psychiatry, 23*(1), 58–90. https://doi.org/10.1002/wps.21160

Kirsch, J., Kitchens, K., Kerr, K. & Sivakumaran, S. (2024). Group-based intervention models in treating refugee mental health in high-income countries: A systematic review. *Trauma, Violence, & Abuse, 25*(5), 4173–4187. https://doi.org/10.1177/15248380241270039

Knox, R., Murphy, D., Wiggins, S. & Cooper, M. (Eds.). (2013). *Relational depth: Contemporary perspectives*. Palgrave Macmillan.

Konkolÿ Thege, B., Petroll, C., Rivas, C. & Scholtens, S. (2021). The effectiveness of family constellation therapy in improving mental health: A systematic review. *Family Process, 60*(2), 409–423. https://doi.org/10.1111/famp.12636

Lammers, M.W., Vroling M.S., Crosby R.D. & van Strien T. (2022). Dialectical behavior therapy compared to cognitive behavior therapy in binge-eating disorder: An effectiveness study with 6-month follow-up. *International Journal of Eating Disorders, 55*, 902–913. https://doi.org/10.1002/eat.23750

Langmuir, J.I., Kirsh, S.G. & Classen, C.C. (2012). A pilot study of body-oriented group psychotherapy: Adapting sensorimotor psychotherapy for the group treatment of trauma. *Psychological Trauma: Theory, Research, Practice, and Policy, 4*(2), 214–220.

Lans, O., Gewirtz-Meydan, A. & Reuveni, L. (2024). Addressing the elephant in the room: How erotic transference is identified and understood in therapy. *British Journal of Guidance & Counselling*, 1–13. https://doi.org/10.1080/03069885.2024.2373187

Levitt, H.M., Pomerville, A. & Surace, F.I. (2016). A qualitative meta-analysis examining clients' experiences of psychotherapy: A new agenda. *Psychological Bulletin, 142*(8), 801–830. https://doi.org/10.1037/bul0000057

Linehan, M.M. (1993). *Cognitive behavioral therapy of borderline personality disorder*. Guilford Press.

Linehan, M.M., Comtois, K.A., Murray, A.M., Brown, M.Z., Gallop, R.J., Heard, H.L., Korslund, K.E., Tutek, D.A., Reynolds, S.K. & Lindenboim, N. (2006). Two-year randomized controlled trial and follow-up of dialectical behavior therapy vs therapy by experts for suicidal behaviors and borderline personality disorder. *Archives of General Psychiatry, 63*(7), 757–766. https://doi.org/10.1001/archpsyc.63.7.757

Little, R. (2013). The new emerges out of the old: An integrated relational perspective on psychological development, psychopathology, and therapeutic action. *Transactional Analysis Journal, 43*(2), 106–121. https://doi.org/10.1177/0362153713499541

Liu, W.M., Liu, R.Z. & Shin, R.Q. (2023). Understanding systemic racism: Anti-Blackness, white supremacy, racial capitalism, and the re/creation of white space and time. *Journal of Counseling Psychology, 70*(3), 244–257. https://doi.org/10.1037/cou0000605

Luo, T. (2025). *FloatMind*. https://www.tingtingluo.work/floatmind

Mckenzie-Mavinga, I. (2016). *The challenge of racism in therapeutic practice: Engaging with oppression in practice and supervision*. Palgrave Macmillan.

Mearns, D. & Cooper, M. (2005). *Working at relational depth in counselling and psychotherapy*. Sage.

McManus, M.A. & Ball, E. (2020). COVID-19 should be considered an adverse childhood experience (ACE). *Journal of Community Safety and Wellbeing, 5*(4), 164–167. https://doi.org/10.35502/jcswb.166

McMillan, M., & McLeod, J. (2006). Letting go: The client's experience of relational depth. *Person-Centered & Experiential Psychotherapies, 5*(4), 277–292. https://doi.org/10.1080/14779757.2006.9688419

McNeil, J. (1976). The parent interview. *Transactional Analysis Journal, 6*, 61–68.

Macneil, C.A., Hasty, M.K., Conus, P. & Berk, M. (2012). Is diagnosis enough to guide interventions in mental health? Using case formulation in clinical practice. *BMC Medicine 10* (111). https://doi.org/10.1186/1741-7015-10-111

Madre de Deus de Sousa, F., Banbury, S., Phillips, O. & Lusher, J. (2024). How counselling psychologists address issues of race with clients from Black Asian and minority ethnic backgrounds: A discourse analysis. *World Journal of Advanced Research and Reviews, 21*(1), 1209–1219. https://doi.org/10.30574/wjarr.2024.21.1.0115

Mahoney, A., Karatzias, T. & Hutton, P. (2019). A systematic review and meta-analysis of group treatments for adults with symptoms associated with complex post-traumatic stress disorder. *Journal of Affective Disorders, 243*, 305–321. https://doi.org/10.1016/j.jad.2018.09.059

Mann, D. (Ed.). (1999). *Erotic transference and countertransference: Clinical practice in psychotherapy*. Routledge.

Mann, J.J., Michel, C.A. & Auerbach, R.P. (2023). Improving suicide prevention through evidence-based strategies: A systematic review. *Focus (American Psychiatric Publishing), 21*(2), 182–196. https://doi.org/10.1176/appi.focus.23021004

Menchon, J.M., Mestre-Bach, G., Steward, T., Fernández-Aranda, F. & Jiménez-Murcia, S. (2018). An overview of gambling disorder: From treatment approaches to risk factors. *F1000 Research, 9*(7), 434. https://doi.org/10.12688/f1000research.12784.1

Millard, L.A., Wan, M.W., Smith, D.M. & Wittkowski, A. (2023). The effectiveness of compassion focused therapy with clinical populations: A systematic review and meta-analysis. *Journal of Affective Disorders, 326*, 168–192. https://doi.org/10.1016/j.jad.2023.01.010

Miller, W.R. & Rollnick, S. (2002). *Motivational Interviewing: Preparing people for change* (2nd ed.). The Guilford Press.

Miller, M.J., Keum, B.T., Thai, C.J., Lu, Y., Truong, N.N., Huh, G.A., Li, X., Yeung, J.G. & Ahn, L.H. (2018). Practice recommendations for addressing racism: A content analysis of the counseling psychology literature. *Journal of Counseling Psychology, 65*(6), 669–680. https://doi.org/10.1037/cou0000306

Mitchell, S.A. (1988). *Relational concepts in psychoanalysis: An integration.* Harvard University Press.

Mitchell, S.A. & Aron, L. (Eds.). (1999). *Relational psychoanalysis: The emergence of a tradition.* Analytic Press.

Monsen, K. & Monsen, J.T. (2000). Chronic pain and psychodynamic body therapy: A controlled outcome study. *Psychotherapy: Theory Research Practice Training, 37*(3), 257–269. https://doi.org/10.1037/h0087658

Monticelli, F., Massullo, C., Carcione, A., Tombolini, L., Guerra, F., Liotti, M., Monticelli, C., Gasperini, E., Russo, M., Novaretto, S., La Vista, L., Mallozzi, P., Imperatori, C., Del Brutto, C. & Farina, B. (2025). Differentiating self-disclosure interventions from self-involving interventions based on the assessment of the short-term therapeutic effects: preliminary results. *Research in Psychotherapy: Psychopathology, Process and Outcome, 28*(1), 800. https://doi.org/10.4081/ripppo.2025.800

Morris, V., Mamak, M. & Moulden, H. (2024). Cognitive behavioural therapy for anger and aggression in forensic mental health populations. *Journal of Forensic Psychiatry and Psychology, 35*(2), 291–313. https://doi.org/10.1080/14789949.2024.2326641

Morrison, P.K., Hawker, L., Cluss, P.A., Miller, E., Fleming, R., Bicehouse, T., George, D., Burke, J., Wright, K. & Chang, J.C. (2021). The challenges of working with men who perpetrate partner violence: Perspectives and observations of experts who work with batterer intervention programs. *Journal of Interpersonal Violence, 36*(7–8), 3524–3546. https://doi.org/10.1177/0886260518778258

Moursund, J.P. & Erskine, R.G. (2004). *Integrative psychotherapy: The art and science of relationship*. Thomson: Brooks/Cole.

Mullan, J. (2023). *Decolonizing psychotherapy: Oppression, historical trauma, and politicizing your practice*. W.W. Norton.

Nakeyar, C. & Frewen, P.A. (2016). Evidence-based care for Iraqi, Kurdish, and Syrian asylum seekers and refugees of the Syrian civil war: A systematic review. *Canadian Psychology/Psychologie Canadienne, 57*(4), 233–245.

NHS England. (2025). *Staying safe from suicide: Best practice guidance for safety assessment, formulation and management*. https://www.england.nhs.uk/long-read/staying-safe-from-suicide/

NICE. (2009). *Borderline personality disorder: Recognition and management: Clinical guideline: CG78*. https://www.nice.org.uk/guidance/CG78

Norcross, J.C. (Ed.). (2011). *Psychotherapy relationships that work: Evidence-based responsiveness* (2nd ed.). Oxford University Press.

Norcross, J.C. & Goldfried, M.R. (Eds.). (2005). *Handbook of psychotherapy integration*. Oxford University Press.

Norcross, J.C. & Karpiak, C.P. (2017). Our best selves: Defining and actualizing expertise in psychotherapy. *The Counseling Psychologist, 45*(1), 66–75. https://doi.org/10.1177/0011000016655603

Norcross, J.C. & Lambert, M.J. (Eds.). (2019). *Psychotherapy relationships that work (Vol.1): Evidence-based therapist contributions*. (3rd ed.). Oxford University Press.

Norcross, J.C. & Wampold, B.E. (Eds.). (2019). *Psychotherapy relationships that work: (Vol.2): Evidence-based therapist responsiveness*. (3rd ed.). Oxford University Press.

Nwosu, P. (2024). Integration of refugees: The role of networks in facilitating the social integration of refugees in the Netherlands. *International Journal of Applied Research in Social Sciences*, 6(12), *2949–2967*. https://doi.org/10.51594/ijarss.v6i12.1778

Ogden, T.H. (1992). *Projective identification and psychotherapeutic technique*. Routledge. (Original work published 1982.)

Olaniyan, F.V. & Hayes, G. (2022). Just ethnic matching? Racial and ethnic minority students and culturally appropriate mental health provision at British universities. *International Journal of Qualitative Studies on Health and Wellbeing, 17*(1). https://doi.org/10.1080/17482631.2022.2117444

Orange, D.M. (1995). *Emotional understanding: Studies in psychoanalytic epistemology*. Guilford Press.

Orbach, S. (2003). Therapy from the left: Interview with Susie Orbach. *The European Journal of Psychotherapy, Counselling & Health, 6*(1), 75–85. https://doi.org/10.1080/1364253032000157080

Orbach, S. (2018). *In therapy: The unfolding story.* Profile Books.

Ostinelli, E.G., Schulze, M., Zangani, C., Farhat, L.C., Tomlinson, A., Del Giovane, C., Chamberlain, S.R., Philipsen, A., Young, S., Cowen, P.J., Bilbow, A., Cipriani, A. & Cortese, S. (2025). Comparative efficacy and acceptability of pharmacological, psychological, and neurostimulatory interventions for ADHD in adults: A systematic review and component network meta-analysis. *The Lancet, 12(1),* 32–43. https://www.thelancet.com/journals/lanpsy/article/PIIS2215-0366(24)00360-2/fulltext

Park, C.J. & Shields, J. (2023). Childhood attachment insecurity and shame-proneness in adulthood: Implications for clinical social work practice. *Journal of Human Behavior in the Social Environment, 34*(7), 1089–1105. https://doi.org/10.1080/10911359.2023.2237091

Porges, S.W. (2011). *The polyvagal theory: Neurophysiological foundations of emotions, attachment, communication, and self-regulation*, W.W. Norton & Company.

Proctor, G. (2018). *The dynamics of power in counselling and psychotherapy: Ethics, politics and practice* (2nd ed.). PCCS Books.

Racker, H. (1957). The meanings and uses of countertransference. *The Psychoanalytic Quarterly, 26*(3), 303–357. https://doi.org/10.1002/j.2167-4086.2007.tb00277.x

Röhricht, F., Papadopoulos, N. & Priebe, S. (2013). An exploratory randomized controlled trial of body psychotherapy for patients with chronic depression. *Journal of Affective Disorders, 151*, 85–91.

Rolland, L., Costa, B. & Dewaele, J.-M. (2021). Negotiating the language(s) for psychotherapy talk: A mixed methods study from the perspective of multilingual clients. *Counselling & Psychotherapy Research, 21*(1), 107– 117. https://doi.org/10.1002/capr.12369

Rønnestad, M.H., & Skovholt, T.M. (2003). The journey of the counselor and therapist: Research findings and perspectives on professional development. *Journal of Career Development, 30*(1), 5–44. https://doi.org/10.1177/089484530303000102

Roper-Hall, A. (1998). Working systemically with older people and their families who have 'come to grief'. In P. Sutcliffe, G. Tufnell, & U. Cornish (Eds.), *Working with the dying and bereaved: Systemic approaches to therapeutic work* (pp. 177–206). MacMillan.

Rosati, F., Lorusso, M.M., Pistella, J., Giovanardi, G., Di Giannantonio, B., Mirabella, M., Williams, R., Lingiardi, V. & Baiocco, R. (2022). Non-binary clients' experiences of psychotherapy: Uncomfortable and affirmative approaches. *International Journal of Environmental Research and Public Health, 19*(22), 15339. https://doi.org/10.3390/ijerph192215339

Rosendahl, S., Sattel, H. & Lahmann C. (2021). Effectiveness of body psychotherapy: A systematic review and meta-analysis. *Frontiers in Psychiatry, 12*, 709–798. https://doi.org/10.3389/fpsyt.2021.709798

Rouf, K. & Waites, B. (2023). *Guidance on responding to disclosures of non-recent (historic) child sexual abuse: Safeguarding and support implications.* British Psychological Society. https://doi.org/10.53841/bpsrep.2023.inf258b

Samuel, N.K.S. & Simonds, L.M. (2025). Disclosing racial trauma in psychological therapy: Exploring the experiences of racially minoritised people in the UK. *Psychology and Psychotherapy: Theory, Research and Practice.* https://doi.org/10.1111/papt.12592

Sander, R., Laugesen, H., Skammeritz, S., Mortensen, E.L. & Carlsson, J. (2019). Interpreter-mediated psychotherapy with trauma-affected refugees – A retrospective cohort study. *Psychiatry Research, 271*, 684–692. https://doi.org/10.1016/j.psychres.2018.12.058

Savenije, A., van Lawick, J. & Reijmers, E. (2022). *Systemic perspectives in mental health, social work and youth care.* Routledge. https://doi.org/10.4324/9781003272038

Schaverien, J. (2011). Boarding school syndrome: Broken attachments, a hidden trauma. *British Journal of Psychotherapy, 27*, 138–155. https://doi.org/10.1111/j.1752-0118.2011.01229.x

Schaverien, J. (2021). Revisiting boarding school syndrome: The anatomy of psychological traumas and sexual abuse. *British Journal of Psychotherapy, 37*(4), 606–622. https://doi.org/10.1111/bjp.12677

Schiavo, R. (2023). Embracing cultural humility in clinical and public health settings: A prescription to bridge inequities. *Journal of Communication in Healthcare, 16*(2), 123–125. https://doi.org/10.1080/17538068.2023.2221556

Schore, A.N. (2019). *Right brain psychotherapy.* W.W. Norton & Company.

Schwartz, R.C. (1995). *Internal family systems therapy.* Guilford Press.

Schweitzer, R.D., Rosbrook, B. & Kaiplinger, I. (2013). Lost in translation, found in translation: A case study of working psychodynamically in an interpreter-assisted setting. *Psychodynamic Practice, 19*(2), 168–183. https://doi.org/10.1080/14753634.2013.778487

Sedighimornani, N., Rimes, K. & Verplanken, B. (2020). Factors contributing to the experience of shame and shame management: Adverse childhood experiences, peer acceptance, and attachment styles. *The Journal of Social Psychology, 161*(2), 129–145. https://doi.org/10.1080/00224545.2020.1778616

Shah, D. (2023). *The analyst's torment: Unbearable mental states in countertransference.* Phoenix Publishing House.

Shapiro, F. (2001). *Eye movement desensitization and reprocessing: Basic principles, protocols, and procedures* (2nd ed.). Guilford Press.

Shivanath, S. & Hiremath, M. (2003). The psycho-dynamics of race and culture. In H. Hargaden & C. Sills (Eds.), *Ego states (Key concepts in transactional analysis: Contemporary views)* (pp. 169–185). Worth Publishing.

Shuker, R. (2010). Forensic therapeutic communities: A critique of treatment model and evidence base. *The Howard Journal of Criminal Justice*, *49*(5), 467–477. https://doi.org/10.1111/j.1468-2311.2010.00637.x

Siddiq, H., Elhaija, A. & Wells, K. (2023). An integrative review of community-based mental health interventions among resettled refugees from Muslim-majority countries. *Community Mental Health Journal*, *59*(1), 160–174. https://doi.org/10.1007/s10597-022-00994-y

Siegel, D.J. (2020). *The developing mind: How relationships and the brain interact to shape who we are* (3rd ed.). The Guilford Press.

Spinelli, E. (2007). *Practising existential psychotherapy: The relational world.* Sage Publications Ltd.

Stoffers, J.M., Völlm, B.A., Rücker, G., Timmer, A., Huband, N. & Lieb, K. (2012). Psychological therapies for people with borderline personality disorder. *The Cochrane Database of Systematic Reviews, 8*. https://doi.org/10.1002/14651858.CD005652.pub2

Stoffers-Winterling, J.M., Storebø, O.J., Simonsen, E., Sedoc Jørgensen, M., Pereira Ribeiro, J., Kongerslev, M.T. & Lieb, K. (2022). Perspectives on dialectical behavior therapy and mentalization-based therapy for borderline personality disorder: Same, different, complementary? *Psychology Research and Behavior Management, 15*, 3179–3189. https://doi.org/10.2147/PRBM.S342257

Stolorow, R.D. (2014). Undergoing the situation: Emotional dwelling is more than empathic understanding. *International Journal of Psychoanalytic Self Psychology, 9*(1), 80–83. https://doi.org/10.1080/15551024.2014.857750.

Storebø, O.J., Stoffers-Winterling, J.M., Völlm, B.A., Kongerslev, M.T., Mattivi, J.T., Jørgensen, M.S., Faltinsen, E., Todorovac, A., Sales, C.P., Callesen, H.E., Lieb, K. & Simonsen, E. (2020). Psychological therapies for people with borderline personality disorder. *The Cochrane Database of Systematic Reviews, 5*(5). https://doi.org/10.1002/14651858.CD012955.pub2

Stratton, P (2016). *The evidence base of family therapy and systemic practice.* Association for Family Therapy.

Sue, D.W. (2023, episode 251). *Speaking of psychology: How to combat* microaggressions [Audio podcast]. APA. https://www.apa.org/news/podcasts/speaking-of-psychology/microaggressions

Sue, D.W., Alsaidi, S., Awad, M.N., Glaeser, E., Calle, C.Z. & Mendez, N. (2019). Disarming racial microaggressions: Microintervention strategies for targets, White allies, and bystanders. *American Psychologist*, *74*(1), 128–142. https://doi.org/10.1037/amp0000296

Sue, D. W., Sue, D., Neville, H.A. & Smith, L. (2022). *Counseling the culturally diverse: Theory and practice* (9th ed.). Wiley.

Sutton, J. (2023, April 4) Understanding therapist burnout: 12 symptoms & recovery tips. *Positive Psychology.* https://positivepsychology.com/therapist-burnout/

Tasca, G.A., Sylvestre, J., Balfour, L., Chyurlia, L., Evans, J., Fortin-Langelier, B., Francis, K., Gandhi, J., Huehn, L., Hunsley, J., Joyce, A.S., Kinley, J., Koszycki, D., Leszcz, M., Lybanon-Daigle, V., Mercer, D., Ogrodniczuk, J.S., Presniak, M., Ravitz, P. … & Wilson, B. (2015). What clinicians want: Findings from a psychotherapy practice research network survey. *Psychotherapy*, *52*(1), 1–11. https://doi.org/10.1037/a0038252

Turner, D. (2025). *Decolonising counselling and psychotherapy: Depoliticised pathways towards intersectional practice*. Routledge.

Vesentini, L., Van Overmeire, R., Matthys, F., De Wachter, D., Van Puyenbroeck, H. & Bilsen, J. (2022). Intimacy in psychotherapy: An exploratory survey among therapists. *Archives of Sexual Behavior*, *51*(1), 453–463. https://doi.org/10.1007/s10508-021-02190-7

von Sydow, K., Beher, S. & Retzlaff, R. (2024). Systemic psychotherapy: An introduction to its theoretical foundations and clinical practice. *Dtsch Arztebl Int. 121*(23), 783–792. https://doi.org/10.3238/arztebl.m2024.0194

Wampold, B. & Imel, Z. (2015). *The great psychotherapy debate: The evidence for what makes psychotherapy work*. Routledge.

Welch-Moring, S. (2025). Ancestral Constellations: Healing the tears and fears of our mothers, grandmothers and great-grandmothers. In H.P. George (Ed.), *Black women, trauma & therapy: Revolutionising therapeutic thought and practice (pp. 128-139)*. PCCS Books.

Westland, G., (2018). A study of significant moments of change in body psychotherapy. *Body Movement and Dance in Psychotherapy*, *13*(1), 17–32.

Williams, M.T., Holmes, S., Zare, M., Haeny, A. & Faber, S. (2023). An evidence-based approach for treating stress and trauma due to racism. *Cognitive and Behavioral Practice*, *30*(4), 565–588.

Winnicott, D.W. (1960). Ego distortion in terms of true and false self. In D.W. Winnicott (Ed.), *The maturational processes and the facilitating environment: Studies in the theory of emotional development* (pp. 140–152). Karnac Books.

Wojnar, D.M., Swanson, K.M. & Adolfsson, A.S. (2011). Confronting the inevitable: a conceptual model of miscarriage for use in clinical practice and research. *Death studies*, *35*(6), 536–558. https://doi.org/10.1080/07481187.2010.536886

Wojtara, M., Syeda, Y., Singh, H., Rana, E. & Sabeer, S. (2023). Examining adverse childhood experiences and attention deficit/hyperactivity disorder: A systematic review. *Mental Health Science*, *1*(2), 104–114. https://doi.org/10.1002/mhs2.26

Wojtkowiak, J., Lind, J. & Smid, G.E. (2021). Ritual in therapy for prolonged grief: A scoping review of ritual elements in evidence-informed grief interventions. *Frontiers in Psychiatry*, *11*, 623835. https://doi.org/10.3389/fpsyt.2020.623835

Wyatt, J.P. & Ampadu, G.G. (2022). Reclaiming self-care: Self-care as a social justice tool for black wellness. *Community Mental Health Journal*, *58*(2), 213–221. https://doi.org/10.1007/s10597-021-00884-9

Yalom, I.D. (1985). *The theory and practice of group psychotherapy.* Basic Books.

Yalom, I.D. (1989). *Love's executioner: And other tales of psychotherapy*. Basic Books.

Yalom, I.D. (2001). *The gift of therapy: An open letter to a new generation of therapists and their patients.* Piatkus.

Yalom, I.D. (2015). *Creatures of a day and other tales of psychotherapy*. Piatkus.

Yehuda, R. & Lehrner, A. (2018). Intergenerational transmission of trauma effects: Putative role of epigenetic mechanisms. *World Psychiatry: Official Journal of the World Psychiatric Association (WPA), 17*(3), 243–257. https://doi.org/10.1002/wps.20568

Žvelc, G. (2009). Between self and others: Relational schemas as an integrating construct in psychotherapy. *Transactional Analysis Journal, 39*, 22–38.

Žvelc, M. & Žvelc, G. (2020). Supervisees' experience of non-disclosure in psychotherapy supervision. *Ljetopis Socijalnog, 28*(1), 231–255. https://hrcak.srce.hr/file/379889

Name index

Subject index

U

V

W

Z